THE HEADHUNTING BUSINESS

The Headhunting Business

Stephanie Jones

Foreword by Sir Peter Parker

MACMILLAN

First published 1989

Published by
THE MACMILLAN PRESS LTD
Houndmills, Basingstoke, Hampshire RG21 2XS
and London
Companies and representatives
throughout the world

Typeset by Footnote Graphics,
Warminster, Wilts

Printed and bound in Great Britain at
The Camelot Press plc, Southampton

British Library Cataloguing in Publication Data
Jones, Stephanie, 1957–
The headhunting business.
1. Great Britain. Companies. Executives. Recruitment.
Role of executive search firms
I. Title
658. 4'07111'0941
ISBN 0–333–51941–8

To D.W., T.C.

Contents

List of Plates

Foreword

Headhunting is a serious, growth business which – until now – has not had the serious study it deserves.

The pace of the internationalisation of companies is quickening; take-overs and deals are the order of the day. The impact of the globalisation of markets means that managements are on the move, East and West. And in all the turbulence, the quality of managers is critical. The boom business of search involves at its best professional judgement based on skilled and thorough research. The prizes for the best placements may sometimes seem glittering and spectacular, but if the appointed person delivers the goods, the search company's human contribution to success and prosperity is decisive. The modern corporation knows the value of this expertise in seeking quality in the internationally competitive world.

This is the first systematic and thorough exercise into executive search, from its origins in the USA to its wide-scale development all over the world. Not least, this book provides a directory of the major UK companies covering their history, size, turnover, style and specialisation. Dr Jones has the good sense to suggest how to choose and use search services.

Management selection is a matter for the professionals: to go about it in any other way is as inadvisable as amateur bullfighting. That is why the headhunting business is growing, and that is why the industry and its standards need to be explicit and visible.

SIR PETER PARKER

Preface

The Headhunting Business concentrates mainly on the top end of the headhunting market; an analysis of the entire executive search – and selection – business, which now involves several hundred firms in Britain, would be unwieldy in length and inevitably inadequate and piecemeal in coverage. Here, we focus on the recruitment of executives and managers receiving salaries over £50,000 per annum, generally by search rather than processes of selection, advertising and out-placement.

If we see the entire recruitment industry in Britain as a Christmas cake, then the headhunters we are discussing here are the icing. The cake itself, or the bulk of the business, comprises the permanent and temporary staff recruitment agencies, such as Alfred Marks, Reed Employment, Blue Arrow, Manpower, Brook Street and Kelly Girl, who have a large volume of business dealing in secretarial, technical and computing jobs. The marzipan layer between the icing and the cake – into which we occasionally dip here – includes PA and MSL and the search and selection businesses which have emerged from management consultancies, advertising agents and accountancy firms, where a mixture of advertising and search is used.

Existing literature on headhunting in Britain is confined principally to three sources. John Byrne's very detailed and readable account of the American search business, *The Headhunters*, includes seven pages describing the impact of the Big Bang on high-level recruitment in Britain. Robert McKinnon's book of the same name, about headhunters in Britain (also the work of a newspaper man), emanates almost entirely from the industry itself without detailed analysis; it ranges widely over all aspects of recruitment and, written at the end of 1981, now seems dated. Finally, there is *The Executive Grapevine*, an annually updated directory of firms and consultants names, addresses and basic details.

In contrast, *The Headhunting Business* seeks to provide an in-depth, critical and perceptive insight into the origins, progress and perform-ance of the top-level search industry in Britain, based on research into the experiences of candidates and the users of search, as well as the industry's practitioners themselves. It systematically dissects exactly how headhunting works in practice, based on a range of case studies, practical fieldword and extensive interviewing. It considers the work-ings of the business internationally, arguing that a search firm cannot offer a fully effective and comprehensive service without a global network. It attempts various projections of the directions in which executive search is likely to move in the future. This book also offers a rough and ready *Which*? -type guide to the principal headhunting firms, providing as much detail as private partnership firms are prepared to divulge, and incorporating a comparative appraisal of their ranking in the market, areas of specialism and style of approach.

As such, this book has been written for all those coming into contact with search, both employer and employed; often they are one and the same, as a headhunted candidate may become in due course a head-hunter's client. More generally, it is aimed at the observer of the British business scene, who looks both backwards over the last generation and forwards into the future.

STEPHANIE JONES

Acknowledgements

I was first asked to write a book about headhunting in Britain back in December 1986, based on an article I had written for *Management Accounting*; at the time, this was the only article I had written on the subject and was, in fact, my first-ever foray into serious journalism. During 1987 and 1988, my researches and fieldwork into headhunting were often put on the back-burner whilst I finished another – completely different – book and taught modern economic history at the London School of Economics and the School of Oriental and African Studies.

My interest in headhunting was sustained by the series of very impressive, charming, suave, witty, energetic, egotistical and even outrageous characters I met in the course of writing this book. There is certainly no such thing as a typical headhunter. This study would not have been possible without the interest, help and – in some cases – actual written contributions of, in particular, John Viney of Heidrick and Struggles; Miles Broadbent of Norman Broadbent; Mark Weedon, then of Egon Zehnder; David Kimbell and Nigel Dyckhoff of Spencer Stuart and Roddy Gow of Russell Reynolds. Thanks are also due to the many users of executive search within a variety of companies, who commented more or less freely about the service they had received.

Two others helped enormously. Dominic Endicott, an ex-student of mine, now with the Boston Consulting Group, was a very imaginative, intelligent and enthusiastic research assistant. David M. Williams, friend and fellow economic historian, read and commented thoughtfully on the manuscript, as he has done for every literary effort I have produced over the last nine years. Both are now hoping to be headhunted!

STEPHANIE JONES

List of Companies
Participating in Chapter 3

3i
BICC plc
British Airways plc
British & Commonwealth Holdings plc
Cadbury Schweppes plc
Grand Metropolitan plc
Kingfisher plc (Woolworth Holdings)
Midland Bank plc
Midland Montagu (the international and investment banking arm of
Midland Bank)
Nomura International plc
Phillips & Drew/UBS
The Plessey Company plc
Procter & Gamble Ltd
J. Sainsbury plc
SBCI Savory Milln
Shell UK Ltd
Standard Chartered Bank
Tesco plc
Unilever plc

and eleven other companies which preferred to remain anonymous.

Introduction: The Economics of Search

The concept of headhunting may be introduced by a simple cost-benefit analysis of the reasons why a company should employ a search consultant in the first place. It suggests that – depending on the salary level of the appointment – headhunting generally costs marginally more than do-it-yourself recruiting, but it saves time and cuts risk in the long run. Thus we may see that on purely economic grounds, for specific needs, search has established a niche in the consultancy market; in later chapters we tackle the wider question of whether or not headhunting actually adds value, and can make a positive contribution to a company's performance.

To make a cost-benefit comparison between headhunting and other forms of recruitment, let us take as a real case study: the search for a Deputy Chief Executive of an important civil service department dealing in land and property, who was to receive a salary of £50 000.

If the would-be employers had undertaken the search themselves, they would be faced with several direct and indirect costs. In the first instance, advertisements would need to be placed in a variety of prestigious newspapers and periodicals. For adequate media coverage, three would be a bare minimum. A sixth of a page, or four 15 cm columns in *The Sunday Times* – any smaller advertisement might go unnoticed and would not reflect the importance of the appointment – is likely to cost £4800 before VAT. The *Financial Times* charges £2940 for a similar space. A half-page advertisement in *The Economist* would cost another £2200. The employers would have to produce artwork and text for the advertisement in each case, in consultation with their advertising agents, which would cost an average of £600 for three.

Other direct costs, incurred in any case, would include a doctor's fee for a medical, and candidates' travelling expenses: a total so far of £11 000.

Indirect costs, i.e. executive and secretarial time spent in the selection process, are equally significant. This does not take into account any business lost whilst executives are tied up interviewing at all stages in the procedure. Time will have to be spent either way on the job specification: normally around four hours. But the employer handling the search him- or herself will have the added problem of devising the advertising text, and discussing it with the advertising agents, which could take another three hours.

The heaviest indirect costs come with the time-consuming work of

1

sifting the applications, interviewing perhaps twelve promising candidates and second-interviewing at least three finalists. The secretarial
work in responding to possibly 200 applications – not an exaggerated
number in personnel experience for a position of this salary level and
status – can easily take 50 hours, even though the great majority will go
straight into the bin. Including final negotiations to the point of signing
on the dotted line, at least 100 man-and woman-hours will have been
spent on tracking down this Deputy Chief Executive. At a blanket rate of
£80 per hour, covering executive and secretarial time, indirect costs
would reach £8000, so that the total bill for the recruitment would be
£18 000.

Of course, not all companies handling their own senior recruiting
spend money on advertising, but it is impossible either to quantify the
costs of personal contacts made on the old-boy network, or evaluate
their effectiveness. Neither is necessary in the case of a company with a
well-developed succession hierarchy, but even the most careful
successor-grooming can come unstuck, and few businesses have
enough talent instantly available to provide new managements for
companies they have just taken over. It would hardly be economic for
them to do so.

By comparison, how much would an executive search consultant
charge, and what would the Chief Executive (or, in this case, Commissioner) within this particular branch of the civil service get for his or her
money?

In the first instance, after meeting the consultant a detailed brief was
drawn up summarising the assignment. This was more than a job
specification: besides outlining the primary areas of responsibility of the
position, the headhunter attempted to analyse the significance of the
appointment and presented a profile of the ideal candidate. To establish
his own credentials, the consultant then outlined his firm's experience
and track record in this particular area of business, with names of other
clients for whom they had successfully completed assignments, in an
attempt to convince the Board that they could do the job. The consultant
then requested further meetings with the client's executives to develop a
plan for the whole search programme.

So, from the beginning, the client employing the headhunter should
receive detailed confirmation of exactly what is needed and how the
consultant will approach the search. From both points of view, it is vital
from the outset that every aspect of the position to be filled is understood.

The standard fee charged by the particular search firm in this case was
slightly less than the costs incurred by the organisation doing the
recruiting itself: £17 500 compared with £18 000. This would be the
minimum charged by a leading executive search firm: few would go

below it. Many search firms do not charge fees based on the final remuneration figure agreed with the successful candidate as it might be felt that this would compromise objectivity in the final, delicate stages of negotiation, which inevitably includes discussion of the salary package. Many search firms prefer to base fees upon time and difficulty of the assignment. Many will undertake an individual arrangement which best suits the client. But the majority charge a standard fee of 35% of the agreed notional gross remuneration of the candidate appointed, which sometimes includes a proportion of a joining bonus or 'Golden Hello' package.

In this case, the fee was charged in three stages. The first 30%, or £5250, was paid after the briefing and acceptance of the assignment, and after the submission of an outline plan and agreement over the job specification and search process. A further 45% – £7875 – was payable upon presentation of the report on the completed search programme, with evaluation on each of the four short-listed candidates produced for the client. The balance of £4375 was, in this case, paid on the appointment of the successful candidate, but this is not to imply that head-hunters work on a contingency basis. No major executive search firm in Britain will work on the basis that their fee is contingent on successful completion.

Overall, it does cost marginally more to employ a search consultant because, as mentioned above, there are several direct and indirect costs incurred in any case, such as medical fees and candidates' expenses, as well as some executive time in agreeing the brief and interviewing the short-listed candidates. Using the same cost structure, this could add another £1000 to the bill. Also, most headhunters charge extra for expenses incurred travelling to interview candidates and referees, and entertainment costs, which can reach 30% or more of the total fee. There has been much media interest in 'power breakfasts' and ritzy – or Ritzy – lunches and dinners, but the maximum budget for entertaining for the whole assignment quoted by the executive search firm in this particular case was a fairly modest £300. The headhunter also charged separately for courier, long-distance telephone, telex and air freight charges. The final bill, when the successful candidate started work, was £19 000.

Although it has been estimated by the leading search firms that 75% of executive appointments at the highest level involve the use of search consultants, many companies still opt out. The use of headhunters is not necessarily justified or excluded on the grounds of cost for a position at this high level and strategic importance, since the differences in such costs are, as we have seen, marginal and not the main issue at stake. Many companies pride themselves on the effectiveness of their in-house training and personnel functions, and prefer not to divulge corporate information to any third party, even if by handling the assignment themselves they are not necessarily assured of as precise a market coverage as possible of the likely candidates.

The cost-benefit analysis does not take account of any positive input above and beyond the scope of in-house methods that a headhunter might provide, through their market experience and objectivity. A good headhunter can help with background management consultancy advice on the organisation's whole structure, and the nature of the position the client seeks to fill; in this particular case, the Board admitted that the consultancy had helped to define their problems and objectives in a manner clearer than had been achieved before. A search consultant can also be employed to look at the existing team, to see if the best person for the job can be found on the inside, comparable with those available outside.

The headhunter can act as a confidential middleman, keeping the client's identity and details a secret from candidates and referees alike until the appropriate agreed moment, and only then home in on carefully selected candidates. The company using advertising, on the other hand, must sit back and wait for the replies to the advertisements to come in. Executive search consultants, with some justification, regard their methods as proactive rather than reactive. Advertising inevitably fails to catch many ideal candidates who are not actively looking for a new appointment and do not read newspaper appointments columns. On the other hand, it tends to bring in a vast and random trawl of many small fry, with relatively few big fish of the right species. To use a different metaphor, ideally the search consultants are firing precise, accurate shots, rather than using scatter-gun techniques. Of course, the precision of their searching depends on the quality and detail of their research, which can vary enormously.

To a greater or lesser extent, headhunters can try to persuade a potential candidate to move, or at least describe the position on offer in a more informed manner, thereby making it seem more attractive than any newspaper advertisement could. Perhaps most significantly, and this is one of the strongest arguments for using search as far as many chief executives are concerned, the search firm guarantees to complete the assignment in hand. This often takes the form of reinstating the assignment for expenses only if the candidate leaves in six months, and/ or continuing the search beyond a specific time scale on the same basis. Few top professional headhunters would agree to a brief if they were not convinced that they were sufficiently experienced and had the resources to complete the task satisfactorily. They are, or should be, conscious that their professional reputation depends on fulfilling their promises, as many clients – quite justifiably – tend to see consultants as being only as good as their last assignment.

In the particular case study discussed above, the plan and search strategy was submitted within two weeks of the original briefing. It was quickly agreed with the selection committee, and a short list of four candidates was presented less than two months later. An interview programme, with candidates, the consultant and the commissioner, was in full swing in the following two weeks and the successful candidate signed contracts less than three months from the date of the first communication between the client and the headhunter.

Employers doing their own recruiting are dependent on replies to advertisements, and cannot avoid the mammoth task of examining scores of totally unsuitable applications before meeting any suitable candidates. The alternative, the old-boy network, although perhaps not producing such a plethora of possibles, is even less certain of finding the ideal candidate, as in these random circumstances it is never known when a likely person might crop up.

Whatever is spent on alternative recruitment methods and whoever is produced as a result, there is no guarantee that the chief executive concerned, who probably has little experience of interviewing, will pick the best person or, much worse, avoid choosing someone completely inappropriate and even disastrous. Of course, there is always a strong possibility that no one remotely suitable will emerge from advertising or other in-house methods at all. It is always possible that the ideal person for the job just does not exist, but at least by employing a professional search consultant – at comparatively little extra cost – most avenues will utimately have been explored.

In the USA today, it is seen as positively unprofessional, even slightly suspect, not to use search consultants when a senior recruitment problem arises. American Board directors have no desire to leave themselves open to accusations that they are favouring their own candidate as a future ally against the others. However, this goes beyond the economics of search into the politics of search.

1

The Emergence and Growth of the Headhunting Business

THE ORIGINS OF HEADHUNTING IN THE USA

Since the Second World War, executive search in the US has developed from a small cottage industry into a $ multimillion, multinational business which has deeply penetrated American corporate life. During that time, as in the case of many other trappings of modern America, it has crossed the Atlantic and subsequently emerged in Britain. But the reasons for the origins and growth of headhunting in the USA are significantly different from those which explain the establishment and continued development of the search industry in Britain. American search is examined here as an introduction to the arrival of this phenomenon in Britain; this analysis owes much to research published by John Byrne in *The Headhunters*.

Headhunting in the USA is a product of the post-war boom. A sudden and unprecedented demand for a large number of new executives to accommodate and take full advantage of this growth coincided with a need for technical experts at management level to develop further the new products and technologies stimulated by the demands of war. At the same time, military service had taken its toll in many American Boardrooms: inevitably, far fewer returned than had originally joined up, their ranks thinned by death on active service, by the desire to stay on in uniform and by retirement.

The great demand for executive talent brought about by the wealth of opportunities created under the post-war Pax Americana soon exhausted the supply. This was experienced by the largest and most outstanding US corporations, all manner of industries grouped together as 'smokestack America', and by the powerful banks and finance houses. All had prided themselves on training and nurturing their own people, and all boasted many employees who had notched up decades of faithful service. Now, for the first time, they found they needed large numbers of new people, with new skills, and they needed them quickly. There was no time to hand pick and develop enough trainees, and the only solution was to capture them from other firms. This immediate post-war shortage ushered in what may be identified as the first phase of the emergence of headhunting.

This emphasis on the demand by companies for executives, as

opposed to a demand from would-be executives for jobs, marked a crucial turning point in the origins of the executive search business. Before the war, the most common intermediary between a potential employee and an employer was the employment agency. The first real headhunting firms – in the first phase of headhunting – insisted that they were working for the company, not the candidate, and the company was paying the bill. The early history of headhunting in the USA, in terms of the individual companies, is discussed in greater detail in John Byrne's *The Headhunters*.

THE FIRST HEADHUNTERS

The first firms, such as Boyden and Handy, who emerged to accommodate this demand did not appear overnight. Their roots lay in another relatively new corporate phenomenon, that of management consultancy, which was gaining credence at the same time. Booz, Allen & Hamilton and McKinsey & Co. dominated this business, which sought to find guidelines for company regeneration and solutions for management problems. Their suggestions often begged the question as to who would actually implement the necessary corporate revolutions which they recommended.

This led to the second phase of the emergence of headhunting, in which management consultants, and with them accountancy firms, developed their own in-house headhunting functions. Boyden and Handy arrived on the scene just as this was beginning to happen. Jack Handy had been with McKinsey in the 1930s before setting up his own management consultancy and 'executive recruitment' business as early as 1944. Handy had left McKinsey over the issue of the status of the executive search function within the organisation. He complained that recruitment was being carried out under the banner of a management consultancy service without being accounted for or charged for separately. Handy, an ex-stockbroker with a respectable, almost aristocratic, background and connections, did much to establish the credibility of executive search as a valuable business tool in its own right. But he established another less welcome precedent which became common in headhunting firms in the future: he took a professional, workmanlike and effective attitude towards solving the corporate problems of others, but at the same time failed to keep his own house in order. For this reason, Handy was forced to sell out in the late 1960s.

Sydney Boyden, after seventeen years with mail-order giant Montgomery Ward, had joined Booz, Allen & Hamilton's executive recruitment division, rising to become its manager by 1941. A powerful, outgoing character, he felt cramped in a large organisation, and had much greater confidence than his employers in the future of headhunting. The formation of his firm in 1946, like Handy's two years before, showed a shrewd sense of timing.

Both firms had been influenced to a certain extent by an even earlier headhunting business, started by one Thorndike Deland in 1926, which proved to be considerably ahead of its time. Deland, a dapper and sophisticated character whose varied career included a stint as a part-time magician, came to executive search through working for an upmarket recruiting agency. From 1920 he ran an 'executive placement bureau' for the Retail Research Association, a trade group of retailers, placing over a thousand managers and executives within the buying and merchandising sector. Setting up on his own six years later to provide a service for companies recruiting people in this field, he charged a $200 non-returnable retainer, which was subsequently deducted from his commission: 5% of the successful candidate's first year's salary. Deland evangelically promoted his firm and its concept to a public not quite ready for it, but his moment came when war broke out and he was summoned by the US War Department to help recruit executives for the Army Service Forces. Deland's business survives to this day but, then, as now, it concentrates on lower-level search rather than on chief executives and Board directors.

Boyden and Handy were more successful than Deland in spreading the idea of headhunting among the higher reaches of corporate America; but it was never easy to convince clients of the independent and unique value of their work. Running his business from his own apartment in Bronxville, New York, Boyden – despite his preference for receiving fees on a retainer basis – was forced to operate on the contingency principle, whereby his fees were contingent on the success of the search. Thus he found himself working within the grey area between employment agencies and headhunters. That many of his clients saw him in the former category is suggested by the fact that they frequently passed to him details of their restless and unsuitable executives in the hope that he would redeploy them.

THE ORIGINS OF THE BIG FOUR

The third phase of the emergence of headhunting in the USA was marked by the formation of the Big Four headhunting firms, the search industry's equivalents of the Seven Sisters of the oil world and the Big Eight of the accountancy profession: they are Heidrick and Struggles, Spencer Stuart, Russell Reynolds and Korn/Ferry. Fundamental to the development of headhunting was the general acceptance of the payment of fees on a retainer basis, so that employing a search consultant was rendered comparable with that of engaging accountants, solicitors, or any other outside professional advisers. This requirement was formalised in the official policy of the Association of Executive Recruitment Consultants, headhunting's first professional body, formed in 1959.

The Big Four emerged from the second phase of headhunting: they developed from the search departments of the major management consultancies and accountancy firms. Heidrick and Struggles, formed in 1953, originated, like Boyden, from Booz, Allen & Hamilton, as did Spencer Stuart three years later. Korn/Ferry, set up in 1969, came from Peat Marwick Mitchell; Russell Reynolds was the exception with a banking background. Several other firms emerged at the same time and by the same process, such as Lamalie Associates in 1967 from Booz, Allen & Hamilton, and Ward Howell and Canny Bowen, in 1951 and 1954 respectively, from McKinsey.

The fourth phase of the development of headhunting may be identified as the splintering of individual consultants from existing firms, to set up on their own, such as Haley from Ward Howell and Egon Zehnder from Spencer Stuart, both in 1964. This fourth phase, which reflects a desire for equity and a fairer distribution of the proceeds on the part of consultants *vis-à-vis* the founders and managing partners, also occurred – and still occurs – in Britain.

THE EARLY GROWTH OF THE BIG FOUR

The development of fully-fledged headhunting firms owes much to a growing conflict of interest between different sectors of their business experienced by the management consultants and accountants who operated headhunting departments. Booz, Allen & Hamilton was forced to close down its executive search division in 1980, when serious problems surfaced as a result of trying to carry on a recruiting business whilst at the same time having 3000 management consultancy clients on their books, who were more or less off-limits from the point of view of providing candidates for headhunting. McKinsey and Price Waterhouse also left the search industry, with only Peat's – of all the firms identified as forming the second phase of the history of headhunting – remaining in the business. Their role in executive search is no longer of much significance, with only 5% of their headhunting clients ranking within the *Fortune* 500 companies. David Smith, one of Korn/Ferry's top New York consultants, left Peat's in 1979 on this very issue. Accused of a conflict of interest between its headhunting business and other functions, Peat's were subjected to investigation by the American governing body for accountants, with the result that they decided to turn down headhunting work for their existing accounting clients. Smith, who had managed much of Peat's search activities, found his volume of business reduced to a fraction overnight.

Another powerful factor behind the early success of the Big Four – and the mushrooming of nearly a thousand individual headhunting firms in the USA alone by the mid-1970s – was the scarcity of managerial talent due, quite simply, to the low birth rate in America during the Depression. By the mid-1970s, managers and executives in the late 30s to late 40s age group were thin on the ground.

Third, the personnel function within many companies was becoming more complex, with recruiting seen as increasingly time-consuming. Problems were encountered when personnel officials – generally lacking in senior and especially Board status – were being asked to advertise for, interview, help select and then appoint executives to positions considerably higher than those they held themselves. These officials also soon discovered that direct approaches to rival firms for executives could be embarrassing, especially when they were turned down. Such experiences clearly demonstrated the need for search consultants, and not surprisingly many new headhunting firms emerged and existing businesses flourished in this atmosphere. Simultaneously, Boardrooms across the USA began to accept that it was not always possible or desirable to rely entirely upon home-grown talent, and that managers and executives could be interchangeable between apparently quite different types of business. A similar sea change in corporate thinking was to take place, much later, in Britain.

Fourth, American government regulations protecting the privacy of the individual became significantly more stringent in the late 1960s and early 1970s. A candidate could refuse to answer certain personal questions posed directly by a potential employer, a problem partially overcome by employing a search consultant as an intermediary.

A fifth factor favouring an increase in business for search firms was the spread of American multinationals overseas. Not only has this phenomenon led to a concomitant spread of branches of the major search firms overseas to the major world capitals – which will be discussed at greater length in Chapter 6 – but also the pressure on multinationals to employ local executives has caused a world-wide reverse diaspora. Increasingly, American expatriates are finding themselves returning home and, as part of the same process, many US executives have found opportunities with European and other foreign firms based in the USA who also favour the employment of nationals.

Between 1967 and 1977 the number of American executive appointments in which headhunters played a part quadrupled from 4000 to

16 000 per year. Over a quarter of these were handled by the Big Four, who dominated the top end of the market, being responsible for over 50% of searches for the $100 000 + positions. Since then, the number has continued to increase, with the Big Four consolidating their lead in top-level recruiting.

THE FIRST MODERN HEADHUNTING ASSIGNMENT

Ironically in view of their later slip down the headhunting league table, the firm of Boyden was responsible for one of the first major searches, a landmark in the history of executive search and a vital precursor of the work of the Big Four. The theory that success breeds success is particularly appropriate to the rise of headhunting: the early searches played a crucial part in promoting the concept of executive search as a necessary tool of modern business, acceptable in even the most conservative American Boardrooms.

This historic search of 1959 was an assignment to find a Chief Executive for ITT, the powerful but then rather dormant telephone equipment corporation, which had been run by a dynasty of ex-service leaders. The incumbent ex-military man, General Edmund Leavey, who had succeeded founder Colonel Sosthenes Behn on his death in 1957, did not welcome the arrival of the headhunters. He did not relish the prospect of his impending retirement two years hence, and refused to consider any of the candidates whom Boyden put forward. Boyden was considerably surprised when, instead of losing the assignment, he discovered that the determined ITT Board had dismissed Leavey and the search was still very much on. As many search consultants were to become after him, Boyden had been the instrument by which a group of directors had removed an unwanted leader.

This search also marked the payment of large headhunting fees for the first time. Boyden received $25 000, equal to 20% of his successful candidate's starting salary. He had originally charged only 10% back in 1946, at a time when he was principally concerned with much lower-level searches, and had frequently experienced total losses when he had been unable to complete an assignment satisfactorily.

The ITT job of 1959 was also the first instance in which headhunting was shown for all to see as directly proving its value. This point is emphasised by John Byrne in *The Headhunters*, who described how the carefully-chosen new chief executive, Harold Geneen, 'the General Patton of American Industry', effectively turned ITT around. By the time he retired in 1977, ITT's sales had reached a record $17bn with earnings of an unprecedented $562m.

HEIDRICK AND STRUGGLES

The first of the Big Four to be established was Heidrick and Struggles, in Chicago in 1953. They emerged as the early leaders of the still embryonic search industry, but were not to maintain this dominance for very long. Gardner Heidrick, like Sydney Boyden, originally came from Booz, Allen & Hamilton, having joined them in 1951; John Struggles, also like Boyden, had been Vice-President of the mail-order house Montgomery Ward. Heidrick took the initiative in persuading his more cautious partner to take the plunge and set up their own headhunting operation; he chose an opportune moment. In 1953, start-up costs were still low, and the partners were able to begin business on a capital of less than $25 000, from a tiny office, employing their wives as secretaries. Their initial growth was slow. Seven years passed before they opened their second office, in Los Angeles.

Heidrick and Struggles' business took off only with the advent of Gerry Roche, a fiercely ambitious, restless, workaholic whizz kid of the 1950s who had gained a night-school MBA taught by Peter Drucker. Discovered by Heidrick in the course of a search, he rose quickly from associate in 1964 to partner by 1968, in charge of the recently-opened New York office. By 1973, Roche was running Heidrick and Struggles' entire East Coast operation. His reputation as a superstar of search, as the king of Manhattan headhunters, grew rapidly, partly through effective self-promotion but mostly because of a series of prominent, high-level successful search assignments, in the course of which he placed more CEOs and presidents of top American companies than any other consultant. He showed immense energy in completing assignments and generating new business, and was especially successful at convincing clients of the wisdom of his choices and candidates of the importance of the opportunity on offer.

Working at the top end of the market as he did, Roche was taking on the most difficult assignments, but they were also the most remunerative and had the greatest publicity value. One of Roche's most famous clients was the mighty CBS, for whom he undertook four CEO searches in the nine years between 1971 and 1980.It is unusual for a major organisation to change its chief executive four times in less than a decade and the fact that they chose Roche each time – in a highly competitive market – is an impressive record in the headhunting world. His reputation, style and personal charm enabled him to recover from serious mismatches, such as the ill-advised moving from ITT to RCA of Maurice Valente, who lasted a mere six months in his new job. In the end, it is always the client who has to carry the can, and fortunately RCA backed up Roche by continuing to retain his services.

By 1978, thanks largely to Roche, Heidrick and Struggles were earning higher total fees than any other search firm; charging 33.3% of the successful candidates' remuneration, these reached $13.5m. They then seemed destined to suffer the same fate as Jack Handy's firm: a sharp decline due to financial extravagance and a lack of closely controlled management. Ironically Roche, who was so effective at creating business, appeared unable to manage it, and almost drove the firm to bankruptcy when he became its President. He was over-ambitious in his programme of opening new branches; he installed a new computer system costing $100 000 which many considered to be inferior to the previous manual system; and he imposed a rigid form of hands-on management without a fair distribution of equity.

Dissatisfaction, exacerbated by the non-payment of the usual bonuses, led to a mass exodus and mutiny. This eventuality was almost inevitable, given the independent, entrepreneurial spirit of Roche and many of the new consultants he appointed, who felt they were not receiving a fair share of the profits. One was heard to complain 'we were shipping the money to New York in boxcars and getting it back in tips'. Roche was forced to return to search work only and take the title of Chairman, to the relief of all, and not least himself.

The firm had been profoundly shaken: it had lost $½m. on its overseas branches, suffered a decline in profits of 80%, and had lost 25 consultants in thirteen months. Both the founders sold out, and over the last decade Heidrick and Struggles has undergone a long and painful reorganisation. Its recovery has been helped by the incentives provided by a fairer distribution of earnings, and Roche's old skill in winning prestigious assignments. His recruitment of John Sculley from Pepsi to Apple was a headhunting coup as historic as the ITT job of 1959. By 1983 Heidrick and Struggles' fee income had recovered to $20m., only marginally behind Russell Reynolds, Spencer Stuart and Egon Zehnder. By 1985 it had overtaken the latter, reaching $25m., and retained its position in 1986 with $30m. and in 1987 with $35m. In the 1987 figures published by *Fortune*, Heidrick and Struggles ranked fourth worldwide with $38.9m. and third in the USA with $27.8m. *Business Week*, in February 1989, also ranked them in fourth position, with 1988 revenues of $55m. earned from 1185 searches by 118 consultants.

SPENCER STUART

One of Heidrick and Struggles' early recruits to its ranks of consultants was one Spencer R. Stuart, yet another former employee of Booz, Allen & Hamilton. Stuart stayed only ten months before setting up on his own in 1956. The firm's pattern of growth, as in the case of Heidrick and Struggles, was very dependent on individual personalities, and also suffered from the fact that the most successful headhunters are usually the worst managers. Stuart was more committed to the establishment of an international network than his rivals, and in this was considerably more successful. By 1973, the overseas offices accounted for more than half of the fee income, but the firm found itself poorly represented in the USA with only two of its nine branches established there. Some of its expansion plans backfired, including a subsidiary set up to recruit minorities – women and non-Americans – which was perhaps too far ahead of its time; it folded after four years, having made heavy losses. These were to some extent offset by the firm's success in pre-empting new markets. For example, Spencer Stuart's Australian office opened in 1970 with virtually no competition and is now, with Egon Zehnder, dominant in the local search market.

In the early 1970s, Spencer Stuart himself considered selling out to a general consulting business. A group of senior Spencer Stuart consultants raised with him the possibility of a sale to the consulting staff instead. In 1973 a deal was concluded: although 'Spence' left, the firm could continue to use his name and the ownership of the business would be widely spread amongst all the existing consultants worldwide. Peter Brooke (who had opened the London office) became Chairman and Jean Michel Beigbeder (then manager of the Paris office) became Chief Executive. From this point on, Spencer Stuart became a genuinely international firm owned by its own consultants (none of whom may hold more than 2% of the stock) and managed by a Chairman and a Chief Executive, each of whom is elected to the position for a defined period.

Spencer Stuart is the only firm which has, so far, achieved the full transition to a structure where control of the business and the appointment of its management is genuinely in the hands of its consultants. This has been a major factor in the stability which Spencer Stuart has achieved in its offices. Beigbeder was elected Chairman in succession to Brooke in 1979 and Thomas Neff, then manager of the New York office, became Chief Executive.

Neff built up the firm's business in the USA not by dint of one overwhelming individual personality, as Roche had done for Heidrick and Struggles, but by exemplifying the success of the Spencer Stuart method of problem-solving in management crises across a range of corporate sectors. Neff's approach was to produce corporate performance charts of his firm's most successful clients, indicating that their fortunes had been turned around by the strategic recruitment of executives headhunted for them by Spencer Stuart. This, and the extensive publicity which Roche attracted to his most celebrated assignments, is in great contrast to the nature of the executive search industry in Britain, where the majority of clients are most reluctant to be publicly associated with named headhunting firms. Yet advertising their track record in detail worked for Spencer Stuart, especially in one particularly significant shoot-out in which they beat four other firms competing to win the assignment to find a chief executive for the American Council of Life Insurance. Neff's presentation, videoed for posterity and for future Spencer Stuart trainees, enabled his firm to break into the insurance sector. It was especially important for Spencer Stuart to enter a new field because they were already facing the problem of blockage (too many clients in one sector and insufficient companies left in which to search).

Spencer Stuart have never suffered the violent fluctuations in fortune experienced by Heidrick and Struggles, and have maintained a pattern of steady – if unexciting and generally unpublicised – growth and expansion. Total fee income doubled between 1977 and 1983, and Spencer Stuart firmly established its position as third of the Big Four by 1985, with $33m. maintained in 1986 with $43m. and in 1987 with $56m. Figures published by *Fortune*, for the calendar year 1987, show Spencer Stuart's recruiting fees worldwide as over $56m.; they are marginally behind Heidrick and Struggles in the USA with $26.2m. *Business Week* ranked Spencer Stuart in third place for 1988 with revenues of $81.7m. based on 1800 assignments carried out by 137 consultants.

RUSSELL REYNOLDS

Both Russell Reynolds and Korn/Ferry were founded in 1969, and now dominate the top end of the global search business. From a slow start, Russell Reynolds emerged as a strong second to Korn/Ferry in terms of fees generated worldwide. If Heidrick and Struggles may be identified as the most individualistic and entrepreneurial search firm, Spencer Stuart as the most discreet and quietly professional – in this sense closely related to Egon Zehnder – and Korn/Ferry as the most aggressive, then Russell Reynolds may be seen as the most elite, preppie and, according to Byrne, even arrogant, of headhunting firms.

Indeed, this is precisely what Russell Reynolds himself set out to achieve in modelling his business on top service organisations like Morgan Guaranty – where he had worked before entering search – and Morgan Stanley and McKinsey. The firm has generally attracted Ivy League types, Reynolds having originally set up with $130 000 contributed partly by himself and partly by old Yale friends. Known for its blue-blooded, polished, privileged, yuppie snobbery, the carefully-cultivated image of being the best has been generally convincing. However, although Reynolds' headhunting PR is effective enough in the USA, it could be argued that the firm has not achieved quite the same level of consistent quality as Spencer Stuart in all its overseas branches.

Reynolds – a particularly single-minded, determined entrepreneur – quickly gained a reputation for headhunting in the financial services sector, gaining large fees on large salaries. He always charged the full 33.3% fee, however enormous the successful candidate's remuneration – a policy shared by Gerry Roche – to the extent that Byrne quoted an observer as saying 'he has never been known to leave a nickel on the table'.

Unlike the founders of the older firms, Reynolds did not come from a management consultancy background; after his early financial services work, he spent three years with William H. Clark, a headhunter from the Price Waterhouse fold. He introduced the taping of telephone calls – then seen as unprofessional, now absolutely the reverse of this – and brought in so much business that he bluntly asked Clark for the presidency of the firm. Clark refused, thinking that Reynolds' increase in salary from $22 500 to $75 000 over three years was sufficient to mark his contribution.

Specialising in the financial sector has given Russell Reynolds class and style, and provided them with prestigious contacts reminiscent of the British old-boy network, but has also been the cause of its major problems. Their Rolls Royce image was dented for a while by accusations of unethical behaviour in raiding from clients, but was restored once the business had expanded into other sectors and gained a name as a generalist.

Reynolds' strategy for developing and maintaining his prized elitist image was an obsessive attention to detail, high standards and team spirit; but his practice of circulating all the office paperwork as a system of mutual quality-control, combined with Roche-style hands-on management on occasion, occasionally backfired and some consultants left. The awarding of cash credits to consultants helping their colleagues on searches was one effective way in which Reynolds could imbue his firm with team spirit. He also developed the concept of 'assists', whereby detailed records were kept of all international and interbranch assignments, showing which consultant was responsible for which aspect of the search; those 'mentioned in dispatches' in this way received due credit.

Russell Reynolds suffered another knock with the arrival of Windle Priem at Korn/Ferry, who effectively took much of the firm's vital financial services business in New York in the late 1970s; but they recovered as a result of the build-up of their overseas branches, and several successful big name searches. A particularly controversial assignment, which added a new dimension to headhunting and was a foretaste of things to come, was the recruitment of Thomas Barrow from Exxon to Kennecott in 1978. Barrow was a White Knight – headhunted to fight off a corporate raider – for whom Kennecott had to pay over

$1m. in order to match a clause in Barrow's contract with Exxon which allowed him bonuses in line with the rising price of the company's stock. Russell Reynolds were to take on a not dissimilar problem when their London office headhunted Ian McGregor for British Steel in 1980.

Hobson Brown, in Russell Reynolds' New York office, maintains that his firm, more effectively than the other headhunters, has attracted the first real career-search consultants, graduates from business schools who have deliberately chosen to make a career in executive search; it was always the goal of Reynolds himself to build up a business as prestigious and high-powered as Morgan Guaranty, in which an ambitious graduate would seek to work right through to retirement. Reynolds wanted new consultants from business schools and commerce or industry, not from other headhunting firms.

Russell Reynolds' predominance in headhunting in Britain, and its spectacular increase in business with the Big Bang, has contributed to its continuing growth of fee income. By 1983, with world fees totalling $22m., it was battling equally for second place behind Korn/Ferry. This position was assured by 1985, when Russell Reynolds earned $37.5m. to Korn/Ferry's $50m., and confirmed a year later when the total world earnings were $45m. and $60m. respectively. Worldwide recruiting fees reached $67.7m. by the end of 1987, with $44m. in the USA, according to *Fortune*. Revenues rose to $91m. for 1988 (*Business Week* figures), with 181 consultants handling 2000 searches.

KORN/FERRY

If Russell Reynolds' position in world headhunting has become assured by its reputation for quality and its elite image, Korn/Ferry's premier standing is maintained by dint of sheer hard work, aggressive marketing and the building of a large volume of business. Korn/Ferry perhaps appeals more to aggressive, fast-growth conglomerates than to old-fashioned, traditional companies. It has, overall, captured less big-name, big-salary work than Russell Reynolds, but it has become well known for the efficient and speedy handling of a wide range of assignments within its pioneering structure of speciality divisions. The Korn/Ferry name is most widely known and publicly quoted of all search firms – Lester Korn is seen as the man who brought headhunting out into the open – and thus the firm can guarantee almost instant interest from potential candidates. It is famous for its tremendous resources and ability to get the job done, but other firms suggest that it has a less than enviable success rate.

Korn/Ferry is still majority-owned by the founders, two former Peat Marwick Mitchell partners, Lester Korn and Dick Ferry, who hold 27.5%

of the equity each. Korn became the front-man of the organisation whilst Ferry was in charge of the back room; both were previously involved in Peat Marwick Mitchell's headhunting branch. Korn may be seen as in considerable contrast to Reynolds; he was no Ivy Leaguer, and learnt the principles of economics and entrepreneurship in his parent's grocery store. He developed the classic personality of the tycoon: huge ambition combined with enormous charm and total ruthlessness. His apprenticeship was in the Big League, as a trouble-shooting whizz-kid at the Bank of America, and he then became Peat Marwick Mitchell's youngest-ever partner in 1961, aged only 30. Korn met Ferry when the former was directing Peat Marwick Mitchell's West Coast headhunting division; Ferry had arrived from Haskins & Sells and the Financial Corporation of Arizona. By the late 1960s, Peat Marwick Mitchell's headhunting division was earning $2m. annually with 20 consultants, an impressive performance considering the much lower salaries paid at that time; but it clashed with their accountancy clients, and the top management did not care much for Korn's apparently pushy style.

When the two partners first set up on their own – according to Byrne, with only $5000 capital and giving up a secure future – they did so under the guise of an employment agency, so that they would not appear to be in direct competition with their ex-employers. But this was merely a cover, and the partners began in search from the start, subsequently headhunting many of their ex-colleagues, despite Peat Marwick Mitchell's threats of legal action. But they, with other accountants, were soon to leave the search business – which they found '10% income 90% headache' – and the field on the West Coast was left wide open for Korn/Ferry, whose only competitors were Heidrick and Struggles in Los Angeles. Korn/Ferry's strategy was to maximise their profit margins by handling all aspects of the work, and they were fortunate to gain such prestigious clients as Rockwell and Norton Simon in their early days; but the concept of headhunting was less well-established on the West Coast than in Manhattan and the partners, fighting for all the fees they could earn, were forced to undertake contingency work to help build up their volume. Yet, more so than the other major search firms at this time, Korn/Ferry was established as a structured business, with six levels of professionals, offering formalised career development to new consultants.

Within three years their efforts paid off. In the period November 1969 to April 1970, Korn/Ferry had made profits of $56 000 on a fee income of $281 200; by 1973, when the firm employed a staff of 42, they were earning profits of $431 200 on total revenues of $3.5m. These figures were revealed when Korn/Ferry decided to go public and sell 25% of their equity to outsiders; but when the stock price fell soon after, they took fright and bought their shares back.

Once Korn/Ferry's annual fee income – growing at an annual rate of 30% – had overtaken that of Heidrick and Struggles by 1978 and Boyden by 1979, they sought overseas expansion. This was initially achieved by taking over existing firms, such as G. K. Dickinson in London and Guy Pease in Sydney, and there was much speculation about a possible merger with Egon Zehnder, which came to nothing.

With success inevitably came enemies, and Korn/Ferry, disliked by its competitors and seen as interested only in quantity, not quality, was banned from the headhunters' club, the Association of Executive Recruitment Consultants. In an attempt to offset these attacks on its image, the firm employed top PR consultants to supply prestige media coverage, published a three-monthly *National Index of Executive Vacancies* and sponsored Yale and UCLA business schools.

In a business dominated by personalities, Korn/Ferry benefited considerably by the arrival of Windle Priem in New York in 1976, who fought and unseated Russell Reynolds' consultants as the leaders of headhunting on Wall Street. But Korn/Ferry have not developed the teamwork approach that has become a hallmark of Russell Reynolds. Why does Priem – who dominates his firm's East Coast financial sector – stay with Korn/Ferry? If anyone had the individual headhunting kudos to survive as a one-man band it would be Priem or, of course, Roche. He stays – he says – mainly for the access to the resource base, and he no doubt receives a generous salary and has future payments and bonuses guaranteed.

Korn/Ferry, whose world fee income achieved a fivefold increase between 1977 and 1986, and is confidently expected to pass the $100m. mark by the 1990s, is sometimes criticised in the USA for being dominated by the central management, for its 'big factory' image where the seniors do the selling and the juniors do the work, and it has also suffered much at the pen of headhunting newshound Jim Kennedy, who produces *Executive Recruiter News*. Yet with its impressive lead in fee income over other firms worldwide, such criticism must inevitably contain an element of sour grapes. Its growth can only continue with the now almost entirely entrenched position that headhunting has achieved in American corporate life. As Lester Korn – never at a loss for a quote – told *Fortune*, 'Business has become too complicated, and the stakes have become too high, for a board chairman who needs executive talent to rely on his friends or his friends' recommendations. He wants the best man available, not the best man visible.' The firm's stand has been borne out by the earnings figures published by *Fortune*: for the calendar year 1987, Korn/Ferry's recruiting fees reached $64.6m. worldwide, of which $45.2m. was generated in the USA. The 1988 figures confirm Korn/Ferry's leading position with $91.5m.; although now facing strong competition from Russell Reynolds, they have far more consultants

(258). The fact that they carried out substantially more searches (2350) for very similar revenues suggests a lower level of work than their rivals.

THE EMERGENCE OF HEADHUNTING IN BRITAIN

The executive search industry in Britain has come of age. Although it has not yet achieved an acceptability on a par with headhunting in America, it has now established a recognised niche in British business, and is thrusting deeper into the corporate jungle. But, despite the fact that headhunting originated in the USA, and that the Big Four have gained a strong presence in the British search market, the headhunting business in Britain has evolved not by aping the American fashion but in its own way, with its own style, priorities, emphasis and approach. It is now a very different business from its transatlantic equivalent, and arguably always has been.

In what way was the economic environment which fostered search in Britain different from the preconditions of headhunting in the USA? What role did the Big Four play in the beginnings of headhunting in Britain, compared with home-grown firms?

The origins of the search business in Britain may be explained by a combination of long-term and short-term factors. In the long term, there has been a gradual but clearly identifiable change in the attitude of British business since the Second World War, which may be summed up in a single word: management. In the short term, acting as a catalyst, there was the creation of a specific demand for executive search skills by a number of enterprising and determined individuals, working both at the behest of the Big Four and on their own personal initiative.

There are parallels here with the beginnings of search in the USA, but in Britain the concept of headhunting, as indeed with other features of modern business practice, was pushed, not pulled. It did not spontaneously emerge with the need to solve specific management problems; those management problems had first of all to be defined and identified. In Britain, there had to be the recognition that a problem existed long before that problem could be effectively tackled; American businessmen had already reached this point and had gone beyond it.

Headhunting in Britain was imposed – seeming alien at first – in the search for remedies for Britain's national corporate ills; in America it had burgeoned at a time of growth and prosperity. Search in Britain has achieved maturity during the turnaround in economic conditions of the 1980s – as discussed in the following chapter – but it began in entirely different circumstances.

THE DEMAND FOR HEADHUNTING: THE LONG-TERM PERSPECTIVE

So, what were the long-term preconditions for headhunting in Britain? The most crucial were the appreciation and acceptance of, first, the significant role of management in the economy and society and, second, the belief that individual skill in business and management could be nurtured by appropriate training and was thus transferable.

These developments in British economic thinking are shown by the publication of two remarkable business texts, which were widely read and discussed in the early 1960s. First, appearing under the title *Management's Mission in a New Society*, were 20 provocative papers, originally written in celebration of the first 50 years of the Harvard Business School. The opening chapter and most pace-setting of these contributions was by the only Englishman featured in the book, Arnold Toynbee. He examined the problems of 'How Did We Get This Way – And Where Are We Going?', arguing that since the last war Britain especially has presented management with a host of entirely new problems.

Second, an equally influential management text of this period was international businessman Roger Falk's *The Business of Management*. He quoted a remark frequently heard 20 years before, in Britain in the 1930s and 1940s, that 'You can't train managers! They're born, not made.' 'The provision of the men who were eventually to take over responsibility for the management of an enterprise was regarded as a matter of making sure that enough young men entered business at the foot of the ladder,' wrote Falk of the old days. 'When the need arose, those who became managers were the people who had best survived the struggle up the rungs to the top. Character was the main help up the ladder and character was the main qualification for management.' Significantly, Falk then wrote, 'And yet today the training of managers is one of the liveliest topics of discussion.'

The recognition of management techniques underlay a new trend of employing external consultants: a parallel in government, closely related to industry, was the advent of Lord Beeching in British Rail. Once the plunge had been taken to call upon outside expertise for a temporary and specific problem, employing outside expertise on a regular basis was not such a great mental jump. The recognition that managers needed training in order to acquire the necessary skills to manage effectively implicitly accepted that such skills could be moved around and injected into businesses when required. This explains why British industry, which had never conceived of employing professional consultants to recruit and select executives and managers, came to terms psychologically with the idea of using headhunters.

The professionalisation of management in the late 1950s and early 1960s coincided with other economic trends, which may be seen as providing fertile ground for the seeds of the search industry. British companies were, generally speaking, increasing in size through mergers and consolidation, so the stakes were that much higher and they could not afford to get things wrong; they needed new management teams to run taken-over businesses; industrial plants were growing in scale; finance was becoming more complex; business was tending to be more and more international; American operations were penetrating many European markets; and Britain was facing a host of unprecedented economic pressures and new competition with the post-war recovery of Germany and Japan. British industry suffered a major crisis and needed to reorganise and rationalise at all levels. The long-term prerequisites for headhunting were, in the case of Britain, negative rather than positive.

THE DEMAND FOR HEADHUNTING: THE SHORT-TERM VIEW

In the short term, the development of the British executive search industry owes much to a mixture of both demand and supply factors. Arguably, the growth of headhunting in Britain stemmed from the success of the sales and publicity efforts of individual headhunters themselves, operating in newly responsive market conditions where a need for change had already been recognised. There entrepreneurs identified the existence of a seller's market just waiting to be developed, and created their own demand, which gathered its own momentum and benefited from a snowball effect. At the same time, technological changes were encouraging increased scale, pressures and stakes. But, at the end of the day, selling companies to people and people to companies requires an ability to sell oneself too. Promotion is the name of the game in headhunting in more ways than one.

Much of this form of headhunting impetus obviously came from the USA after the opening of branches in London by the Big Four. They were eager to capitalise on the partial Americanisation of British business and the acceptance in many quarters of American management approaches and techniques; they also closely followed and matched the globalisation strategy of their major multinational clients.

Yet British search firms played an equally, if not more, important role in the emergence of the headhunting business in this country in the 1950s, 1960s, 1970s and 1980s. These firms had either splintered off from American companies – as in the case of Norman Broadbent – or they had been set up on their own from scratch, in a variety of forms such as MSL, EAL, Tyzack, Alexander Hughes, Goddard Kay Rogers, John Stork, Merton and Whitehead Mann, to name but a few. How did the individuals behind these businesses manage to promote their services so effectively? How many more fell by the wayside in the process?

THE INTERNATIONAL HEADHUNTERS COME TO BRITAIN

Spencer Stuart

Spencer Stuart was the first of the American headhunting giants to open a branch in London, in 1960–1. Peter Brooke, who left the firm to enter politics in 1979 and became Chairman of the Conservative Party, set up the firm's British base in prestigious but not overtly showy offices in Park Lane. Followed by John Broadbent Jones, Christopher Wysock Wright, Kit Power, Tim Scriven and David Kimbell, Spencer Stuart have discreetly and subtly developed a sound reputation without seeking wide publicity, enjoying many very senior assignments and a high level of repeat business. The firm is well known for its painstaking re-search, which may mean that assignments are completed less quickly than by rival headhunters, but they are certainly carried out more thoroughly. Spencer Stuart's success rate – proportion of assignments successfully completed to the client's satisfaction within the specified time – has been independently estimated at 80%, much higher than many rival firms.

Unlike most of its competitors, the firm has tended to inspire loyalty on the part of its consultants – who, since Stuart sold out in the 1970s, may enjoy a share in the equity – and has achieved a remarkable stability of gradually improved performance, still at a rate of 35% per year. One drawback of Spencer Stuart's long-established position in London and its low turnover of consultants – otherwise seen as great advantages – is the inevitable ageing of its directors and the problem of regeneration. The average age of Spencer Stuart directors is older than that of other Big Four consultants, but is being lowered by new recruits.

The firm and its individual consultants have not unduly specialised in any one sector, and have made inroads into the new headhunting fields of working for non-profit-making organisations and the recruitment of non-executive directors. By 1980 the firm already had eleven consultants in the UK in addition to its directors, and this has since increased to twelve. Spencer Stuart has been variously estimated as holding a market ranking of fourth position, with its annual fee income now exceeding £4m. Like Egon Zehnder, fees are charged on the basis of time and difficulty of each assignment, and not on the successful candidate's salary; a minimum fee of £20 000 is quoted. Despite its unhurried style and careful attention to detail, the firm achieved 170 placements with eleven consultants in 1979; now, with thirteen consultants, the firm annually completes far more, but is not necessarily seeking to maximise its volume, and certainly not at the expense of quality of service.

Spencer Stuart's business in London and Manchester owes much of its success to its Britishness, to the fact that its consultants are at home in even the most conservative Boardrooms; the firm works in direct contrast to the style apparently adopted by Korn/Ferry, for instance. Thus Spencer Stuart has not been unduly dependent on the multinational business it originally brought with it, and has many loyal British corporate clients on its books. If ever the Royal Warrant were to appear on a headhunter's letterhead, it would be Spencer Stuart's, except that they would be too modest and discreet to make it public knowledge.

Boyden

Boyden followed Spencer Stuart in 1965–6 but has suffered varying business fortunes since then. Few of Boyden's early British headhunters have survived to the present, and its level of business declined and failed to take off significantly in the late 1970s and early 1980s. For instance, during 1979, with three consultants only 30 placements were achieved in the UK, compared with Egon Zehnder's 80 and Spencer Stuart's 170 in the same year. The number of placements had marginally increased by 1981 to 40. The business did grow after the arrival of Michael Curlewis in 1982 when billings were still below £300 000; according to the accounts filed at Companies' House, in 1985 Boyden, with only three consultants, achieved a turnover of £490 258. This increased to £779 750 for the year ended 30 June 1986, but the firm was still substantially behind the Big Four and Egon Zehnder. However, billings have risen to £1.06m. for the year ended 30 June 1987, reflecting a dramatic recovery. The modest premises in Buckingham Palace Road have been deliberately maintained to keep Boyden's minimum fee down. Instability and lack of direction from Head Office may explain the absence of growth in the early 1980s. Other explanations suggested have included lack of a share of the increased City work with Big Bang. The decision to avoid this sector was consciously taken, but now Boyden is moving into recruiting in investment banking. Boyden worldwide has become stronger, with revenues of $34.6m. earned from 1150 searches by 100 consultants; this may lead to an increased presence in the British market.

Heidrick and Struggles

In 1968 – the same year that Gerry Roche became a partner – Heidrick and Struggles arrived in London, as part of a perhaps ill-advised and over-ambitious strategy of global expansion, and the London office encountered considerable difficulties in trying to achieve an impact on the British market in the face of profound instability back in New York. It too lost many early consultants – including Michael Curlewis, who went to Boyden – and did not achieve significant profitability and an important stake in the headhunting business of the capital until taken over by Dr John Viney, then aged 37, in 1985. Previously with the prominent British executive search firm of Whitehead Mann, he had spent eight years in industry, and had worked in general consulting with HAY–MSL after a distinguished academic record at Cambridge. Keen on promoting venture capital, Viney owns a chain of wine bars as a sideline. Other headhunters, he has pointed out, have similar outside business interests, such as Stephen Rowlinson's (Korn/Ferry) bicycle company and David Norman's tennis racquet import agency.

Since 1985, Heidrick and Struggles in London has more than tripled its number of consultants – from five to fifteen – most of them at first new to search and comparatively young. As a result of the Viney Revolution fee income per year has increased four-fold to over £4m., based on over 150 assignments annually. The structure of ownership allows the individual consultants a high level of personal profit; they can receive almost half of the billings. This rapid growth has been achieved by dint of strong and imaginative leadership pushing the firm into new areas, reflecting an almost evangelical aim to break down the old-boy network and cut out the dead wood from British industry. The firm's estimated successful assignment completion rate of 80% compares well with other leading firms.

Heidrick and Struggles places a strong emphasis on research, employing as many researchers as consultants, and has successfully promoted researchers to become consultants. New consultants are thus coming from the ranks of the research consultants as well as from industry and, recently (with less success), from rival headhunters. The firm is looking for further growth, especially overseas, chiefly by acquisition and joint venture; now with several clients in Australia and elsewhere in the Far East, the London office is feeling the lack of branches in that area, despite its comparative strength in the USA. Heidrick and Struggles in London is an entirely different organisation from what it was 20 years ago. This transformation has been consolidated by the firm's move away from gloomy Old Burlington Street to literally 'Ritzy' 100 Piccadilly.

Egon Zehnder

Egon Zehnder was founded in Switzerland by the still-practising Dr Zehnder, who was originally with Spencer Stuart. As a strongly international business it is more appropriate that it appears beside the Big

Four rather than with the British consultancies. Established in London in 1970 in King Street, St James', then from 1975 operating in upmarket Jermyn Street, the firm is in many ways similar to Spencer Stuart. Egon Zehnder has established a reputation for high quality and absolute discretion, charges fees based on work to be undertaken and not on a contingency or percentage of salary basis, and has retained practically all its senior staff. The five Zehnder consultants of 1979 have now doubled in number but, nearly ten years later, the original partners are still loyal to the firm. Egon Zehnder has only ever employed 140 consultants, and 100 of those are still with the firm. Two of the few consultants lost were Michel Carre and Georges Orban, who went on successfully to form their own firm, Carre Orban. Another rare loss has been that of Mark Weedon, the Managing Director in London until the autumn of 1988, now at Heidrick and Struggles. Bearing in mind that Egon Zehnder's London office was established almost ten years later than Spencer Stuart, they do not face the same regeneration problem; only now are their oldest consultants coming up to retirement.

Egon Zehnder is currently the most powerful in Europe (in terms of number of offices, consultants and fee income) of all the London head-hunters, with a strongly European culture and, in keeping with its Swiss origins, has gained a reputation for being very expensive and ultra-professional. Egon Zehnder consultants tend to play down the head-hunter image, now freely accepted by most of the Big Four's directors, and see themselves, like their European colleagues, as management consultants. Their research resources clearly play a vital role, and the firm takes a great interest in the latest technical developments which can facilitate this department's work.

The firm's number of assignments has doubled since 1979 – from about 70 carried out by five consultants to around 150 handled by nine – and its annual fee income in London now exceeds £3m. Profits are shared equally by the partners worldwide, and all new consultants are taken on with the view that they will ultimately become partners. The firm is perhaps more strongly committed to growth than Spencer Stuart, recently taking on more new consultants and expanding into the stylish Devonshire House development opposite the Ritz Hotel in Mayfair Place. The emphasis on research, however, is less marked than at Heidrick and Struggles, and there is no movement upwards from the ranks of researchers.

Korn/Ferry

Korn/Ferry came to London in 1973, and was unique among the Big Four in taking over an existing British firm rather than setting up its own branch, a policy since dispensed with. One advantage of acquiring G. K.

Dickinson, however, was the older, distinctly British roots this provided: the firm had been founded six years earlier by a group of ex-Spencer Stuart consultants. The connection proved useful as Korn/Ferry was initially strongly dependent on the multinational clients that its American offices supplied. However, the Dickinson team had been left to run their own show, and the London office failed to match the pace of expansion of the rest of Korn/Ferry. With the arrival of Stephen Rowlinson as London Managing Director in May 1985, total staff were reduced from 42 to 24, and consultants were replaced, mostly by other McKinsey people: Rowlinson had spent seven years with McKinsey and had been CEO of a group of manufacturing companies. He brought to the London office the sort of uncompromising determination that has been Korn/Ferry's trademark everywhere else.

By determined marketing Korn/Ferry has now developed and maintained a high and increasing level of placements and fee income, moving into more high-earning assignments. It apparently sets great store by creating business and completing assignments relatively quickly.

As part of an international group, Korn/Ferry's accounts have been filed at Companies' House, which show an impressive rise in fee income during the present decade. Fees in 1981 totalled £501 461; in 1982, £698 507; and in 1983, £1 106 446. An accounting change then took place, with the fee figure substituted by that of turnover; this totalled £1 278 120 in 1984, £1 761 405 in 1985 and £2 060 979 in 1986.

Yet, despite its prominence in headhunting in the USA and its global dominance as the highest-earning executive search firm in the world, Korn/Ferry is still a long way from being number one in fee income in Britain. Despite the efforts of Rowlinson and his undoubtedly substantial contribution to the growth of the UK business over the last few years, Korn/Ferry has not yet adapted to the British corporate scene quite as successfully as Egon Zehnder or fellow members of the Big Four. Rowlinson's latest move – in December 1988 – was to merge with John Stork International's London and Scandinavian offices, a return to the earlier growth-by-acquisition strategy.

Russell Reynolds

Russell Reynolds was the last of the Big Four to enter the London market – in 1972 – but has been far and away the most consistently successful. It was helped enormously by its expertise in financial services at a time when the demand for headhunting services in this sector was reaching unprecedented heights. This enabled it to survive the mass defection of four consultants – equal to almost half their team – led by David Norman in 1982–3. The annual fee income, now approaching £6m. in the UK alone, has been helped by its success not only in handling high-salaried

financial appointments, but also in its many chief executive assignments. As we shall discuss later, David Norman, head of Russell
Reynolds in 1980, was responsible – helped by international teamwork –
for finding Sir Ian McGregor for British Steel, the first time in Britain that
headhunters had been called in to find a new boss for a nationalised
industry. Russell Reynolds also handled the celebrated search on behalf
of Lord Keith of Beecham which resulted in the appointment of Bob
Bauman, then one of the most highly-paid CEOs in Britain on a £1m.
salary. In 1984 an impressive 59 assignments, accounting for 42% of
Russell Reynolds' fees, were for CEO and MD appointments, each
receiving salaries in excess of £50 000; by 1986 the firm handled 65
assignments in this category, with over half of their placements that year
for positions receiving at least £60 000.

The elitist image that Reynolds himself so carefully nurtured has been
successfully transplanted in British soil, principally through the efforts
of David Norman, David Shellard and, more recently, Roddy Gow, ex-
Trinity College Cambridge, the Scots Guards and Barclays Bank: clearly
the British equivalents of the Ivy Leaguers back in New York. Russell
Reynolds has achieved the highest fee income in the British market
through adapting to the British way of doing things whilst retaining an
American approach to marketing and business development; it has
achieved the former as effectively as Spencer Stuart and the latter as
profitably as Korn/Ferry, to produce a combination more successful than
either. It does, however, share Korn/Ferry's possible future problems of
the need for a wider distribution of equity, and blockage from too many
clients in one sector. Russell Reynolds' premier position in the British
search market seems assured. Its closest competitors are not only other
members of the Big Four, but a number of successful home-grown
British firms. How and why is this the case?

THE ORIGINS AND GROWTH OF HOME-GROWN BRITISH EXECUTIVE SEARCH

In addressing the problem of how British headhunting firms, in competition with the multinational search companies, were able to create
and develop a sustained demand for headhunting services, it would be
unnecessarily long-winded and tedious to examine every one in detail,
yet at the same time it would be sketchy and uninformative to list them
all briefly without analysis, and the basic information is given in the
Select Directory. So individual examples have been chosen as representative of many others, followed by a statistical appraisal of the entry and
drop-out rate of all firms in the British headhunting business over the
last four decades.

THE 1950s: MANAGEMENT CONSULTANTS AS THE PRECURSORS OF SEARCH

There are many contenders for the title of first headhunter in Britain, and claimants include Charles Owen and Harry Roff, of EAL and MSL respectively, who entered the business in the mid-1950s. These two pioneers were followed soon after by John Tyzack and by four of the big management consultancies: PA, PE, AIC and Urwick Orr.

Yet Owen, Roff and their contemporaries were not at this point working as real headhunters in the American sense of the word. They adamantly believed that 'at that time it was not done to "poach" settled executives in any direct or overt way'; but they may be seen as the precursors of headhunting in Britain, in so far as they acted as consultants in executive selection and advertising, within a general management consultancy practice. They entered the pure search industry much more recently, and still offer their previous range of services. MSL forms the principal recruitment consultancy of Saatchi & Saatchi plc, one of the world's largest business services groups. Charles Owen sold his interest in EAL in the mid-1960s. The firm now concentrates on search, only occasionally using selection.

There were two main hurdles to the development of headhunting in Britain in the 1950s, besides that of the perceived need for completely undercover operations. First, press advertisements were traditionally used for all levels of appointments. This was not a problem which American headhunters – working in a vast country with few national newspapers read throughout the land – had had to face. Second, the old-boy network offered a time-honoured alternative to advertising, particularly for the most senior appointments. Such a system, based on social class and the old school tie, had never become quite so entrenched across the Atlantic in the first place, and had largely broken down by the end of the 1950s.

THE 1960s: THE BEGINNINGS OF 'PURE' SEARCH

This decade, which saw the arrival in London of Spencer Stuart, Boyden and Heidrick and Struggles, also witnessed the origins of the first home-grown headhunters. Tyzack, Clive & Stokes and Alexander Hughes were formed by enterprising individuals seeking to enter this still largely untried market. The birth of the search industry in Britain was officially recognised in the media, with the first authoritative article on search appearing in *The Director* in 1961.

The early search firms were dominated by two types of individuals. First, there were the blue-blooded man-about-town types who had perhaps not – generally speaking – enjoyed the greatest success in their commercial and professional careers, who were restless, and saw executive search as an institutionalised old-boy network, in which they could make the most of their old contacts and make money without the need for major capital investment, and who misguidedly thought that it would be an easy living.

By the end of the 1970s, such of these early headhunting characters who still survived could be found occupying the positions of non-executive directors and chairmen of search firms, lending respectability and weight but not necessarily being called on for practical help; by the 1980s most had disappeared. Yet they played an important part in providing an entrée for headhunting to the Boardrooms of Britain. Cricketing celebrity and journalist Robin Marler is a good example of this genre. Korn/Ferry had Viscount Montgomery of Alamein and Sir John Trelawney; Boyden had Viscount Slim. The consultants referred to in the earliest issues of *The Executive Grapevine* include many hyphenated surnames, aristocratic titles and senior military, naval and air force ranks. The best of this breed were able to break down bastions of prejudice against headhunting, and show that the systematic and research-based recruiting of executives could be combined with sensitivity and an appreciation of the corporate culture; the worst were incompetent and snobbish.

The second type of individual headhunter was the practical, down-to-earth type with more management experience at different levels than the blue-bloods, who identified the existence of a demand for skills in senior recruiting but who was not pretentious or elitist about it in any way. Executive search was a more scientific – and more profitable – rarefied form of more general appointment selection, a natural corollary of management consulting. A client prepared to bring in management consultants could, in theory at least, be interested in headhunting. This second interpretation of the originally American concept of search, and how it could be applied to Britain, sees the business more from the client's point of view than that of the would-be consultant.

Alexander Hughes, 1965

An example of this second type of headhunter is Bert Young of Alexander Hughes. Although he spent his early career teaching, including seven years as a headmaster, he moved into management consultancy work at the beginning of the 1960s, using a variety of selection firms on behalf of his clients. Frequently dissatisfied with the results, he argued that the need for scientific executive search was already apparent. When Young subsequently became the Chairman of Alexander Hughes, then in its original guise as an insurance company advising pension fund managers, he pushed them into entering the headhunting business. He formed Alexander Hughes & Associates in 1965, which was hived off when the parent company was sold to Hogg Robinson in 1967.

Young maintained contact with his previous management consultancy clients who were already half-way convinced of headhunting, but he was prepared for much knocking on familiar and unfamiliar doors and cold-calling to drum up more business in a practical way. As soon as he had completed a few successful assignments, word was passed around and more business came his way. The appointment of an executive search firm to an assignment was very largely dependent on that firm being recommended by a satisfied client within an informal corporate network; shoot-outs were rare in the 1960s and many companies were loath to give business to a firm on the basis of their literature and/or presentations by consultants; so the success of early searches was crucial.

Young found that the potential clients most amenable to the idea of headhunting were those who had a particularly confidential recruitment problem on their hands, situations when it was essential that no one either inside or outside the company knew what was going on, 'the real cloak and dagger stuff'.

Headhunting 1960s-style tended to make consultants feel conspiratorial, shady and slightly suspect even if, like Young, they were wholly convinced of the ultimate value of executive search to a company's efficiency and performance. Many clients saw headhunters as taking on the dirty work, and many candidates obviously shared this view. Those on the receiving end of Young's telephone calls, instead of enthusiastically welcoming the possibility of a new opportunity, were frequently openly rude and abusive; many immediately cut him off and contemptuously slammed down their receivers. Meanwhile, the consultants did all their own research, both by telephone and in libraries. It was not until 1970–1 that Alexander Hughes established its own research department.

Unlike the large international headhunting firms, Young never sought to develop as much business as possible, preferring to maintain tight control of a specialist practice which also offered a form of management consultant-type counselling. By the end of the 1960s, the firm had established a reputation in the electronics and motor industries, and in the early 1970s it expanded into oil, petroleum and chemicals, and established a foothold in the merchant banking sector.

By the end of the 1970s, Alexander Hughes' seven consultants were undertaking between eight and twelve assignments per year each, achieving between 60 and 70 placements annually, and have maintained this level of work, based on at least 70% repeat business. The greatest changes have occurred in the average salary of candidates placed – from £25 000 to £70 000 – and in the firm's international links, which have extended from two European offices to membership of the globally spread E. S. International Group.

Alexander Hughes has survived, when many like firms have disappeared, through a combination of timing, a practical approach, a realisation of the need to specialise yet take advantage of special demand – as in financial services – and the provision of international contacts. It has been lucky in its track record, having apparently never had the necessity of reinstating a completely failed assignment. The fees, based on time and difficulty rather than on salary level, have been kept competitive; the firm's offices, first in High Holborn, then in New Cavendish Street, then in Harley Street and back to new Cavendish Street again, are presentable and functional rather than opulent or 'space age'. Perhaps a final factor has been the differing styles of the individual consultants, so that the firm appeals to a wider spread of clients. If Young is an example of the second type of early headhunter identified, then the firm also has a representative of the first, in Vice-Admiral Sir Ian McIntosh.

THE 1970s: EXECUTIVE SEARCH COMES OF AGE

The third type of headhunter, more appropriate to the increasing professionalism of the business, is epitomised by David Kay and Dr Anna Mann, who entered executive search with strong commercial, professional and academic qualifications, and set about forming businesses which would continue to grow and capture an important stake in the British – if not the greater world – market. Especially towards the end of the decade, the third type of headhunter was viewing the search business as a profession in its own right, as dynamic as the talent they were seeking, rather than as just an extension of management consultancy. This was a function of the increasingly competitive international economy, and the crises which many stalwarts of British corporate life were facing.

Goddard Kay Rogers, 1970

Goddard Kay Rogers (GKR) is now among the leading eight firms in the British search market. Although much of its growth may be accounted for by the rapid increase in headhunting in financial services in the mid-1980s, the firm's capability and success in this market stemmed from its secure reputation established over the preceding decade. In the 1980s, search won many new customers; but these were precisely the companies who had been most reluctant to call on headhunters, and most cautious in using them. GKR – long established, entirely British, and with a name for utter discretion and high quality work – was able to win over the most conservative and privacy-obsessed Board directors. GKR's consultants were then, and are now, similar in style, qualifications and background to those at Russell Reynolds and Spencer Stuart, but without any of the American trappings, and certainly without the aggressive marketing and obsession with business development which marks many of the international firms. At the same time, GKR has not been sold out and swallowed up by a larger organisation, as have MSL by Saatchi & Saatchi and Norman Broadbent by Charles Barker, although there is an element of outside shareholding.

When David Kay, Roy Goddard and Fred Rogers established their business in 1970, they were one of the first British firms to operate in the same way as Spencer Stuart, Heidrick and Struggles and Egon Zehnder. From the outset GKR concentrated exclusively on executive search, unlike Alexander Hughes and many other 1960s contemporaries, who clung either to management consultancy or selection as a sideline. Again in contrast with many firms of the 1960s, GKR sought a general business coverage rather than specialisation in any particular sector. If it did specialise, it was more by function, concentrating especially on CEO and MD assignments. Advertising was practically never used, even in the early 1970s when the use of search by companies was much less widespread. Like its multinational headhunting rivals, GKR aimed to deal with assignments with some speed, with eight consultants making over 80 placements by 1979, a rate later much increased.

GKR was able to avoid the problems of the pioneering phase of headhunting in the 1960s, and appreciated the importance of a strong research department from its foundation onwards. Like some of the multinational headhunters and unlike many other British firms, researchers are encouraged to accompany consultants at client briefings and become closely involved in the assignment, rather than being treated as a mixture of secretary, librarian, PA and headhunting dogs-body. GKR claim to have developed a uniquely effective research procedure, but it is such a closely-guarded secret that its uniqueness and efficacy is impossible to judge.

GKR laid the foundations of a world network in the 1970s which broadened in the following decade from Europe to the Far East. Besides these wholly-owned GKR offices, the firm established links with American affiliates. Now the lack of more overseas offices is perceived as a weakness, and the firm is particularly interested in a greater US presence. GKR's business in London dominates its income, although it has Northern and Southern offices, in Leeds and Bath respectively.

GKR's growth in terms of fee income and number of consultants, although showing modest progress in the 1970s, did not take off dramatically in this particular decade. The rate of entry of new firms in executive search was increasing and the business was becoming more competitive, but there was not yet the demand to support them all. However, GKR began to flourish in the early 1980s, not so much in financial services as across the board in industry. It is one of the very few search firms whose results are published in *Kompass*, which reveals not only the firm's rapid rise in turnover but a striking rate of return on capital employed, indicating the potentially very profitable nature of the headhunting business. From August 1982 to August 1984, GKR's turnover increased from £963 000 to £2.5m., and profits from £46 000 to £439 000. Capital employed increased from £152 000 to £591 000, and the return on capital employed, (ROCE) from only 30% in 1982 to 74% by 1984. The firm's turnover by mid-1987 reached at least £5m., with a pro rata rise in profits and ROCE. Total worldwide fee income exceeded £6m. by 1989.

The impact of Big Bang on GKR was especially profitable for the firm because it was well prepared. Ronald Begley, a consultant working in this sector, explained that back in 1981 GKR began establishing a team – they recruited three new consultants – to work specifically in financial services. The team was able to win some very prestigious senior assignments during this time, deliberately dissociating itself from the wholesale movement of dealing and broking teams, an aspect of search of which GKR strongly disapprove. So keen are GKR not to be identified with the less ethical and aggressive end of the search market that it maintains it frequently turns down business; from any other search firm, this statement might be questionable, but GKR's standing in the market, and the obvious importance of its untarnished reputation in gaining that position, suggests that it is probably the truth.

John Stork, 1973

John Stork, until recently also an entirely British-owned search firm, has established a significant niche in the British headhunting business but, unlike GKR, it has concentrated less on building up a large volume of business in London and more on expanding into Europe. It now has wholly-owned offices in Paris, Amsterdam, Brussels, Frankfurt, Geneva, Stockholm and Gothenburg, is a shareholder in a well-established US firm and has associate arrangements in the USA and elsewhere, enabling it to sustain an annual growth rate of between 20% and 30% which is now generating annual total fees of up to £5m. Although John Stork International became, to all intents and purposes, a pure search business, this was not always the case, and it still maintains other interests, including two management assessment firms, who employ several psychologists.

John Stork – when in his mid-30s – became aware of headhunting when he found himself on the receiving end of a headhunter's call for the first time; in due course he became the successful candidate, but did not take the job, staying on as a member of the international Board of Masius Wynne-Williams advertising agency, where he had earlier been head of research. The agency was enjoying considerable success on a worldwide basis at the time and, when there was a change in owner-ship, he considered starting his own business in marketing consulting.

The headhunting business as a whole, although it promotes the idea of systematising personal networks, still owes much to chance, coinci-dence and Lady Luck. In this context, Stork came into contact with headhunting again, through his leisure interest in sailing. At the time he was racing a boat on the international circuit and his crew member's cousin was none other than David Kay of GKR; Stork followed up the contact and, because of his research, marketing and overseas experi-ence, the newly-established GKR offered him a job to develop their search business in Europe. Stork was attracted to the idea of headhunt-ing, but less to the idea of working for GKR, so he decided to set up on his own, working at both headhunting and marketing consulting.

Stork was not entirely sure how the headhunting process worked; indeed, there were no guides to the subject and all the existing purveyors of search are more or less self-taught. With his international research and marketing background Stork (and a number of his contem-poraries) argued that there must be a more effective approach than the 'who you know' networking in current use in the 1960s and early 1970s. Stork's approach, as it has evolved, is marked by a preference for more experienced consultants with line management experience rather than younger graduates who just have MBAs; and for sending two consul-tants on every assignment, who handle the job 70/30%. Stork maintains that researchers should be strictly focused on research, working on one assignment at a time, with little movement of staff between researcher and consultant, believing that distinctly different skills are involved.

Stork set up the firm in 1973, becoming operational with three employees in 1974. The investment of £25 000 was returned in profits in just over twelve months. The 1970s saw considerable growth, the decade ending with Stork employing nine consultants, an increase of four from the previous year, completing at least 60 assignments annually, charging fees on a retainer basis, with a – now slightly ridiculous – minimum fee of £5 000. The number of consultants overseas continued to grow and the emphasis of the business moved more and more to Europe.

Stork until recently has personally maintained his hold on the majority of the equity in order, he says, to help set the direction of the firm. He initially did not appear worried that he might lose staff as a consequence, in the way that Egon Zehnder left Spencer Stuart and Norman, Broadbent *et al.* left Russell Reynolds. He argued that consultants were tending to stay put by the mid-1980s because of the much higher start-up costs now involved in setting up an executive search firm, which he estimated as at least £250 000, or ten times the figure he invested back in 1973. However, John Stork & Partners Ltd (as it was then styled) itself suffered a disastrous blow in the autumn of 1986 when two of its star consultants, Anthony Saxton and Stephen Bampfylde, suddenly left with no warning, taking one of the two senior researchers, Tim Roberts, with them.

Yet the firm recovered and continued to grow, generally due to a high level of repeat business and its role as an alternative to the large international search firms in shoot-outs for European-based assignments. This emphasis on its international business was officially recognised by a change of name to John Stork International. In a surprising development in December 1988, John Stork merged his London and Scandinavian offices with Korn/Ferry; the European businesses would appear to be still operating independently.

Although there are few certainties in the headhunting business, those firms which survived the 1970s are largely still in existence, and will probably continue to prosper, through building up a loyal client base. Many companies prefer to hand search assignments to consultants they know, and thus will continue to support a firm, whatever happens. As experienced by the largest international headhunting companies, the value of a 'name' to act as an umbrella, providing clients, research services and inter-consultant support, is vital and is becoming increasingly important. Yet ambitious and confident consultants, especially those good at business development and successful at winning shoot-outs, are still able to branch out on their own, and it would not be healthy for the industry if this were otherwise.

Merton, 1976

This hitherto little-known independent British firm has recently gained considerable prestige and a dramatic rise in fee income – of over £2m. for 1988 – through specialising in a limited range of sectors. Merton's success in its principal specialty, the London property world – the firm undertook search assignments in connection with Rosehaugh Stanhope's celebrated Broadgate development, for example – suggests that such a strategy of specialisation may become more and more common in the British headhunting business in the future.

Merton is the second of two major ventures in the recruiting business which have been set up by entrepreneurial Michael Silverman. Well connected in the city and an enthusiastic supporter of the Conservative Party – he is the Librarian at the Carlton Club – Silverman's professional career began with Procter & Gamble. In the early 1960s – as John Stork had done – he joined Masius Wynne-Williams, a leading British advertising agency, and developed a strong belief in the value of qualitative market research. (His claim to fame in these years was the slogan 'Kleenex Kitchen Towels mops up like a sponge' for client Kimberley Clark.)

This influenced Silverman's first commercial venture, a forerunner in the search consultancy business, Lloyd Executive Selection, which offered a contingency service, employing market research techniques and limited advertising to recruit specialist managers in accountancy, law, banking, insurance and marketing. Operating from one room above Bishopsgate Fire Station from 1968, by the time Silverman sold out in 1976 it occupied five floors in High Holborn, employed nearly 100 staff and was earning nearly £1m. annually. He also set up two associated businesses, Lloyd Advertising Agency and the Lloyd Institute of Management. Lloyd Executive Selection had risen in this period to become a major contender alongside MSL and PA.

Merton itself, as a result of Silverman's experience in selection, advertising and research, was first conceived as a high-level recruitment consultancy which then evolved into a management consultancy and executive search practice; he based his approach – ahead of its time in Britain in the mid-1970s – on the concept of building up a profile of 'the ideal candidate' by using the most sophisticated industrial market research techniques, approaching a recruitment programme in the same way as he had devised and implemented a marketing plan.

One of Silverman's earliest partners, who is now Merton's chairman, was Air Vice-Marshal Bill Gill; as head of manpower for the Royal Air Force, he was one of Merton's early clients. First based in Queen Victoria Street, by 1977 Merton had moved to Grafton Way, near many other independent British firms elsewhere in W1; the overheads of Piccadilly and St James' are affordable only by the large multinational firms.

Now with a total of twelve consultants in London and an office in Leeds, Merton has doubled its business since the mid-1980s through its policy of specialisation, according to the experience of its partners. But this is not as narrowly based as it might first appear. For instance, Air Vice-Marshal Gill has handled a large number of controversial searches in the defence and aviation sectors. One, reported in *Flight International*, was to find three senior aerospace engineers for Canadair, the leading Canadian aeronautical manufacturer, well known for its Challenger corporate jet, CL–215 water bomber and advanced military surveillance systems. Gill naturally began probing top British Aerospace personnel who, facing redundancy and compulsory relocation away from the Home Counties to the North of England, were interested in the opportunities on offer. Not surprisingly, the switchboard at British Aerospace, alerted to what was happening, refused to put through any of Gill's telephone calls; the positions were filled after Gill strategically leaked the story to the local press covering the area near the British Aerospace factories.

Michael Silverman himself, who handles assignments in the firm's property sector – which now accounts for over a quarter of its business – has also established a reputation in the retail industry. His firm was called on by Tesco plc, now one of Britain's leading supermarket chains, when Ian MacLauren was building up his new team. The transformation of Tesco in the mid-1980s owed much to the company's new finance director, headhunted from International Stores, and the new productivity director, who was recruited from Safeways.

One problem of working in limited specialty areas is that existing clients might be averse to the idea of employing the same search firm as their rivals; so Merton, approached by another major retailer with an assignment, cleared the matter with Tesco first. Specialisation can also result in blockage, with so many clients in a narrow field that the scope for search is limited; this problem can be solved by specialising only in large sectors, and also widening the range of services on offer, such as management consultancy products, including manpower planning advice, executive assessment and salary surveys. Even-more significant for their future growth, Merton has expanded the field of candidates open to them by being able to search globally, as a member of Transearch, a group of internationally affiliated consultancies in fifteen major business centres. Silverman argues that no British-based search firm can offer an effective service and earn substantial total fees without the support of an overseas network; few would dispute this.

Whitehead Mann, 1976

Whitehead Mann has established a very professional and assertive business, now generating an annual fee income of over £4m. It is among the least publicity-seeking and therefore among the least well known of the major firms, but enjoys a very high reputation within the executive search industry itself.

Dr Anna Mann – her PhD is in psychology – is clearly one of the pioneers of high-quality search in Britain. She was only 28 when she set up on her own in 1976, after starting her career as a researcher.

In the mid-to-late 1970s, while building her business, she had to cope not only with prejudice against headhunting, but with prejudice against her as a woman. When faced with one 'old boy type' executive, who on meeting her with a view to beginning an assignment declared that there was no place for women in his business, she announced that as he was obviously only looking for someone just like himself, he could do that better than she could. He changed his mind and called her back, and is now one of the firm's most long-standing clients.

Dr Mann's attitude is tough, determined, meticulous and very businesslike. She has strong views on ill-informed observers who think that headhunting must be a glamorous life of leisurely meetings with prestigious clients and candidates, punctuated by breakfast at the Savoy, lunch at Claridges, and dinner at the Ritz. As she told a journalist on the newspaper *Today* – who was obviously rather disappointed – 'I never feed my candidates. If they want to meet me at 8am, they can have breakfast before they arrive – they don't need breakfast at the Savoy. It is far more efficient and professional to do business in my office or theirs.'

Whitehead Mann has built up an enviable concentration in the top end of the market, attracting some particularly senior and thus highly remunerative assignments. The firm's profits are the subject of some speculation in the business, because of its comparatively small number of employees and relatively modest premises in Welbeck Street. Whitehead Mann has taken on some of the highest salaried job searches in Britain, comparable with Russell Reynolds' recruiting of Bob Bauman for Beecham; an assignment on behalf of a major British company looking for a chief executive to run their operations in Australia earned the firm £333 000, according to the popular press (on the basis that the successful candidate was to be paid an annual salary approaching £1m.). Dr John Viney, now managing director of Heidrick and Struggles in London, who originally worked at Whitehead Mann, estimated that with modest overheads Mann herself personally bills at least £1m.

Whitehead Mann's prominence shows that it is not necessary to wholly own a large number of overseas offices to gain and handle top assignments successfully; its membership of the Ward Howell Group covers its international search needs without incurring the capital expenditure and risk that the Big Four have undertaken. This is one of the largest, most effective, and most highly reputed of the global inter-headhunter associations, with over 100 consultants in 29 offices in seventeen countries including Australia and Japan. In the USA it has recently slipped in rank to eighth position.

The firm has achieved such a profitable business largely through its efficient and meticulous research, on which Whitehead Mann places much emphasis. This has enabled a low-profile firm to have one of the highest profiles in terms of revenues. The strategy of teamwork on each assignment of a director, consultant and a researcher has worked well in producing an impressive completion rate and concomitant large amount of repeat business. Whitehead Mann's dynamic and determined style and no-nonsense approach have appealed to the most sophisticated users of search; Dr Mann is seen as the thinking businessman's headhunter.

THE 1980s: HEADHUNTERS THRUST DEEPER INTO THE JUNGLE

The fourth type of headhunter combines the professionalism of the third with a practical and dynamic 1980s entrepreneurialism. This is manifested in a strong desire to break away from corporate environments seen as financially restrictive, especially those businesses which are obviously very profitable but where the profits are not fairly shared out among those who are helping to generate them. Many headhunters see setting up on their own as an ultimate ambition, despite the risks of flying from the safe nest of a large firm with many clients and a high level of repeat business. Although individual client executives tend to favour dealing with known consultants, if those consultants leave their firms, they are not necessarily then seen in the same light, or as having the same resources at their disposal. Yet the dramatic increase in the volume of headhunting business in the 1980s has enabled many individual consultants to make this leap. Norman Broadbent and Saxton Bampfylde may be regarded as 1980s examples of the same trend which influenced Dr Egon Zehnder to leave Spencer Stuart in 1964: a desire both for autonomy and for profit. A second phenomenon within the headhunting business in the 1980s is the transition of firms from advertised/selection-based recruitment to search; this was achieved by the old-established British firms Clive & Stokes and Tyzack & Partners.

Clive & Stokes, 1980

Clive & Stokes was originally founded at the beginning of 1959 when John Stokes, who had been in personnel management in ICI and Courtaulds and was later to become the MP for Halesowen and Stourbridge, joined Robert Clive Associates, a small recruitment company. Clive, descended from Clive of India, together with Stokes developed close personal working relationships with a number of blue-chip companies and did not plan to expand the firm.

Their approach was to run a business similar to a small City firm of solicitors, maintaining close relationships with a few senior people for whom they would provide a personal service and gain good repeat business. Robert Clive had family ties with Banque Worms, an influential French private bank, and worked in the City mainly for the clearers, but also had close working relationships with companies such as Distillers and Bowater. The practice included recruitment through advertising and personnel management consultancy besides recruiting through a direct approach. In the early 1970s Charles Barker, who handled all their advertising, took a 25% interest with the aim of developing a consulting division. Although Clive & Stokes took on one partner from Barker, Peter Bingham (who had been Personnel Director of Bowater), the strategy was not successful and in 1986 the connection with Barker was severed.

Clive and Stokes then took stock of their position: Clive was now over 65 and looking to retire; John Stokes was 61 and very much involved in public life as the MP for Halesowen and Stourbridge. They felt they should either bring in new blood or sell the company. Hamish Kidd – previously with Heidrick and Struggles – was introduced to them in 1978, and it was agreed that he would work with them for a year with the aim of establishing that a sale could be arranged. This was finally effected in the spring of 1980.

The meeting was timely because Hamish Kidd, a Cambridge chemical engineer who had spent a long period in general management consultancy with P–E Consulting Group, had developed systems to introduce executive search into P–E when it was sanctioned as an allowable technique by the Management Consultants Association (MCA). Prior to 1972 the MCA had strictly forbidden member firms to use executive search when recruiting for their clients. Kidd reflects that at the time he was not given the unqualified support by other members of P–E who felt that the search approach was still inappropriate for a consulting firm with resident consultants on client premises and that it could injure the firm's consulting practice. P–E had on occasions recommended clients to Lyn Brua, an American who had founded the London office of Heidrick and Struggles, and it was through that connection he decided to join the executive search industry. After two years in the London office of Heidrick and Struggles, Kidd felt that he would prefer to work for a British firm and employ the systems he had designed.

At Kidd's arrival Clive and Stokes concentrated solely on executive search, but it has since undertaken organisational consulting assignments. The practice has a strong industrial and commercial base and has progressed steadily, investing most of the profits in sophisticated research and information systems. Bryan McCleery, previously the Otis Personnel Director, joined in 1980, followed by Malcolm Campbell in 1981, who joined from Touche Ross. The firm was but rarely in the area of financial services until Michael Springman joined in 1986 to head a City practice. He had moved earlier from Heidrick and Struggles to found the executive search division of MSL. In 1987 Alan Tipper also joined from the London office of Heidrick and Struggles. In order to maintain a close relationship with northern clients, a small office was opened in Manchester in 1985 and a Leeds office was opened in 1988.

It was apparent in the 1980s that, to provide a complete service to multinational clients, it would be important to match their international spread with a network of offices. In conjunction with several American firms, Clive and Stokes has been involved in developing ISA (International Search Associates) which aims to find firms who will adhere to

a strict set of rules and co-operate in a manner which will enable the
client to have the benefit of local know-how, with less restrictive off-
limits constraints, but at the same time have an international outlook.
The firms which have joined ISA have usually been formed by consultants with experience in the major international search firms, who wish
to remain independent but adhere to the same ethical standards of the
majors. It is actively seeking to extend its network: currently it has been
in discussion with firms in Austria, Greece, Italy, Spain and South
Africa. The Far East is also an important area but it has been difficult to
find firms of the requisite standard who are independent. Clive and
Stokes has survived in business for nearly three decades only because of
its adoption of modern search techniques, as in the case of Tyzack.

Tyzack, 1981

Founded by its eponymous chairman in 1959, who had previously
started up MSL with Harry Roff, the business enjoyed a pre-eminent
position in senior recruitment through advertising until the end of the
1970s. Tyzack's advertisements, especially in the *Financial Times*, were
eagerly studied by those seeking better opportunities in the pre-
headhunting days. John Tyzack provided for his comfortable retirement
in Oxford by selling the business to Henderson Administration, the
well-known investment trust. Management was passed to Tony Barker,
a law graduate of Yale, who had formerly worked with BOC. By the turn
of the decade, the partners and a specially created employee trust
bought the business back from Henderson Administration – by way of a
cash payment and a short-term fixed interest debenture – long before
the term 'management buy-out' became part of everyday business
vocabulary. The arrival of a few younger consultants prompted the
decision to change Tyzack into a totally executive search business, in
order to maintain its market position. In the nadir of the recession in
1981 the strongest brand name was removed from the recruitment
advertising pages and became, for the first time for 20 years, an unseen
operator. After twelve months of reorganising and repositioning,
Tyzack began to emerge as a contender in the top echelons of executive
search.

During this transition, the retirement age was brought down by five
years, staffing numbers were reduced, the unprofitable office in Edinburgh was closed, procedures were modified and attitudes changed, a
research department was established, some shuffling of the partners
took place, and the youngest of them, Nigel Humphreys, was appointed
Managing Director. An Oxford graduate, he had moved into general
management in manufacturing and then into international construction

and consultancy from which he had been headhunted by Richard Addis, now one of his senior partners.

Since that time, the research department has grown to twelve, and several new partners (for example, Peter Bryant from Eurosurvey) have been appointed from competitors; chief executives from major institutions like Chemical Bank – Alex Gibson – and Grand Metropolitan – Peter Ohlson – have been hired to add weight to operational skills. Nevertheless, there is considerable stability in this firm, and average partner service exceeds seven years. Despite the passage of time since 1981 – their biggest billers are those of the original core who remain.

As far as Humphreys is concerned, firms which occupy the high ground in executive search are not necessarily limited in the variety, volume or type of search work that can be undertaken; for example, Tyzack's recent work includes finding the chairman of London Transport, looking simultaneously for three chief executives for an international trading company in the Far East, Europe and the US (none of whom was to earn less than US$450 000), searching for the chairman of the Monopolies & Mergers Commission, tracking down the chief executive of a building society and the MD of a conglomerate which, during the search, was defending itself against likely take-over bids. Assignments can be especially challenging as in the case of the Director-General of a national charity, the chairman of a county council, the MD of a small airline perilously close to the Official Receiver, the chief executive of gunmakers Holland & Holland and – last but not least – the *chef de cuisine* for one of London's most famous eating places.

In order to serve corporate decentralisation and nascent prosperity outside the South East of England, Humphreys believes in regionalism. In addition to London, Tyzack has an office in Bristol and will shortly be opening a third UK branch in the North. It has also now established a network of offices – some of which it owns and others to which it is closely affiliated – in New York, Paris, Frankfurt and Hong Kong. Assessment by psychometric testing, according to Humphreys, will become either an intrinsic part of more searches or a stand-alone service contributing further to management development and appraisal techniques. Remuneration planning remains an activity of growing importance for search firms such as Tyzack, as companies agglomerate and national compensation characteristics clash.

Tyzack's UK turnover in 1988 was £2.5m. and world-wide billings around £7m. Heavy investment in research, data base management and information systems has been made in anticipation of continued growth in a wider, more international, but more competitive market. The company came a long way in the 1980s, but only because the leopard changed its spots by making the transition from selection to search.

Norman Broadbent, 1983

David Norman – a graduate of Eton, McGill and Harvard Business School – had already made a controversial impact on the British search business before setting up his own firm, which now enjoys an annual fee income of over £5m., ranking in second place behind Russell Reynolds in the pecking order of Britain's highest-earning headhunters.

In 1980, when Norman was UK Managing Director of Russell Reynolds, he was approached by Sir Peter Carey, then Permanent Secretary to the Department of Trade, to find a new chief executive for British Steel. When Norman recruited Sir Ian McGregor, this marked the first time in Britain that a nationalised industry chief had been appointed through executive search. The impact of this assignment on the history and development of headhunting may be compared with that of the ITT job of 1959. John Byrne, in *The Headhunters*, describes the British Steel search in detail: more than a hundred candidates from Europe, North America, South Africa and Australia were interviewed over the course of ten months. The difficulties of persuading a businessman to take on the running of such an ailing industry – it was losing at a rate of £2m. a day – and handle its relationship with the Government and the unions was exacerbated by the comparatively low salary on offer.

Norman had pointed out from the beginning that this financial package would not necessarily be sufficient to attract the highest quality executive, and warned the Government that they should be prepared to pay more. But he could not forestall a major parliamentary outcry on the news of McGregor's appointment. It was not the issue of his salary alone. McGregor, aged 67, had recently retired as Chairman and Chief Executive of AMAX, Inc., but was still a partner of Lazard Freres & Co, a New York investment bank. Although McGregor was to be paid £50 000, the same as the man he replaced, the British government had to pay Lazard Freres $4.1m. over five years to compensate them for losing McGregor. MPs described the payment as 'monstrous', 'farcical' and 'disgraceful', but the appointment showed an official acceptance of headhunting as the only practical solution to recruiting at such a high level, and an acknowledgement that top-quality executive talent was worth paying for. The fees charged by the search firm were arguably minimal in this context. As far as Norman was concerned, the British Steel job marked 'the first coming of age' of executive search in Britain.

Assignments such as this – and the recruitment of Colin Marshall from Avis to the newly-privatised British Airways for Lord King by Miles Broadbent – made an important contribution to Russell Reynolds' global earnings, and especially to the growing personal wealth of Reynolds himself, still holding a 60% stake in the equity. This drove Norman to consider putting the reputation and earning power which he had developed for the company to his own use, and in 1982 he formed Norman Resources Limited. A year later – by mid-1983 – three of his former colleagues – Miles Broadbent (who replaced Norman as London managing director of Russell Reynolds), Julian Sainty and James Hervey-Bathurst – also defected, and Norman Broadbent International was formally established, helped by the credibility they had acquired from these prestigious assignments.

An accurate picture of the growth of the business was revealed when the partners – although maintaining their day-to-day management intact – sold their equity to Charles Barker in 1986, for an initial consideration of £3.16m., finally equal to £9m. This has provided a rare insight into the profitability of headhunting in Britain in the 1980s, which is now on a vastly larger scale than ever before. In 1985, Norman Broadbent's chairman and seven consultants were responsible for the completion of 143 assignments – 53% in financial services and 47% in industrial and commercial services – which, at an average of £23 000 per assignment, produced a turnover of £3.3m. and a trading profit of £1m. This reflects an eightfold increase on their first year's business, when turnover was £416 000 and the trading profit was £111 000. This growth rate has continued, with 224 assignments in 1986, a 51% increase in volume on the previous year. The following year 202 assignments were completed, with a further 109 in Hong Kong; 24% of Norman Broadbent's business is now of an international nature. Profits have continued to represent about one-third of the turnover; this is seen as not necessarily the highest proportion of profits to income in the headhunting business as a whole, where estimates of 60% have been made in some cases.

The particularly rapid growth of Norman Broadbent owes much to the partners' skill and luck in their sense of timing in the formation of the company; it is unlikely that this could now be repeated quite so successfully. They entered the business and developed a reputation at a time of unprecedented and unique demand, offering an independent British alternative to Russell Reynolds, with a younger and more up-market, polished and highly qualified team than GKR seemed to have. Their income rocketed with the Big Bang demand for specialists in sales, trading, research and corporate finance. Of Norman Broadbent's City assignments 21% were for jobs paying over £100 000, and 14% of their industry business was also at this level. This rose to 35% and 20% respectively by 1987. During 1986 and 1987, more than two-thirds of their work was repeat business; in 1985 it had been 80%, so much of the increase in volume was due to winning new clients.

Norman Broadbent has been more successful in offering the benefits of an international network than its rivals GKR, through a combination of its own companies – as in the manner of the Big Four – and membership of a well-known established group (as with Whitehead

Mann). Through cross-shareholdings in The International Search Partner-
ship, Norman Broadbent are represented by their own offices in New York,
Hong Kong, Tokyo and Sydney, and share those of Eurosearch in
Dusseldorf, Milan, Paris and Zurich.

Besides City work, Norman Broadbent has continued to attract the
same high-powered assignments which came its way when it was with
Russell Reynolds: 40% of its assignments were at CEO and MD level in
1987, compared with 24% in 1986. Thus it has been able to overcome the
major hurdle of the possibility of losing top contacts and clients when it
was set up on its own. For instance, in May 1987 it found John Craven of
Phoenix Securities to be the new chief executive of Morgan Grenfell,
another assignment on behalf of Sir Peter Carey, who has since moved
from the Department of Trade to become chairman of this major
merchant bank.

Saxton Bampfylde, 1986

Saxton Bampfylde represents a more recent example of a breakaway –
this time from John Stork – suggesting that there is still scope for start-
ups in headhunting.

Anthony Saxton's management training began with a major international cosmetics company, and he became Managing Director of an
advertising agency before joining John Stork in 1978, where he ran the
UK division. Saxton, a doyen of British headhunting, is Chairman of the
Executive Recruitment Association, formed in 1985 to link together a
variety of search firms; as yet, it would appear that few of the largest are
interested, but this body could form a foundation for a professional
association of headhunting in Britain.

Stephen Bampfylde is by far the younger of the partnership, and
contrasts Saxton's industrial and commercial experience with strong
academic qualifications. His First from Cambridge was followed by a
short career in the Civil Service, commercial experience with IBM, and
work with another search firm before he joined John Stork and met and
worked with Saxton.

In the autumn of 1986, when Saxton and Bampfylde abandoned their
previous employers, they had already prepared their future strategy: to
work with only a selected and comparatively small number of clients in
certain market sectors only, with an emphasis on finding the people
needed to satisfy a client's strategic needs rather than on the level of
appointment. The market sectors in which the partners are most keen to
establish an impact revolve mainly around services such as retailing,
advertising and finance. Most of their work to date has been with blue-
chip companies, but they have also handled assignments from leading
merchant banks and fashion retail houses.

Saxton Bampfylde's office in Westminster is staffed by five consultants and eight researchers. Three consultant psychologists are on hand
to provide independent assessments of short-listed candidates. It thus
has a strong research bias to its approach. From the beginning, the
partners set out to offer a global service, establishing a European and
North American network of associated consultancies, shortly to be
extended to the Far East.

In offering any new product on the market it is essential to have
something which is new and different; with the number of headhunting
firms now established, how can any one firm be really unique? Saxton
Bampfylde tries to be extra sensitive, open and considerate, not only to
the clients who are its bread and butter, but also to candidates, who
frequently feel they have been ridden roughshod over and hard-done-
by in the search process. Perhaps Saxton Bampfylde's approach is an
indication of the new style executive search of the 1990s and beyond?

AN OVERVIEW: THE ENTRY AND DROP-OUT RATE OF FIRMS IN EXECUTIVE SEARCH

As outlined in the Introduction, this book specifically and deliberately
concentrates on the upper end of the British search market, and is not
concerned with firms specialising in lower-level appointments, selection
and advertising, except when this accompanies some higher-level work,
as in the case of MSL. The following analysis is based on an annual
guide to search and selection firms published since 1979, *The Executive
Grapevine*. This source can provide an approximation of the number of
firms in Britain but cannot allow a differentiation of firms according to
their standing in the senior recruitment market. For 1986, *The Executive
Grapevine* listed 324 firms, compared with only 212 in the previous issue,
in 1984. Forty-eight of the firms listed in 1984 had dropped out by 1986;
the real increase in new firms between 1984 and 1986 – fuelled by the Big
Bang – was thus 160. This represents a rate of new entries of 80%,
compared with a fall-out rate of 23%. Such a rate of increase has not
lasted, however; 357 appeared in the 1987 issue of this guide, most of
them representing new growth, but at a steadier rate. The 1988–9
volume lists 583 including many firms previously omitted and many
newer, lower-level selection firms. The 1989–90 volume is even larger
with nearly 700 entries; presumably the same applies, but there is an
expanded European section.

Which years saw the greatest growth in headhunting? According to
this source, and obviously excluding those firms who did not give a year
of formation, only fifteen firms were established in the 1960s. Nine were
set up in 1970 alone, and this rate was maintained through the decade of

the 1970s, rising to fourteen in 1973 and dropping to seven in 1977. But the first real headhunting boom began in the late 1970s and early 1980s, when the recession really began to bite; executive search may be seen as one of the few industries which grew in this period. Between 1979 and 1981, 39 new search firms emerged, and thereafter the rate declined. It is impossible to analyse from this source the rate of entry in the last few years, because brand-new firms are reluctant to advertise their newness in case this dissuades clients and candidates from trusting them and taking them seriously.

CONCLUSION: LONG TERM OR SHORT TERM, CHICKEN OR EGG?

It is clear that although the long-term factors which favoured the professionalisation of British management and the acceptance of using outside consultants helped to prepare the ground for the spread of headhunting, the leading executive search firms themselves played a vital part in creating this new business out of nowhere.

The Big Four provided the patterns of organisational structures and methodologies in an untried and untested industry, but they did not provide people. From the start, it was realised that for the branch of an American headhunting firm in London to gain credibility and attract clients unused to search, it was necessary to appoint British consultants and researchers rather than Americans, but nevertheless with strong support and detailed advice from the corporate headquarters across the Atlantic.

As in the case of the early home-grown British firms, many of the Big Four's consultants were of the first two types of headhunter we have identified: either the aristocrat with the old-boy network contacts or the practical selection and management consultant type whose experience was more in personnel than commerce and industry. Therefore it took some time to penetrate the Boardrooms of British industry, because many of the early headhunters did not really speak the businessmen's language. At the same time, the shake-out of British industry did not gather momentum before the late 1970s.

The emergence of more professional search consultants coincided with the increased need for headhunting services to help rationalisation and reorganisation; but arguably as the search industry was maturing, headhunting could attract better-qualified candidates, and as their earnings rose and headhunting became more profitable, executive search was increasingly being seen as a viable alternative to a line-management job.

Headhunters were also forced to become more professional because of the growing complexity of the corporate problems they were called upon to solve; those consultants who were less sophisticated than their clients soon went out of business. British companies rarely welcomed headhunters positively; they engaged them out of desperation, but it gave the good firms the chance to rise to the occasion. Many clients became disillusioned with search in the 1970s, receiving some indifferent service and assuming that all headhunters were the same; this view is rapidly disappearing in the 1980s, although many search practices current during the Big Bang gave search a bad name, such as wholesale movement of trading and broking teams, for instance.

Overall, headhunting did create its own demand, and it is still arguable that many companies can do without it; indeed, many do. But except for the very largest corporations with the most extensive resources, the majority of organisations have seen the wisdom – and overall cost-benefit – of bringing in outside experts when required. It has become a recognisable stage in the growth process to use external consultants. Single entrepreneurs just starting up, with little capital, may prepare their own advertising literature and letterheads; do all their own bookkeeping; organise their own promotion campaigns; carry out their own market research on new products; find out for themselves about new customers and, when the business begins to grow, handle their recruiting problems by advertising or asking around. As a business becomes more sophisticated, as the founder is more pressed for time and is earning more money, the concept of outside help becomes more acceptable and, ultimately, desirable.

The real achievement of headhunting in Britain, which indicates the new maturity of the industry, has been a gradual but discernible change in the attitude of the majority of users of search. At first, economic pressures pushed clients to a grudging, reluctant use of search consultants, and a realisation that they were acceptable and tolerable on the grounds that they could save time and hassle and ultimately even money, and could carry out confidential corporate dirty work in tight spots. Therefore long-term factors played a strong part in convincing client companies to experiment with headhunting for the first time. But the greater professionalism of the top search consultants and their measurable success in the business by the 1980s has influenced a significant number of clients to go beyond a basically negative attitude; and in the words of one regular user of search, to see headhunting not just as a convenient time and money saver, but as an objective, imaginative, innovative, creative and even indispensable management tool.

2

The Nature of Headhunting in Britain in the 1980s

The 1980s have seen a significant change in the fortunes of the major executive search firms in London. Although most of the major firms now at the top of the executive search market were present in London before 1980, their position, structure and influence was relatively small compared with their growth in importance in the 1980s. The London market may be seen to be increasingly dominated by eight firms, five of whom are true international firms – owning and controlling a wide network of offices worldwide – and three local firms. The international firms are Egon Zehnder, Russell Reynolds, Spencer Stuart, Korn/Ferry and Heidrick and Struggles; the UK firms are GKR, Whitehead Mann and Norman Broadbent. A number of smaller British firms are also making an important contribution, such as Tyzack, Merton, John Stork and specialists like City headhunters Baines Gwinner.

The recession of the early 1980s did much to improve the fortunes of executive search firms. The downturn in business in a wide variety of sectors called for outstanding management talent in order to regenerate British industry. It called – on the whole – for people different from those associated with the old-boy network, generally different from the type of people who responded to advertisements, and required a new approach to recruitment. It came to focus on a headhunting approach to find this talent, not necessarily people who had gone to the right schools and universities. Rather, the recession called for candidates who were above all young, sharp, bright and who had the necessary track record of success to turn businesses around. It required fewer people who could pass the port in the right way, and more people who would have the drive, energy, initiative and sheer guts actually to make money for the shareholders and themselves in a recessionary environment.

Once a number of these people were in place, naturally they wanted to build teams in all the major functions – finance, marketing, personnel, production, R & D – more in their own image. Thus the hunt was on for heads of functions who could deliver results, and executive search was seen to be the only truly effective way to actually define and attract this key talent.

During the recession of the early 1980s, many traditional British firms began using executive search in a significant way. Executive search consultants became, for the first time, acceptable rather than an odd, maverick collection of people that most companies did not really like to admit using. It also marked the beginnings of a true differentiation between the advertisements placed in the *Financial Times, The Sunday Times*, the *Daily Telegraph* and those jobs that were sourced by head-hunters. Prior to this, in the 1960s and 1970s, most senior jobs had in fact been advertised and senior people, even at chief executive level, would expect to find their next opportunity by looking in *The Sunday Times*. In the 1980s it became apparent that an increasing number of the senior jobs were handled by executive search and this increased during the decade until the late 1980s, when 80% of all senior jobs in the UK sourced outside the company were covered by the search firms. If one looks at the newspapers one rarely sees jobs advertised at over £80 000. In addition to the traditional British company using headhunting firms, the financial services community (always a large user of executive search) was pulling even more strongly. High-technology (hi-tech) businesses, with an open attitude to recruitment, have also been large users of executive search and today almost all sectors of British industry use this facility to some extent. In the USA the not-for-profit sectors dealing with heads of major museums, art galleries and universities are increasingly searched by headhunters and this may well be a sector in Britain that uses search in the future, particularly if more of those organisations continue to receive increased levels of funding from the corporate sector, as would seem to be the case.

Another reason for the increased acceptability of the use of executive search firms by a wide range of industries has been a noticeable improvement in their quality. In the 1960s and 1970s, the ranks of executive search consultants included many people who had largely failed at what they had previously undertaken. A not untypical background of an early headhunter was someone who had had general management experience and had worked in one or more functional roles, and then found themselves, for the best of reasons, on the market. Many thus went into executive search as it seemed an attractive, lucrative and not unpleasant way to earn a living. These people had little training in interviewing, in handling client relationships and in understanding what a service business was about, and many clients were understandably put off by such individuals. In the 1980s, however, things have changed. The large executive search firms in the UK have attracted many high-quality people from a diverse range of backgrounds. One of the notable features is that executive search consultants are a good deal younger than previously. Many have strong academic qualifications, such as an MBA, and a significant number have experience in general consulting as well as a number of line management roles. However, the great difference is that the executive search consultant of today sees this as a career rather than just something to move into because they have failed in one or more previous jobs. A significant number of the executive search consultants in the major firms have chosen, for the best of reasons, to come into this role and find it a challenging and stimulating career in itself.

SPECIALISATION OF EXECUTIVE SEARCH SERVICES

A further feature of the growth of the executive search market has been specialisation. With increasing professionalism and sophistication, the buyers of headhunting services have become more astute, often having a great understanding of how executive search firms operate and the similarities and the differences between them. They are well practised in choosing what they believe to be the right firm to handle a particular assignment and nowhere is this more clear than in the area of specialisation. Increasingly in the late 1980s search consultants who present themselves to clients are being asked about their background, their particular specialisation and what they have to contribute. Specialisation can be seen in two broad ways. Specialisation could be in terms of industry, for instance, financial services; experience in a particular area of banking; in high technology; in consumer products; in working for the international general consultancies; or in working in chemicals, engineering or pharmaceuticals. Knowledge of a particular industry can be a major factor in a specialist firm being selected by a potential client to undertake a search. The only difference here is at the most senior level when search firms are asked to undertake assignments for CEOs, MDs, non-executive directors or, indeed, chairmen. Here, experience of a particular sector is less important as a previous record of achievement in searching for such individuals than having the necessary weight and calibre to be able to attract those people.

The other way that specialisation is becoming apparent is in terms of functional discipline. Many headhunters now specialise in the finance function, recruiting financial directors and financial controllers for a wide range of interests. Other examples in the 1980s include information technology directors, marketing directors, sales directors or, indeed, human resources directors. This form of specialisation is attractive to potential clients, particularly where the executive search consultant has undertaken many assignments successfully and has a functional discipline that works across a diversity of industries. Some search consultants span these two worlds and have both a functional and an industry discipline.

What is increasingly clear is that for a large number of headhunters in the major eight firms – and many of the more profitable smaller ones – this functional or industry specialisation is a key to success. Most of the top-flight executive search consultants who now operate at the very top end of the market have developed their search careers by some functional or industry specialisation and there is evidence that this will continue to be an important factor. It is now becoming difficult for consultants to call themselves generalists covering all functions and all industries, and still be credible in today's highly professional and competent search market.

An example where this is very clear is in the City. Financial services have a diversified range of job openings; some call for broad marketing knowledge, some for human resources management skills and many call for specialists in the area of arbitrage, mergers and acquisitions, swaps, corporate finance, equity trading and research. The financial services community knows more than any other sector of British business which consultants really have that functional specialisation in executive search and will employ them accordingly.

Another factor that has become an increasing part of the business scene in the 1980s is the changing relationship between seniority and salary. It used to be taken for granted that the person who earned the highest salary in an organisation was the general manager or managing director: the one at the top, the one that most people look to as the boss. In this changing world, this is no longer so. There are many cases in service industries, in consultancies, in the financial services and in high technology where heads of functions and sales-driven people who generate tremendous sums of money for their companies are paid more than the person who is actually managing and running the business. Examples of this are nowadays quoted in most of the newspapers – the 25–30 year-old trader who is earning £200 000–£400 000 whilst the person who runs the whole department may be on a salary of only half this. What is not so readily understood is that many of these people are paid extensively on commission. If they make the money they get paid, but if there is a downturn in the market or their performance is not as strong as it was a year ago, then their salary will be reduced accordingly. Likewise the top sales performer in a hi-tech company can earn, by a mixture of base earnings, commission and stock options, more than the sales director and indeed more than the managing director. In many service businesses there is a growing number of people who do not necessarily want to progress in traditional career terms. They would rather continue earning this money for a few years with the hope of becoming financially independent, thus broadening their options and opportunities. Increasingly management is not seen as an end or goal in itself. Headhunters, who mostly have a fee based upon one-third of the first year's guaranteed compensation, did very well for themselves in the 1980s by recruiting many of these people who can make an outstanding contribution in terms of revenue to their organisations. The headhunters' fees are large because of the very real difficulty of attracting key people and because bringing in these outstanding people can add millions of pounds' revenue to client organisations, which makes the headhunter's fee appear small in comparison with the overall potential gains.

COMPANIES THAT NEED SEARCH

The worst possible environment for business for the executive search consultants is a steady state, i.e. one where there is little change in the business climate. With significant opportunities for growth, or even in a recession, all this change provides business for executive search. Search consultants are often called in when an organisation is considering going into a new business sector, as Marks & Spencer did when they went into financial services with their credit card; as when BP were trying to diversify their business and spot winners by developing new technology; as financial services institutions do when they wish to launch a new product or enter new markets. Similarly organisations that find themselves in difficulty; where the profits are not coming through, where there is pressure from shareholders for a significant improvement in profit performance; here again, the chairman and the Board are likely to reach out to executive search consultants to find them new talent.

A further example is when an organisation which has been trading for many decades finds itself increasingly out of touch with the market and the organisation's internal culture and style is no longer appropriate to the markets it is trying to address. Again, changing the culture of business is no easy task. One of the elements it nearly always requires is a new senior team. Attracting the best possible talent and developing a team of people who can work really effectively together and restore the fortunes of the organisation is a particular province of the executive search consultant.

A further example is when companies wish not only to grow internally, but also to acquire other companies as a means of strengthening their market position or indeed of entering new markets. Often there is insufficient management talent on board to achieve this objective, or it might be stretching the existing team too much so that their existing businesses may suffer. Again, because of the confidentiality and the need to attract the best possible talent, executive search firms are often called in.

A further example where executive search firms are often used is in the question of size of business. If an organisation is market leader and has a size and presence which can ensure that manpower planning is possible so that most jobs can be filled from graduate entry, then the need for an executive search firm is probably limited to a few specialist or technical appointments. If, however, we are talking about the number two or number three in a particular market, they may not be of sufficient size to achieve these objectives. They may have a requirement where they are looking for a very high return on capital employed and need to attract and retain the very best people in order to achieve that. They may be a branded goods company which does not have the strongest brands in the markets in which they operate. To reinforce these brands by attracting and retaining the best talent available is a key objective. If you are the number one in the market and have the strongest brands it could be argued that you do not necessarily need to have the strongest people!

Clients often expect to make a mixture of appointments, some internally and some from outside their organisation. An interesting point here is that certain organisations have won a reputation for attracting and retaining senior management talent. They become known by the headhunters as a likely place in which to find appropriate candidates for other searches. There are a large number of organisations where the converse is true: it is not possible to find much talent and they do not occupy the time and effort of executive searchers. Again a significant point is the culture of the company. Some companies are fairly closed and resist the change induced by bringing people in from outside. This has been the case with many traditional British companies and it is only now that they are really being exposed to greater change. It is also notable that where a chairman or chief executive has been brought in from outside to those organisations, this may be followed by many changes in senior management and so, from the headhunters' point of view, putting a chief executive into an older-style organisation is usually an opportunity for them to work with the newly appointed chief executive to build the new senior management team.

COMPANIES WHO DO NOT USE HEADHUNTERS

There are a number of major organisations who make only very limited use of executive search and yet are successful on a worldwide basis. This is certainly true of many of the largest oil companies, such as Exxon, Shell and BP. It is true to a large extent for IBM and it is true for a branded goods company like Procter & Gamble. All these organisations are mainly targets for the executive search fraternity, as they make only limited use, if at all, of the search firms' services. This is because they are able to attract a wide range of able, graduate-level entrants; they expect to (and do) lose a significant number of those but have the ability to retain the ones that they see as candidates to fill their senior management positions. Their manpower planning is sophisticated enough to ensure that there will be an adequate number of candidates of sufficient calibre to reach the highest levels in those organisations at any future time. They are able to do this because they have a dominant position in many markets and have the financial resources, excellent graduate training schemes, pay competitive salaries and offer a broad range of opportunities for young would-be executives to gain early experience. Middle-sized and smaller organisations find it truly hard to compete. These major companies are very stable, with an organisational structure which has been developed over many years and, like the Japanese Zaibatsu, they have a large-core business which is able to withstand changes in the market place. Smaller and more volatile businesses do not have this luxury and often find themselves unable to attract the best people, and therefore have to go outside to recruit for senior management.

The culture of these non-search-using companies is often very strong, and moulds and forms people in particular ways. Procter & Gamble influences people in terms of quality brand experience, and IBM in terms of broad sales and systems support training in computing and related areas. The secret of these organisations is that they have a power which enables them to keep the key people which they want, even if executive search consultants potentially and actually try to lure them away. It is well known in the executive search world that it is hard to prise really good people out of IBM or indeed attract those out of IBM whom IBM truly wish to keep. However, these steady-state type of organisations, when they enter new markets, do then use executive search consultants to find people with particular skills. There are no ultimate advantages or disadvantages, and such companies offer a very successful but different approach to organisation and management development which minimises the need for executive search consultants.

ORGANISATIONS WITH THEIR OWN IN-HOUSE SEARCH FUNCTIONS

Some organisations have developed their own executive search function internally to cope with their recruitment needs. An example here is Fidelity, the world's largest mutual fund manager, based in the USA. They have their own search company which they have developed as a service business. However, it tends to work for other companies rather than their own, although – not unnaturally – they make use of it. A number of other organisations have their own executive search division, often in broadly-based consultancies or in service businesses. Saatchi & Saatchi bought Hay Associates which has a recruitment business, MSL, with an advertising, selection and search arm. They certainly use MSL for some appointments but, as is well known, they have gone outside to use a number of the major search firms for many of their senior appointments. It is not always easy to use their own in-house people if the chairman or chief executive wants to find a very senior director: then they nearly always go to outside professional advisers for confidentiality, for objectivity and often because the senior headhunters in the major firms are the best, of the highest quality and are paid accordingly. Many of the in-house executive recruitment and search people are paid only relatively modestly and in many cases that is unfortunately a fair reflection of their ability.

THE BUSINESS CULTURE OF THE HEADHUNTING WORLD

The business culture of the large, international headhunting firms working at the top of the market plus a number of leading UK companies varies considerably but may be broadly defined.

Inevitably, in any market where there are competitors, the market, at some stage, will mature. The USA is a mature search market; and the UK is now showing early signs of a maturity of the product. Classic business theory tells us that it is increasingly difficult when the market begins to mature for new entrants to gain a significant position at a realistic cost. The style of many of the executive search firms in the 1970s was entrepreneurial: it had to be, because the market was embryonic and growing rapidly, and the firms run by entrepreneurs grew with the market: for instance, David Norman at Russell Reynolds, David Kay and Roy Goddard at GKR and Anna Mann, founder of Whitehead Mann, are good examples of that style. Another example could well be Peter Brooke who, though not having quite the same entrepreneurial approach, certainly had the business instincts and connections to build a significant position for Spencer Stuart in the UK, principally among the more traditional British organisations. Those firms who did not have one strong business driver building the operation were often unable to establish a business base in the late 1970s. These included Heidrick and Struggles, Korn/Ferry and Egon Zehnder. By definition, any national or so-called boutique business must have a business-mover. Failure to have that person will almost always mean that there is an inability to build the business sufficiently quickly to attract new high-quality people or retain existing staff, and build a profit base.

In the mid-to late 1980s, the position had changed. Russell Reynolds and Spencer Stuart, both with strong UK businesses, had reached a position where being entrepreneurial was not the only thing that mattered. Maintaining their position involved having consultants with a broad range of business and managerial skills. Almost always, where there is a strong market position in a mature consulting environment, the needs are consolidation, client management and strong attention to quality rather than going out and finding new clients.

Egon Zehnder has a not dissimilar approach, but a more cautious and longer-term perspective, putting quality of people and of work above everything else and truly trying to build a worldwide firm with a recognisable cultural identity. Other firms still see themselves as totally entrepreneurial: Korn/Ferry and Whitehead Mann must be seen in that category. The pitch for new business and the winning of new business are being extremely highly regarded and valued within those organisations even now.

Heidrick and Struggles, which had previously never really made much of an impact in the UK scene, although they were strong worldwide, reorganised in the mid-1980s and attracted a strong team which is now giving them a significant presence in the UK search market.

There are other ways of looking at the culture of executive search firms. Some may be characterised as predominantly transaction orientated: that is, obtain the brief from the client and work as hard and fast as possible to fill that particular job, that being both the goal and the result. Other firms have much more of a consulting bias, in particular Egon Zehnder and Heidrick and Struggles, who see themselves predominantly as advisers rather than just recruitment specialists. Their recruitment policy reflects this in the type of people they hire. Another way that firms may be characterised is by their use of research consultants. There is growing use of research consultants by executive search firms, but how they are used shows vast differences between the major firms. Some use researchers mainly as librarians, keeping all the contact with clients and with potential candidates with the consultant who is handling the assignment. Other firms use researchers to do most of the contacting or cold-calling. In particular, four firms are very large users of this latter type of research approach: namely Heidrick and Struggles, Whitehead Mann, GKR and Tyzack. For instance, in Heidrick and Struggles there are more research consultants than there are consultants, and in Tyzack the numbers are about equal. Saxton Bampfylde and Baines Gwinner also put much emphasis on research in this way.

Over and above these differences there are also cultural variations between the firms. It is common currency within executive search that consultants who are successful with one national or international executive search firm may find it very hard to be successful in others just because the expectations and culture, way of operating and behaviour may be vastly different. It is no easy matter to define these differences, but the clients who often use more than one of the major firms notice significant variations. The perception of Dr John Viney of Heidrick and Struggles – and that of the clients with whom he has spoken – is this: to be recruited as a consultant in Egon Zehnder one needs a strong First degree, plus a business degree, usually an MBA. In Heidrick and Struggles there is a strong disposition for potential consultants who have a mixture of general consultancy experience and relevant industry knowledge. In Korn/Ferry, it would appear that the focus is strongly on sales performance. Most headhunting firms, especially Korn/Ferry, will take the view that if people are interested, willing, motivated and tenacious enough to make a success then they will support them. However, if they do not find it an attractive business or one that they are successful at, they are likely to be asked to leave.

A further major difference between many of the search firms is whether a consultant is really working under the umbrella of a big name in the executive search business or working truly as part of a team. One approach – more like traders in financial services – is where they work almost independently, having their own cluster of clients and work with only a secretary. The other end is where there is a strong culture and willingness to integrate the client in the business, put more than one consultant on a search assignment and make sure that all the consultants work together for the long-term future of the business. Two of the international firms with a particularly well-developed cultural identity are Russell Reynolds and Egon Zehnder. Russell Reynolds is characterised by people with a strong educational background in the UK who may well be ex-public school and Oxbridge. This is a blue-blood organisation, very keen on people with style, contacts and a good record in industry usually working for prestige, high-quality organisations. The more well known or international they are, the better. Much emphasis is put on style, class and polish. Egon Zehnder, typical of a Swiss-based search organisation, is more low key. It is clearly prominent among executive search firms in Europe and has a strong, worldwide, one-firm concept. Typical Zehnder consultants will, as mentioned earlier, have a First degree, an MBA and a strong consulting element in their background, as well as successful line experience. Much less flashy and class orientated in a UK sense, they have more of a general consultancy view of the world, with a problem-solving approach rather than just an interest in completing a job. There is a discernible culture in Egon Zehnder, whether one is in Australia or mainland Europe. Their recruitment policy has worked very well for them and they are by far the largest outside America, although they are still having great difficulty establishing themselves in the USA.

A further difference in style between the firms is whether the culture of the organisation is centred around one or two key people or is broadly based and spread across all the consultants. An example of a narrow-based firm is Whitehead Mann, where Dr Anna Mann has a strong market presence and is the visible outward sign of the firm and defines its culture and approach to the market place. The other consultants in the team are expected to integrate around that style and there is pressure for them to be seen to do so. Much the same could be said, though not as strongly, of GKR where one of the remaining founders, David Kay, is attracting most of the business and defines the overall style of the firm. Perhaps it is not too strong to say that in national firms or boutiques the culture is defined by the owner or founder of the business. This is not the case, interestingly, in Tyzack, who are now one or two generations removed from their founder and, although working on a small scale internationally, have managed to create a strong collegial style, with a low turnover of consultants.

With the large international search businesses, inevitably there is no one view. Many of the international firms have a broad range of consultants who have differing styles and philosophies and therefore potentially appeal to a wide and diversified range of clients. In this sense many of the international firms will try to be all things to all people. This has the positive advantage of giving them a broad-based appeal across a diversified range of industries and functions and always having some-body in the team who can potentially suit the chemistry of a particular client. John Viney maintains that the exception to this among the major firms in the UK is his own firm, Heidrick and Struggles. There, the team would attempt to have a narrower range of appeal but a greater oneness with the clients to whom they are trying to appeal. The great advantage to them of this approach is that it has a strong one-firm concept, where most of the values and styles of the consultants are compatible, thus making it potentially easier to integrate as a consultancy team. Here the philosophy is to go and find the clients in a range of sectors which have a compatible style and approach leaving the other clients to seek their executive search needs elsewhere. The aim of Heidrick and Struggles' approach is to build a team that can truly work and integrate together over a number of years.

Much has been written on how to keep a team of consultants in a service sector together. Shared values among the team and a common approach is often at the core of success. Again, Egon Zehnder have, in no small measure, managed to keep their team together worldwide by having one strong culture and recruiting people who really integrate with it.

THE FAILURE AND DROP-OUT RATE OF FIRMS

In any dynamic market there is always a movement of positions and differences in firms measured in fee income. The loss of a top person in an executive search firm can radically alter the business and their fortunes. Many firms that had a significant executive search presence in the market place in the 1970s and early 1980s are now not even visible in the market. However, with the maturity of the business, these changes will become less noticeable and frequent.

WHY BECOME AN EXECUTIVE SEARCH CONSULTANT?

There is no one easy answer to this question. In many cases candidates have been attracted to the search business through being in contact with a search firm while discussing an assignment they are handling. Perhaps the assignment is not appropriate to them but the managing partner of the search firm may well feel that he or she has potential to be an executive search consultant. However, there are always attendant risks with taking people out of an environment where they have been successful and moving them, mid-career, into a completely different style and sector and trying to make them successful there. Every executive search firm clearly has had their failures.

Below is printed the specification for an Executive Search Associate, compiled by Heidrick and Struggles. It is not that different from many of the needs of the top executive search firms.

ASSOCIATE, HEIDRICK AND STRUGGLES

After initial training, the Heidrick and Struggles Associate will be expected to undertake entire search assignments with minimal supervision and coaching from the Office Manager and/or Partners. This involves definition of the job specifications with the client; laying out a search strategy with the Research Department, the development of potential candidates through sourcing, interviewing, making a final recommendation to the client; and handling both client and candidate in the delicate final stages of the negotiation to ensure a positive end of the assignment.

Any Associate is recruited with the prospect that he or she will be eligible for partnership after a few years: business development abilities, superior counselling skills in the field and a deep commitment to the firm and its progress are qualities which will rapidly become determinant. Compensation is made of a base salary and a bonus. Base salary is commensurate with the remuneration this person would earn in a top paying industry in view of his or her educational and professional experience. The bonus is discretionary but linked to performance: billings, acquisition of business (new and repeat), and general quality of work.

- Age: late 30s to early 40s.
- Education: postgraduate degree level from a leading university.
- Languages: all Heidrick and Struggles Consultants should be fluent in English. Persons whose mother tongue is English should preferably have another language. An international attitude and frame of mind are important, including an ability to understand, accept and work with other cultures.
- Experience: persons who have been in other types of consulting seem to adapt more rapidly to executive search and this should be an important source of consultants for Heidrick and Struggles. On the other hand, consultants from other search firms have very often failed in Heidrick and Struggles but this has not always been the case. Some line experience appears a main criterion. Experience in selling goods is certainly a plus.
  The candidate's professional career must show a clear progression and unquestionable achievements. Unusual interests, off the beaten track experiences should be of interest.
- Good presentation: dress standards of a person working at the highest levels of large corporations.
- Above-average communication skills: to the point, concise, convincing without being too talkative: a good listener but not passive. Quick to understand the hidden points of a conversation. A good sense of humour is a great plus.
- Intelligence and intuition. Empathy and judgement. Good critical mind, but not to the point of cynicism.
- Deep-rooted emotional stability. Strong resistance to stress. Resilience. A person who is quickly back on his or her feet after a serious blow.
- Self-motivated and self-starter. Fairly independent and autonomous personality. Achievement driven. Intellectual honesty. Service-minded and strongly dedicated to solving the client's problem. But not a loner. Capacity to attach to a firm, a team.
- His or her ambition should be to become a recognised professional in the field, to handle more and more prestigious assignments rather than to acquire the powers of a line executive.
- Entrepreneurial spirit. Good at managing one's own time. A strong interest in people and what makes them tick.
- Attentive to quality: high standards for oneself and others. Not willing to compromise with what is merely acceptable.

In the 1970s most people who joined executive search firms came from a career in industry. Most were in their 40s to 60s in age and were of an Establishment style and type. In the 1980s there are people from a number of different backgrounds. John Viney at Heidrick and Struggles came from a general consultancy and two other executive search firms before coming to Heidrick and Struggles. Mark Weedon had a period in general management consultancy with McKinsey and experience in a major international company before coming to Egon Zehnder. John Grumbar, who replaced Weedon at Egon Zehnder, is an exception having a financial services background with the Stock Exchange without previous consulting or recruiting experience. David Shellard had previous recruitment experience before joining Russell Reynolds. Anna Mann at Whitehead Mann had a background in research and previous experience in another executive search firm before founding her own firm. Nigel Humphreys, before joining Tyzack, was engaged in international consultancy, advising governments. Thus, the managing partner of these firms of the 1980s usually has either a recruitment or management consultancy background, rather than just having worked in industry. They are also much younger.

WHAT MAKES A SUCCESSFUL SEARCH CONSULTANT?

This is a very hard question to answer but one which the executive search firms would like to answer in a really strong and substantive way. On the one hand ability to sell is needed but perhaps more important is the ability to manage client relationships at a very senior level. That particular task needs a more outgoing personality. However, there are more reflective tasks: for example, interviewing. A headhunter needs to be an excellent listener, receptive, willing and able to see the difference in peoples' backgrounds and how those people might fit into a very different environment. A strong measure of creativity is required, not just an ability to see the obvious. In addition, a strong administrative capability is desirable in order to be able to manage themselves and the large amount of work, in a quality-conscious and timely fashion. Apart from that, a consultant should have the ability not just to be an egotist but to integrate with a team of people; they should also have the strength of purpose to be able to get results and to keep going through adversity. Another important attribute is the ability to work for long periods almost independently and not feel alienated but, on the other hand, also be able to integrate with the team. One of the interesting aspects of the executive search business is that it has enabled some people, who have not been truly successful at other careers they have undertaken, to be more than successful in executive search. A high-quality academic background, experience in consultancy and line management and qualities such as weight and drive are by no means a total guarantee of success.

THE NATURE OF EQUITY HOLDING IN EXECUTIVE SEARCH

In the national executive search companies, the equity holding is principally with the founders of the business. None of the big eight firms in the UK – Heidrick and Struggles, Russell Reynolds, Egon Zehnder, Spencer Stuart and Korn/Ferry (the international firms) or Whitehead Mann, GKR and Norman Broadbent – is directly quoted on the Stock Exchange. Norman Broadbent, 2½ years after they were founded, was acquired by Charles Barker plc, a quoted company, as discussed in Chapter 1. At the time of writing none of the other firms is quoted on the Unlisted Securities Market or the Stock Exchange. In the early 1970s – as we saw – Korn/Ferry had a market quotation for a period but the partners soon bought all their shares back. Thus the equities in these businesses are based at present on net asset value: that is, the value of the leases or freeholds, the furniture, the carpets, computer equipment and so on. That value is small compared with the potential value that a search firm would have if it had a market quotation; there would be a significant number of new millionaires were that to happen. However, with a flotation come outside shareholders and a proportionate loss of control. Also there is more outside scrutiny as to what consultants and owners of the business are paid. In the UK the top six to eight performers in executive search earn well in excess of £250 000 per annum plus a range of benefits. Investing some of this money in pension plans or other equities can – and has – made a number of top executive search consultants financially independent. However, the question of equity and the marketability of equity is a contentious problem and can be looked at in two ways, from the perspective of the international firm and also the national one.

In international firms like Heidrick and Struggles, Spencer Stuart or Egon Zehnder the partners of the firm have equity in the enterprise: that is, they own a proportion of the shares. However, none of these firms is a true partnership in the way that some of the accounting or legal firms are. They are often registered overseas. Partners own equity in those businesses and as they thrive and prosper and grow the value of that equity increases. However, it is based only on the net asset value and there is no market in the shares. When executive search consultants leave or retire, they are forced to sell back the equity to other partners who, on election to the partnership, are encouraged to purchase stock at an agreed rate. Within the major firms this stock has been rising in some cases at over 20% per annum, and has proved to be a very good investment in spite of not being on the market. It does provide an effective way for partners 'to accrue capital'. However, it will never make them rich in the same way that potentially having an independent company and taking that to the market would have.

THE NATIONAL COMPANY

The problem of taking a national executive search firm to the market is that they have been, up to now, a one-product company. The Blue Arrows and Michael Pages of the recruitment world have found it much easier because they have had a variety of products and services, and encompass a number of sectors. The average national executive search firm, in order to come to the market, needs a broader range of products. However, having a broader range of service products creates problems of conflicts and interests. For example, it is very hard to set up a general management consultancy with a broad range of clients and then allow the executive search firm to poach people out of them. If that opportunity is denied the search company then they will have significant problems convincing their clients that they can do a good job. The three major national firms are each trying a different solution. GKR are trying to make the business an international one by opening in Japan and in Germany, and hope to build an international business of wholly-owned subsidiaries of GKR. They believe having an international executive search business is the way to go, although they are late in starting and face formidable competition from the major international search firms. Whitehead Mann take a completely different view and do not see themselves diversifying overseas with wholly-owned subsidiaries. Instead they are interested in building on a range of other products, thus broadening their base. Norman Broadbent, after remaining alone for 2½ years, have, as we have seen, backed their business into Charles Barker, which came to the market in 1985/86. In Charles Barker they are one of a range of public relations and advertising businesses and time will tell if this is a truly successful strategy. Tyzack and other smaller national firms have formed regional offices in the UK and have established international networks, usually through associates.

With the exception of Tyzack, the fundamental difference between these two types of firm is that, at some stage, the owner will have to sell out. They can sell to the other people in the business but will probably require a much higher price than net asset value for their shares. That may put a large and possibly intolerable strain on the firm and may not be an attractive option for the other consultants in the business. Perhaps the Tyzack route of the founder selling to an institution and then the partners and staff buying it back by way of a management buy-out is one that might be followed. Boyden too did this more recently.

The international firms see themselves remaining independent although the founders of Korn/Ferry and Russell Reynolds are still large holders in their businesses, and how these organisations are going to resolve the equity issues, so that the founders of the firm are paid an acceptable return for having started the business is being watched with interest. Russell Reynolds himself is in his 50s, and this is already becoming an issue. Korn/Ferry are likewise addressing this problem. It may yet prove attractive for one of those two international firms to be purchased, and there would be substantial competition in order to acquire an executive search firm with such a famous international brand name. Heidrick and Struggles had a difficult time when the founders, Gardner Heidrick and John Struggles, left the firm in the early 1980s and there was a period of turmoil until an international partnership structure emerged. Spencer Stuart went through this process a few years earlier in a more effective way.

DEFECTIONS FROM THE MAJOR INTERNATIONAL COMPANIES

In the UK, the most notable defection from an international company to set up an independent search business has been that by David Norman and Miles Broadbent, who were both previous MDs of Russell Reynolds in London, and who took with them other colleagues to found Norman Broadbent. Whitehead Mann and GKR are different as their consultants did not come from any of the major search firms. When Heidrick and Struggles had difficulties worldwide in the early 1980s there were many defections, both of individuals starting up their own businesses (principally in the USA), and also key performers defecting to other international search firms.

There is still some poaching between the major executive search firms and Korn/Ferry founded their worldwide business on doing this in a very successful way, but more recently they have had a number of losses themselves both to Russell Reynolds in the States and Heidrick and Struggles in Europe. Most of the good performers in the international search companies enjoy the prestige of being part of a large firm. Many of them do not see the benefits of moving to a smaller, nationally based firm. Moving is always traumatic, especially in wondering whether clients will follow them, although the major firms have strong, legally enforceable clauses regarding poaching of clients. This all goes to dissuade consultants in the major firms from leaving. The spark that does often make people go is when there are changes in the international organisation or indeed a change in the fortunes of the company. However, most of the international firms are getting more practised at this now, and as the major international firms become stronger, brand loyalty from their clients and stronger images worldwide will make it proportionately less attractive for key performers and partners to leave. Top headhunting firms will become, in essence, more like the international law and accounting firms, and to a lesser extent the advertising fraternity. Considerable prestige will increasingly be enjoyed from being part of those international businesses.

THE INPUT OF HEADHUNTERS TO A COMPANY

Why use headhunters? The reasons for using some form of external assistance in recruiting key people are often quite clear: the confidentiality, the know-how and the experience are all obvious factors; why bring in a headhunter rather than use an advertising consultant is sometimes more difficult to explain. Often a headhunter will advise the client to advertise if in his or her judgement it is the most appropriate way of identifying suitable people. The last thing an executive search consultant wants to do is to take on an assignment which is not achievable and which he or she cannot complete. No one is going to be happy with that situation. The job has to be at a senior enough level and it has to be constrained enough to enable the job to be searched. If there are potentially 5000–10 000 people who can do the job, then it is almost certainly more appropriate to advertise, even anonymously. However, when the market is sharp and clear and there is a need for very strong, talented individuals to fill the position, when the client is looking for someone with outstanding ability to run the business or to be a senior director, then talking to a headhunter may well be the best first step. Executive search is one of those products which has a large degree of elasticity. That is, the person who is selling the product and service can persuade potential clients to buy the service, and it is only really limited by the quality of people selling the service.

A good headhunter potentially has significant awareness of how other companies have solved this problem, and knowledge about the market place in which to look for an individual. Often, if they have a disposition to broader problem-solving, the search consultant can provide views on several issues: the potential organisational structure; how the individual would fit in; the likely scope of his or her responsibilities; if the tasks he or she will be set are manageable and possibly whether candidates can be found in the market who meet a particular specification; whether the search can be a UK-based search or needs to be international; whether any of the top candidates can be attracted for the remuneration or does the remuneration of the senior team need reviewing; is the nationality of the candidate important; could a woman do the job; what happened to the last job holder; did he or she move on to a bigger job or was he or she fired, and was that person successful in the role?

The headhunter may well feel that there is a need to bring a more general consulting focus to bear in order to solve the organisational issues before an executive search is undertaken. Sometimes the consultant feels that there is so much ambiguity regarding the appointment that it is unlikely to be successful as presently structured. There may well be differences of view amongst Board members on the matter of the type of person required and the future role. Again the perceptive executive search consultant can help resolve those issues, often working with and alongside the chairman and MD. Sometimes the Board can be changed and the need for the job eliminated. Sometimes the headhunter receives a fee for that advice without even undertaking an executive search.

In the 1980s, the personnel departments of many organisations are a lot slimmer than they were in the 1970s. In fact, many organisations have reduced this and other functions to such an extent that they use consultants for a wide variety of activities whether it be for strategy advice, for marketing, production, organisation development, training or indeed executive search. It is generally true that if organisations try to set up such functions in-house, they are unlikely to keep and retain the best people; thus there is always a gulf between the in-house employees and their performance and what can be obtained in the way of services by using external consultants to undertake the job.

The sophistication and professionalism of the chairman, chief executive or personnel director varies considerably. However, in the major publicly quoted firms and in a growing number of the smaller firms, there is a high level of understanding and increased professionalism. If there is a relationship with an existing search firm the client may well use a known firm when making further appointments. If there are doubts about the search firm's ability to work at a senior level, say to find a chief executive, the client may well invite two or three firms in to pitch competitively and see who has the best overall track record and appears most attractive and experienced to the Board.

Clients are very well aware of levels within an organisation and, if they have a smaller headhunting firm working at one level in the organisation, they may well not use that firm when a very senior appointment arises. This is why, in a large number of instances, the major, large executive searches go to the top firms rather than those that are smaller. It is one thing to trust a middle-management appointment to an executive search consultant within a small firm; it is quite another to trust him or her to find a new group chief executive. Overall, clients are likely to go to the executive search firm they feel most comfortable with, which has the most appropriate range of experience and is closest to the image of the type of people they wish to recruit. It is a truism that the executive search consultant hired has a stronger influence on the person eventually put on the short list of candidates than the client. The search consultant who comes nearest to the Board's idea of the chief executive they wish to hire may well be successful in winning the assignment. The dominant issue in most searches is how well the executive search consultant understands and relates to the culture of the client. It is not easy with new clients to truly understand their culture and to find a range of people for a short list who would truly fit into that organisation. As ever, the acid test for search consultants is not getting the people hired, but whether those people are doing an effective job two, three or four years later. An even better test is whether, after two years, the successful candidate is promoted again or given a larger international role. Bringing a very senior candidate into a new organisation right at the top is always a very difficult matter. There may need to be a large number of meetings and discussions between the consultant and the client even after the candidate is appointed to ensure that things are running smoothly.

HOW IS AN EXECUTIVE SEARCH CONSULTANCY INVITED INTO A COMPANY?

Clearly the firm has to be known, and a well-informed personnel director or even chief executive has often developed a number of relationships with executive search firms. The ones that study the search market even more closely will know who is particularly good at what and who has done recent searches. He or she may even know the number of consultants within a particular firm, how it has been performing, what are its key issues, how it has grown over the past year and generally what it is doing and how successfully. The executive search consultants are usually good at keeping these relationships and informing decision-makers on changes in their organisation as well as general information about the search business. There is nothing more interesting to a busy chief executive or personnel director than knowing what the competition are doing, what they are being paid and who is moving where. The perceptive executive search consultant (a) keeps in contact with clients, both actual and prospective, and (b) is very effective at giving them this sort of information.

When the need arises to review the search firms they are using or when there is a particularly sensitive issue, then which firm is contacted is clearly a very important issue.

In a recent large UK search the company in question called on five of the major search firms, and invited them all in to make a competitive pitch to decide who was going to be successful at finding them a group chief executive. However, having said that, the best way of getting new business is by referrals from satisfied clients rather than completely new assignments with completely new clients.

In summary, it is clear that the nature of headhunting in the UK is changing. It is a great deal more professional than it was a few years ago comparable with the standards of other types of consultancies and partnership firms, and is attracting an altogether higher quality of person than was previously the case. In turn, clients' expectations are growing; they are more informed, more knowledgeable about the process, much more likely to adopt an open style, and want to know the key facts, expecting a high level of overall professionalism. Very few of them believe there is any magic (if ever there was) in the business and almost all of them want to understand the process and expect executive search consultants to provide that knowledge. There is now no room for the amateur or the dilettante in the business.

In conclusion, it is clear that the market in the UK is maturing and the executive search product is starting to come to age. Executive search is becoming the most effective way to recruit senior management talent into organisations. It is expensive for clients but, in relation to the potential benefits which a strong appointment can produce, the fees and expenses involved appear very small.

A future interesting trend may well be the 'poachers turning game-keepers' syndrome on both sides. There is some recent evidence of executive search consultants moving from major positions in search firms to become group personnel directors or even MDs of large firms or service businesses. Some executive search consultants are now becoming non-executive directors in businesses where there is no potential conflict.

The opposite side of the coin is that group personnel directors or chief executives are moving from the corporate world to join executive search firms which can offer a wholly different but very satisfying way of earning a living. After all, having some fun, earning some money and getting better at what one does have got to be three of the key elements in business and, potentially, a career in executive search (in the right environment) offers all three.

3

Client and Candidate Experiences of Headhunting: A Survey

THE QUALITY OF SEARCH FIRMS

Do users of search – a significant sector of British industry – agree that most headhunting firms offer a professional and high-quality service, and thus see no need for the official regulation of the executive search industry? Official regulation of headhunting in Britain, in contrast with the USA, has not been developed and no widely accepted written body of rules exists. Neither is there any organisation to which all the major firms subscribe. Is this situation acceptable, or should it be changed?

Most users of search believe that, on the whole, headhunters do a good job, and that the industry is effectively self-regulating because, given the grapevine spread of information, poor work would quickly result in loss of business. However, an outspoken minority of executives responsible for recruiting felt strongly that the industry has a disreputable, cowboy element that is potentially damaging to client users and to professional and respectable search firms alike.

This was the first problem addressed in the following survey, which also asked the following questions: why do companies use headhunters instead of their own in-house recruiting facilities and personnel function? How much use do individual companies make of headhunters? What is the relationship between companies' usage of large international headhunting firms compared with smaller, specialised consultancies? What is the attitude of companies to headhunters poaching their people? Have they experienced the phenomenon of poacher-turned-gamekeeper or gamekeeper-turned-poacher? Was recruiting by companies affected by the Big Bang and/or the stock market crash of October 1987? How did the companies first come across the headhunting firms they employed? Finally, the survey sought to gauge the views of candidates; this was much more difficult, as very few were prepared to contribute their views, despite an extensive mail-shot. The results of the client survey are appended to this chapter.

On the matter of the quality of search firms, companies were asked: were the candidates selected by headhunters appropriate to the agreed

71

briefs? Would the company comment on the performance of individual executive search firms with whom they had worked? And were they aware of any leaks of confidentiality or illegal use of information by search firms at any time?

The survey showed that, on the whole, most companies reported good experiences of search. The mail-shot received a high response rate of over 43% – 13 replies from 30 enquiries – so a higher number of negative responses was expected, bearing in mind that people are generally swifter to complain than to praise. Yet the questionnaire responses were usually favourable. Most negative criticisms of the quality of search work were expressed verbally on home territory to the author; relatively few clients were prepared to commit themselves to serious discontent on paper, even anonymously. In all, 30 companies contributed; in addition to the 13 questionnaire replies, nine were prepared to speak on the telephone, of a total of 25 called, and eight were visited and interviewed in more detail.

Responses pointing to especially good search work emanated from Grand Metropolitan, Plessey, Kingfisher plc, Cadbury Schweppes, BICC, four companies who preferred to remain anonymous and the majority of the financial services users. Tesco, Midland Bank, an international holding group, two large international banks and three other anonymous respondents commented on mixed performance. Only one contributor, a human resources director, expressed herself as entirely anti-headhunting, during a two-hour interview at British Airways' Heathrow-based central office, and she may be seen as principally involved in lower-level recruitment. Peter White, main Board director of group personnel at Midland Bank, was more justified in complaining that the banks in the City had suffered during the Big Bang as the result of excessive leverage enjoyed by headhunters in a tight market.

David Tagg at Grand Metropolitan, the drinks, hotels, brewing, retailing and food-producing giant ranking number 10 in *The Times 1000* and employing nearly 150 000, spoke cheerfully of his general liking of headhunters. He remarked that if they did not exist he and many others in his position would have to invent them! He believed that combining the selective use of headhunters with sound internal management development was the most effective way to establish a management team. Michael Brookes of Nomura, the leading Japanese securities house, considered that the use of search consultants had helped Nomura to integrate into the London financial market.

Tagg would not classify headhunting firms as good or bad, but spoke of the need to find an individual consultant who would fit into the company's style and culture. He thought that headhunters were kept on their toes by the generally-held view – expressed frequently both inside and outside the headhunting industry – that a consultant is only as good as his or her last assignment. Tagg looked for prompt and well-considered short lists of candidates, shrewd advice and help in drawing up the brief and specification, and some form of guarantee and after-sales service. The few inappropriate appointments in his experience were, Tagg felt, probably more the fault of Grand Metropolitan than the headhunters concerned, and reflected very rapid changes in the organisation at that particular time. He was confident that search consultants stuck to their rules of good conduct and professional service without the need for the kind of official regulation in force in the USA, as laid down by the Association of Executive Search Consultants, (formerly the Association of Executive Recruitment Consultants). Peter White of Midland Bank was less convinced, complaining of the failure of some large firms to adhere to a strict off-limits policy, and described an even worse practice of advancing a candidate who has undertaken to engage the headhunter involved at a later date if he or she lands the job.

Adrian Gozzard, formerly Director of Human Resources of Plessey, the telecommunications and electronics giant (number 93 in *The Times 1000* and employer of over 30 000), who has had long and extensive experience of search, has turned time and time again to headhunting firms, despite having used a full-time, in-house recruitment manager, and working hard on internal management development. Writing in *The Executive Grapevine*, he sees natural competition between search firms as enough to foster and maintain their quality, and considers that the last few years have witnessed a weeding-out of the less professional outfits resulting in fewer and better consultants.

Retail giant Kingfisher – number 51 in *The Times 1000* with over 56 000 employees – has been, according to Peter Samuel, Director of Organisation and Management Development, a wide and extensive user of search. Over recent years, headhunters have helped to make consistently good appointments without major cause for complaint. Confectionery, food and soft drinks manufacturer Cadbury Schweppes – ranked 60 in *The Times 1000* and with nearly 27 500 employees – was also prepared to give credit to headhunters. Graham Shaw, then Group Personnel Director, regarded the quality of search work he had experienced as satisfactory, without leaks or indiscretions; he agreed that headhunters who could not be trusted would soon be finished.

Cable manufacturers and engineers BICC, rated 49 and employing 45 000, considered that there were probably far too many headhunting firms around, but users could learn by experience and then stick to those they knew best. A leading wines and spirits producer and distributor wrote of generally good candidates and satisfactory performance. Two completely anonymous respondents agreed with this view of overall high-quality work, one confidently but paradoxically remarking that the firm would not have been hired otherwise! A large venture capital organisation, who refused to comment on individual headhunter performance, wrote that on the whole good candidates had been put forward, but that they would not know if there had been any leaks or illegal use of information by search firms. Most of the respondents answered this question in a similar manner; it is perhaps disturbing that most companies feel they would have no way of knowing if a head-hunter had abused their trust.

One large car-hire company, who expressed mixed feelings about headhunters, had a suspicion about a possible leak by a search firm: 'we believe there was but we could not sustain it' with any evidence. They also pointed out that headhunters were 'only good if managed tightly'. A past personnel director of an international trading group agreed. He said that a company could suffer bad headhunting experiences if it was not entirely sure exactly what it wanted the search consultant to do. Unsatisfactory results would then be its own fault. Although head-hunting generally was gaining a professional reputation, he continued, in London especially the business was still seen as 'rather dodgy'.

The suspicion surrounding headhunting was not helped by what he and many others saw, and still see, as the frequent movement of individual consultants between rival headhunting firms and in and out of industry. Headhunters are, by definition, enemies of long-term company loyalty and, because they spend so much time persuading people to move, it is hardly surprising that they themselves do not hesitate when they see an exciting new opportunity. Thus many com-panies see them as a threat to their holding on to their good people, and instilling corporate loyalty into new appointees.

The successfully transformed supermarket chain and multiple retailer Tesco – ranked 22 in *The Times 1000* and employing 71 000 – similarly described headhunters as good servants but bad masters: their work should be closely defined and controlled by the client. Although some search firms were undoubtedly first rate, a spokesman felt that it was unwise to stick to just one, especially for a company like Tesco, hitherto unused to search. There was a need for a trusting relationship between client and consultant, he agreed, but he was not prepared to rely on any headhunter completely, maintaining that they pretended to act accord-ing to codes of conduct only when it suited them. He was also involved in lower-level search and was attached to more traditional methods.

The director responsible for recruitment at a leading French bank spoke of generally successful placements through search, but warned that choosing the wrong headhunter could be a disastrous mistake. A Far Eastern bank's personnel spokesman agreed that generally good candidates had been found but, in common with two anonymous respondents, he would not comment on specific firms and expressed a lack of confidence in many of them.

Lynda Philamore, head of assessment and recruitment at British Airways – ranked 26 in *The Times 1000* and employer of 44 000 – was exceptional in this survey in expressing almost entirely negative views about the executive search industry, despite the publicity surrounding the success of headhunted chief executive Colin Marshall.

She called for an exposure of the headhunting industry as a whole, accusing consultants of a variety of sins: of perpetuating another form of updated old-boy network, of ignorance about systematic interviewing practice, of poor report writing, of rushing through assignments as quickly as possible and of an inability to handle complex, highly specialist assignments: they would either fail to find anyone or send someone completely unsuitable. She emphasised that, as far as she was concerned, headhunters were rarely useful to high-quality, prestigious companies – such as BA, presumably – but did serve a function for low-profile businesses with image problems, whom they could puff up, and flatter candidates into joining.

She denied that search consultants observed any professional ethics beside the obvious one of not poaching from clients for at least two years, and noted a complete absence of clear standards of approach and guarantees to do the job properly. There should be official training courses for headhunters, she suggested, and the industry should be properly regulated.

Why did other companies not complain as she was doing? They were loath to attract adverse publicity by criticising headhunters for an unsuitable or even disastrous appointment, or felt it might be a reflection on them if they chose an unsuitable firm. She maintained that bad headhunting practice was thus allowed to continue unchecked.

Such views about the executive search industry are relatively uncommon, yet these views should not be entirely ignored. The feeling of disquiet about the practices and methods of some headhunting firms in terms of ethics, reliability, quality of work and total professionalism is such that the possibility of setting up an official self-regulatory association ought to be investigated. It would be effective only if all, or at least a majority of firms – especially the large international search businesses – agreed to join. Such an organisation could take the form of a formal association which would arrange qualifying examinations and the provision of certificates, like the legal and accounting professional bodies, or at least operate in the manner of the existing MCA.

HEADHUNTING OR IN-HOUSE RECRUITING?

Why do companies use headhunters instead of their own in-house recruiting facilities and personnel function? It should be established at the outset that many large blue-chip companies do not actually use search at all. In this survey, replies were received to this effect from three such businesses. Shell International Petroleum's Head of Group Recruitment, Adrian Loader, wrote that: 'The Shell Group very rarely uses headhunters to recruit and the exceptions are limited to quite specific cases. In fact, in my time in central recruitment we have not used headhunters in any way, and there is little prospect of our doing so in the near future.'

Peter Dutton, Corporate Recruitment Manager at Procter & Gamble's UK head office in Newcastle, wrote: 'We do not use Headhunters at all, because we have a policy of recruiting only at the first level of management (usually graduates direct from university) and filling all more senior management positions by promotion from within.' J. Boyett, Manager of Central Services and Special Projects at Standard Chartered Bank, replied that, 'The Bank's experience in using Head-hunters is so limited that a response to your questionnaire would be worthless.'

Procter & Gamble and Shell in particular, together with several other giant organisations like IBM and Unilever, have their own completely adequate recruiting and training resources, and what is more they follow a policy which actually discriminates against outsiders. Of course, as far as headhunters are concerned, these companies fall into the category of poaching grounds. Venture capital giant 3i had not used executive search at all in the past four years but mentioned that they had lost a number of people through headhunters.

As we have just seen, British Airways also suggested that their need for search was minimal, and that many other large, highly professional concerns felt the same. As companies became more sophisticated, they argued, organisations could handle most, if not all, their recruiting problems. But it is possible – and equally convincing – to argue precisely the reverse: that the most advanced companies recognise the value of the strategic use of consultants generally – including headhunters – in running a business as efficiently and effectively as possible. David Tagg of Grand Metropolitan saw the rise of headhunting as part of a growing trend of employing outside consultants for specific problems. A Phillips & Drew spokesman said that his organisation uses search very rarely but thought that this could well change in the future, especially through the influence of his firm's parent company, the Union Bank of Switzerland.

Adrian Gozzard, ex-Plessey also valued headhunters in their role as external consultants. Through their objectivity, he argued, search consultants were able to provide what he saw as conceptual help in defining a business need and translating it into the sort of people who could fulfil it; actually searching for people was perhaps less important. Most clients were too close to their organisation – they could not see the wood for the trees – to solve many of their senior recruiting problems. Headhunters were also more likely to offer a dynamic rather than a static solution, Gozzard suggested: they would be looking for what was to happen to the company in the future, not just today, and the role of the successful candidate in effecting change.

Indeed, most companies responding admitted to employing head-hunters principally for such strategic positions as Gozzard indicated, so inevitably their usage of search was exceptional rather than everyday. Additionally, management functions attracting a small field of candidates and/or subject to supply volatility, such as financial, marketing and trading positions, were most likely to be recruited by search. BICC spoke of employing headhunters when looking for 'rare birds' for specialised jobs as 'horses for courses'. Sainsbury's, only occasional users of search, would make exceptions in the cases of jobs currently hard to fill, such as top accountants and systems analysts. Other employers referred to the advantages of employing search consultants for particularly sensitive appointments; obviously a personnel director could not be expected to try and find his or her successor. Several companies spoke of the special value of headhunters when moving strategically into new business and/or geographical areas. Gozzard, when he was with Allegheny, called on search consultants to develop its brand-name business, including Wilkinson Sword, Bryant & May, Sunbeam and Rowenta.

The French bank used both search consultants and job agencies – depending on the level of the position – without in-house recruiting at all; this was mainly for convenience, as they had no experience of recruiting or advertising for jobs in Britain. They did not necessarily believe that employing such consultants was more cost-effective than in-house methods, just quicker and easier for an overseas branch. All their offices abroad used outside recruiting consultants as a matter of policy.

They were not the only respondent of the survey who identified another clear advantage of headhunting, especially for the most senior positions: that staff who were prepared to move jobs actually prefer to be headhunted, rather than face the time-consuming task of ploughing through advertisements or the slightly demoralising task of putting their names down with agencies. Many executives who would not consider these second and third options would actively welcome the first. The element of ego-boosting and prestige associated with the headhunter's call has not been lost on employers, even those who were not headhunted themselves.

Many users of search also appreciate the fact that an approach to an executive by an intermediary partly removes any moral dilemma employees may face about being disloyal. After all, the executives cannot then be accused of directly approaching their employers' rivals. This 'poaching' by headhunters – criticised so often by employers on the receiving end – is recognised as a great facility by experienced users of search, one of whom wrote of the value of search consultants in 'winkling out talent which may not respond to advertisements'. Graham Shaw, ex-Cadbury Schweppes, said exactly the same. Peter Cole, Personel Director of SBCI Savory Milln spoke of employing search consultants as intermediaries, not just for the confidentiality and anonymity, but for the benefit of a more structured search.

Those respondents who insisted on strict anonymity – to the extent of removing coding on the questionnaires and sending them back in plain brown envelopes – not surprisingly pointed to the anonymity factor as an attractive feature of headhunting when compared with in-house recruiting. Although, as discussed in Chapter 4, most search consultants encounter difficulties in attracting candidates on behalf of clients who insist on remaining anonymous for at least the initial stages of the search, many clients see this as a real plus in using headhunters in the first place. A large investment conglomerate replying to the survey suggested that the main advantage of employing headhunters occurred 'when the position to be filled is sensitive internally and externally'. Cadbury Schweppes would turn to headhunters when 'we don't want anyone to know we're looking'.

Such confidentiality about the client was also seen as particularly important by Tesco. Similarly, David Tagg of Grand Metropolitan referred to using headhunters when he had an eye on a specific person within another company: a headhunter could discreetly and confidentially find out if that person might consider moving, before the name of the interested party, i.e. Grand Metropolitan, need be revealed.

An indication that the acceptability of the concept of headhunting has made great progress among employers in Britain is the fact that many of the respondents attested to search consultants' knowledge of the executive market place, gained over a number of years, and their expertise in certain specialised sectors. A spokesman for a large nationalised service industry wrote of headhunters being able to provide them with 'the feel of external experience' and an appreciation of the stature in the market place of their existing staff and the organisation itself, together with a more extensive network of contacts than they could possibly have at their disposal.

Sainsbury's, ranking 17 in *The Times 1000* with 82 000 employees, when considering appointing a senior departmental director, chose to use headhunters for 'political reasons rather than convenience or speed' because they could then be informed in detail about the market for candidates. Otherwise, Sainsbury's considered that they had good connections in the retail trade – especially through their joint-venture with British Home Stores – and thus their own recruiting facilities were usually adequate.

As suggested in the cost-benefit analysis of headhunting in the Introduction, the majority of respondents considered that using search consultants was certainly more expensive than in-house methods. Yet many qualified that statement: Peter Samuel welcomed the way that headhunters could put all their resources into one search at a time and avoid Kingfisher having to maintain expensive overhead staff unnecessarily. Other employers thought that on costing their executives' valuable time and all the overheads involved in do-it-yourself recruiting, the differences in total expense were probably marginal. Peter Christie of Midland Montagu said that he would always take a separate commercial decision on each assignment, according to fees quoted. Many others would do the same.

The element of time-saving is seen as significant by many employers, and one respondent identified it as the main motive for taking a recruiting problem to a search consultant in the first place. Tesco agreed that one of the great advantages of using headhunters was their speed in short-circuiting and short-cutting – but not skimping – all the work involved. David Tagg of Grand Metropolitan said the same, fully accepting that his company did not have a research department comparable with that of a major headhunting firm, and neither was this necessarily desirable. An experienced headhunter could narrow the field down to short-list stage much more quickly and cost-effectively, Tagg argued. Adrian Gozzard, ex-Plessey, saw the reduction to its essentials of the complex and time-consuming task of senior recruiting as one of the most important functions of the headhunter.

The human resources director of a large UK wines and spirits business also suggested that once total costs were taken into account, it could be argued that headhunters were not necessarily more expensive than using home-grown methods. An anonymous respondent wrote perceptively that it 'depends on how you cost internal opportunity cost, etc.'. He concluded that the methods probably cost about the same; 'but that's if they [the headhunters] are successful, but they are not always'. Graham Shaw, ex-Cadbury Schweppes, said he always gulped when he received a headhunter's bill, and certainly took cost into account in choosing between the methods. He would always think twice about how to recruit for a position paying £30 000–£35 000, i.e. a job on the borderline between the marzipan and the icing. David Tagg of Grand Metropolitan considered that employing headhunters was probably not economical below this level except in specialised cases. He agreed that headhunters were indeed expensive, but then one is, after all, dealing with an expensive commodity – one's senior personnel – and it is not wise to cut corners on such vital issues. Financial services users of search placed greater emphasis on the costs of headhunting, with more justification, as they were paying out more. Michael Brookes of Nomura suggested that headhunting firms, to justify their charges, should be prepared to accept that part of their fees reflect a performance-related element. A final instalment could be paid when the candidate starts work, or even a year later, if that candidate has stayed with the firm and/or performed well.

In making the choice between headhunting or in-house recruiting, it is clear that the crux of the matter is the level of appointment involved; most employers do see a place for both methods. This factor determines the answer to our next question, that of the frequency and extent to which companies use search firms.

RATE OF USAGE OF SEARCH

How much use do individual companies make of headhunters? It has not been easy to establish the numbers of appointments – and hence fees paid out – for which clients engaged search consultants. Clients are apt to minimise numbers of assignments, whilst headhunters maximise them, and neither are willing to divulge exact figures.

To the question, 'Do you use headhunters regularly or on specific occasions only?', respondents admitting regular usage accounted for only 15% of the companies surveyed. How did they define 'regular' or 'specific' in this case and did this vary over time? This latter consideration seems to be especially important, since fluctuations in headhunting usage by clients would appear not to be constant but to rise and fall with internal and external changes in demand for staff, as one would expect.

In this sense, Peter Samuel wrote that no particular departments of Woolworth had significantly different levels of requirement, but that early in 1988 they had 'made a number of senior financial appointments from external sources via Executive Search Companies'. The large mining conglomerate responding to the survey wrote that none of its sectors made appointments using headhunters frequently; but, on the other hand, the government service organisation questioned spoke of particular usage of search in finance, marketing and information technology. These seemed to be especially important recruiting areas in early 1988; executives in these fields – together with sales – were also being particularly sought by the wines and spirits company in our survey. The large industrial investment group questioned identified 'mainly front line operating departments' as their most frequent users, and an anonymous respondent referred to research and marketing as sources of headhunting demand.

Cadbury Schweppes revealed that the average yearly number of headhunting assignments initiated by the company would be between eight and ten, divided equally between generalists and specialists. Like many other blue-chip companies, Cadbury Schweppes employ headhunters exceptionally and sparingly, giving more attention to internal promotion and internal management development; yet they still acknowledge the value of executive search.

Sainsbury also claimed a comparatively modest rate of usage of headhunting, preferring to concentrate even more on long-term policies of training up graduates. David Tagg of Grand Metropolitan referred to more extensive usage, perhaps on a par or slightly more than Cadbury Schweppes, depending on timing of demand for staff. He considered that there must be very few large firms who never needed headhunters at all. Financial services have long been among the heaviest users of search; Michael Brookes at Nomura referred to 20 major assignments in less than three years with many more slightly lower-level searches.

Headhunting in Britain apparently received a great boost from the deregulation of the stock market, the so-called Big Bang of October 1986, within which the movement of teams of executives between merchant banks and other City businesses received especially extensive media publicity. However, this particular aspect of headhunting activity is very much the exception rather than the norm. None of the companies in this survey – although a number of banks and other City concerns were included – had actually ever employed search consultants to recruit whole teams, although two said that they would if the need occurred. The large government service organisation consulted accepted that although it had not needed to recruit a team yet, 'we may do'. Most other respondents categorically refused to entertain the possibility. The headhunting phenomenon of moving teams gained itself a bad name, and it is clear that such a practice is still scorned by many of the most reputable executive search firms and by many companies too, although it is accepted that it happened comparatively rarely.

The survey also asked companies about the salary level of executives recruited via headhunters. Kingfisher quoted the £30 000–£80 000 range, the large car-hire firm questioned mentioned their policy of maintaining a bottom limit of £30 000, and the international mining conglomerate which responded to the survey stated a top limit of £100 000. The government service organisation quoted a narrower range of £30 000 to £40 000 and the wines and spirits company £35 000 to £50 000. The industrial investment group also employed headhunters for positions at £30 000 upwards, and the two anonymous respondents quoted £30 000 to £80 000 and £35 000 to £80 000.

Cadbury Schweppes and Sainsbury would not consider calling in headhunters to search for jobs paying less than £35 000: Sainsbury once considered employing a search firm for a £25 000 post as manager of a depot, but decided this would be a waste of money, and gave the assignment to one of Britain's largest search/selection/advertising businesses, MSL. As we discovered in asking why clients would use search consultants rather than in-house recruiting, the salary attached to the job has to be above a certain ceiling to justify the fees involved. Exceptions occur when a position is so specialised or obscure that search is the only way; but by the laws of demand and supply, such jobs as these usually attract high salaries in any case. A decision to use search is primarily dictated by the size of the population of candidates in the sector in question, related to the current level of demand. Peter Christie of Midland Montagu uses search for most £40 000+ appointments, and especially for heads of departments, frequently in great demand in the City.

Are the salary levels of those recruited by headhunters likely to go up or come down? To what extent are headhunting firms moving into lower-level recruiting in order to maintain their own momentum of growth, and how is this being incorporated with their higher-level work? Alternatively, are they likely to concentrate even more on the top end of the market, because their fees will rise pro rata with salaries and thus increase their fee income? These and connected questions will be addressed in Chapter 7.

SMALL IS BEAUTIFUL?

What is the relationship between companies' use of large international headhunting firms compared with smaller, specialised consultancies? The top multinational search firms, according to users, have a number of advantages. Obviously, when a post cannot be filled by a British executive because it requires a more cosmopolitan background a client would turn to headhunters with a strong overseas network; and there was a general feeling that in these cases long-established major inter-national search firms were preferable. Such consultancies were seen as being prestigious in the eyes of candidates, having a wider field from which to chose, an extensive research resource immediately to hand, and the largest data banks.

The smaller, specialised firms, on the other hand, offered more personal contact and service; charged lower fees; and, because they had fewer clients than the large consultancies, had access to a wider range of candidates because fewer executives were off-limits. The consultant whom the client first met to discuss the assignment would be the same consultant who would undertake the work. It was widely felt that smaller firms offered a better service for nationally-based positions. Specialised assignments were often given to smaller firms offering particular expertise in that sector, with generally good results.

The balance of usage between the two types of consultancies in the

survey varied according to the salary level and functional area of the
position involved, and the experience of the executive handling recruitment in terms of contact with search consultants. Frequent use of search
was often marked by a period of experimentation with a variety of firms
in the first instance, followed by a settling down to regular work with a
smaller number of firms with whom the client had achieved a *modus
vivendi*. Some users are reluctant to employ more than one search firm.
Peter Cole of SBCI Savory Milln, considering that trust was crucial,
thought that to employ a number of headhunters ran the risk of losing
trust.

The leading French bank in the survey, an experienced and extensive
user of search, worked with a combination of large and small firms.
Russell Reynolds had been called in on occasion, and a smaller firm –
seen as a very good specialist – for specific assignments in commodity
finance. Other specialist firms were employed when required. Michael
Brookes of Nomura and Peter White of Midland Bank did the same,
using one of the Big Four for Board-level work and a specialist firm such
as Baines Gwinner for the level beneath. A spokesman from BICC was
dismissive of the large choice of search firms available, considering that
there were far too many; once he had learned by experience and found
good firms, he would stick to those he knew best, regardless of their size
or type. British & Commonwealth Holdings especially favoured smaller
search firms; they had received generally good service and quick results
from those they had used, and appreciated the personal contact and
cheaper price. The Far Eastern bank interviewed took an entirely
different line; they always worked with the large international firms,
claiming that neither they nor candidates had any confidence in the
smaller firms.

Peter Samuel of Kingfisher, who quoted the names of nine search
firms he had employed (including two major international consultancies, Heidrick and Struggles and Norman Broadbent), argued that he
used both large and small firms because of the variety of assignments he
handled. His choice between the two would depend on his assessment
of each particular position for which he was recruiting, and the relevant
qualities and strengths of each specific headhunting firm. He did not see
size of firm as a particularly important factor in his choice. He also
showed a willingness to give business to new firms, such as Saxton
Bamfylde, as well as more old-established businesses like GKR and
Clive & Stokes.

The large car-hire firm in the survey also used both, but – without
mentioning any names – showed a marked preference for the large
international firms, arguing, perhaps slightly unfairly in some cases, the
'top level targets do not like back-street companies'. An anonymous
respondent, similarly reticent about details of search firms' names,

agreed that 'large buys prestige in the eyes of candidates', but warned that using these firms 'tends to restrict the choice of employer' from which to hunt and find candidates.

All the other respondents referred to specific firms, with the mining conglomerate expressing satisfaction with service from multinational firm Korn/Ferry as well as a number of smaller, British-based firms who nevertheless have overseas offices: Canny Bowen, Tyzack and GKR. MSL were used for a variety of recruitment problems at various levels. The client's choice of search firm in this case depended on the nature of the requirement. The only advantage identified from using the largest headhunting firms was a 'bigger candidate bank'; it is unclear whether or not this means general pool of candidates open to the firm, or the size of their data bank.

The government service organisation questioned would not comment on the quality of the headhunting service it had received but, of eleven firms it cited, mentioned only one top international consultancy, Spencer Stuart. The corporate personnel director concerned stated a preference for employing UK search firms, but accepted that large firms could provide the resources for proper support of the assignment and following through the appointment with a form of after-sales service.

The large wines and spirits business in the survey referred to two UK firms who had shown good performance – EAL and Whitehead Mann – but apparently had no experience of the largest firms. The director involved thought that perhaps larger consultancies offered more credibility among candidates, but he was not convinced. The industrial investment group replied that it had employed both Korn/Ferry and Russell Reynolds, but wrote that although the type of firm used depended essentially on their need, 'our experience is that in our opinion we receive better service from smaller, local firms for positions which do not have an international content to the job'.

An anonymous respondent quoted six firms – Heidrick and Struggles, Spencer Stuart, Tyzack, GKR, MSL and Boyden – and etc., etc., you name them'. The search firm chosen depended on a mixture of the clients own requirements for the assignment, its past experience with individual headhunters – based on how good the particular consultant doing the work had been – and 'how we like their presentation'. The larger firms usually had a 'wider range of contacts and resource immediately on tap', but the respondent did not express a preference for them. This particular client seems to follow the policy of staging a shoot-out or competitive pitch between firms for each assignment, and trying out an increasing range of firms, rather than just sticking to those it has known and worked well with in the past.

Tesco, on the other hand, had received good service from UK-based Merton and had used them again and again. They remarked on the personal service, from the same senior consultant whom they had first met, comparing them with a larger firm who had acted in a heavy-handed way towards them and who had subsequently sent a junior consultant actually to handle the work, after they had dealt with the most senior partner at the beginning. Adrian Gozzard, ex-Plessey, also expressed a preference for consultants who took responsibility for all parts of the search, bringing in the business in the first place and the, closely supervising the research.

Tesco accused the same large headhunting firm with whom they had dealt of adopting a blasé attitude caused by processing a too rapid and too large turnover of assignments, whereas Merton had apparently provided individual attention and a fresh approach to the problem. Large firms generally, they considered, had a conventional outlook and data base whereas small firms could be more imaginative in the range of candidates presented.

Graham Shaw, when at Cadbury Schweppes, also expressed loyalty to particular search firms, quoting regular use of only three. He identified his main recruiting problem as this: the relatively small number of companies in the confectionery business meant that certain search firms would have to declare that certain specific potential hunting-grounds were off-limits, and this restricted his choice of headhunter. In any case, his use of search was not so extensive as to merit using a large number of firms. David Tagg of Grand Metropolitan mentioned a wider range of headhunters, naming Heidrick and Struggles and a number of smaller search firms, used according to the salary level of the appointment. Unlike Tesco, he had not experienced a heavy-handed or demanding manner from any of them, and was convinced by the value of the work they had done, without expressing a preference for any particular one.

Thus there is clearly room for a variety of search firms in the market place, with the smaller firms being able to overcome the disadvantage of fewer contacts and less international experience by offering a cheaper, more personal and more specialised service. Yet, in the case of really senior assignments, the prestige and resources of the top firms are obviously essential. Adrian Gozzard, ex-Plessey, spoke for many executives responsible for recruitment in Britain's largest companies when he argued his preference for broad-based search firms, rather than those specialising by functional discipline. He thought that the latter were potentially too narrow, and their consultants were not experienced enough in business generally. Gozzard wanted to deal with headhunters who were businessmen and businesswomen in their own right, and this was much more important than even the most sophisticated data banks. Nevertheless, good research departments whose staff had conceptual ability as well as research skills would be needed more than ever, and these were more likely to be found in the large, broad-based search firms.

IS POACHING PREVENTION POSSIBLE?

For every company that initiates and completes a search, inevitably there is another which loses an executive. The balance between gaining and losing is by no means even; many infrequent users of search are seen as prime poaching grounds, whereas companies constantly recruiting may not necessarily be losing people, but experiencing rapid growth. The few non-users of search, however, are seen not only as good at training people but also keeping them. Many headhunters frequently speak of the difficulty of extracting people from such strong corporate cultures as Procter & Gamble, Unilever and IBM.

Companies in the survey were asked if they used any mechanisms to protect themselves against poaching by other businesses employing headhunters. Overall, most employers felt that it was impossible completely to prevent an executive from moving. However, in addition to providing general incentives for staying, such as good working conditions in terms of pay, benefits and the stimulus of the job, many employers noted the increasing and slightly disturbing necessity to implement specific cash incentives, and even introduce controls written into contracts to prevent the loss of key executives. The Big Bang has certainly encouraged the trend towards offering Golden Handcuffs – to maintain the Golden Hellos – and the insertion of exclusion clauses in contracts to prevent executives going over to the competition. This is now less prevalent.

Peter Samuel of Kingfisher was prepared to insist on such restraint clauses when necessary. The car-hire company, and one of the anonymous respondents, did not consider such methods and questioned how poaching could be prevented at all. The mining conglomerate, the government service organisation, the wines and spirits company and the industrial investment group simply answered 'No' when asked if they had any poaching-prevention plans. The remaining anonymous respondent wrote of the 'normal contractual requirements, good management and good conditions of employment' as the only strategy for protection against poaching.

Graham Shaw, when at Cadbury Schweppes, spoke in more detail about the problem. He looked at it quite philosophically, seeing poaching as an irritant but also as an inevitable occurrence; in headhunting, all's fair in love and war. The only effective poaching prevention strategy was systematically identifying and nurturing one's most vulnerable executives. In regular manpower audits, Cadbury Schweppes pick out their most susceptible employees – usually around 50 or 60 in number – and watch them carefully, ensuring that they are happy at work in terms of the demands and responsibilities of their jobs, and how well they are paid. Keeping especially useful people – Shaw spoke of an outstanding taxation specialist employed by Cadbury Schweppes – is seen as a challenge rather than a difficulty.

David Tagg of Grand Metropolitan also acknowledged that headhunters will try quite naturally to seduce good people away from such companies as his own; but, he maintained, headhunters overall did a good job for him and he was not frightened that they might take his staff.

Some large companies, unsure if they are rewarding their top people adequately, have been known to commission firms to find out what the competition are paying; who better to ask to undertake this research than the headhunters themselves?

GAMEKEEPERS AND POACHERS

The phenomena of poacher-turned-gamekeeper and gamekeeper-turned-poacher are rare but not unknown. Most headhunters originally left their positions in industry at the behest of a headhunting firm who needed more consultants and saw them as fitting the bill. Comparatively few consultants had directly approached search firms for a job, but this is becoming more the case, especially in the USA, and will become more common as executive search becomes more generally accepted and regarded as an attractive career in its own right.

Poacher-turned-gamekeeper – a headhunter going back to industry, especially via an assignment he or she is handling – is rarer. Only one company questioned, who insisted on complete anonymity, had taken on an ex-headhunter into a position it had been seeking to fill, and admitted that it had been a disastrous mistake. On the other hand, there have been successful cases of poacher-turned-gamekeeper. Spencer Stuart was certainly the loser when one of their senior consultants in Hong Kong, Paul Cheng, was searching for a director of corporate affairs for overseas trader Inchcape and decided to join them.

HEADHUNTING IN THE BIG BANG AND AFTER

In seeking to establish the role of headhunting within the general economic environment, the survey questioned whether or not the Big Bang of October 1986 and the stock market crash of a year afterwards affected companies' recruiting policies and usage of headhunters. Search consultants themselves claimed that their business did markedly increase – in the number of new clients as well as in terms of the number of individual assignments – as a result of the Big Bang, and that the level of their work has continued to grow steadily, in spite of subsequent national economic changes. Is this true from the clients' point of view?

Media reports indicated an enormous increase in headhunting activity on the eve of the Big Bang. A favourite quote was from County Securities: 'We got to the stage in our institutional room where headhunters came on the phone so often we put them over the loudhailer because it was such a huge joke.' Salomon Brothers, who trebled their staff to 600 in less than two years, had employed head-hunters to help fill all their professional posts.

The banks questioned in the survey argued that although the level of headhunting activity had indeed risen with the Big Bang, from their point of view it had then fallen off; whilst many non-financial users of search, such as BICC, suggested that claims of noticeable changes in recruiting as a result of either event were wildly exaggerated. Peter Samuel of Kingfisher agreed, having experienced no direct impact on either occasion.

Many felt that possibly as a result of Big Bang more people generally were changing jobs, and the mining conglomerate questioned wrote that: 'we have had to review salaries etc. of staff vulnerable to approaches from the City. The downturn is too recent to assess from the point of view of recruiting, but it may make people more cautious about moving to the City.' The car-hire firm considered that it was too early to tell.

The government service organisation considered that a shortage of legal and estates professionals may have been influenced by the Big Bang, but nothing was visible as a result of the Crash, and they had not been particularly affected themselves either way. The wines and spirits company thought that the Big Bang had made recruiting more difficult but agreed that the effects of the Crash were hard to discern. The industrial investment group identified a stronger pressure on recruiting candidates with MBAs, and expected recruiting to be slightly easier as a result of the Crash, although it was difficult to judge. Both anonymous respondents claimed that both events had had no impact whatsoever on their recruiting.

External economic changes would seem to have a specific and localised impact on businesses within the particular sectors most im-mediately affected: neither the Big Bang nor the Crash has necessarily triggered off either an expansion or diminution of headhunting across the board in British companies generally. The Big Bang may have encouraged a greater familiarity among companies with search firms, simply because it was the first occasion when they had called on their services, often reluctantly and as a last resort. The personnel director of SBCI Savory Milln, Peter Cole, confirmed that this was his view of headhunters; he would employ a search firm only when he had exhausted his own supply of personal contacts. It is likely that the headhunting business in Britain will continue to expand as a result of its increased acceptability generally, and due to the existence of an increasingly competitive business environment. Overall, use of search is now widespread enough to enable search firms to ride out storms in specific sectors.

SEARCHING FOR A SEARCH FIRM

Finally, because this book seeks to assist users of search in selecting a good headhunting firm for their particular needs, the survey asked how companies had come across the headhunters they had employed. The replies suggested that the choice of consultant and search firm was initially quite random, which partly accounts for the unsatisfactory performance occasionally experienced.

The French bank originally heard about the headhunters they had employed by word-of-mouth contact, and BICC had based their choice – perhaps more dangerously – on a review of headhunting firms' own literature. Peter Samuel of Kingfisher cited two different routes: a recommendation of a consultancy from a referral source, i.e. an executive who has come into contact with the headhunter on a previous assignment; and by direct experience of a particular search firm from the user point of view from a Kingfisher executive who had employed that firm on a previous occasion, before he worked for Kingfisher.

The car-hire company referred simply to 'years of contacts', as did the mining conglomerate, the wines and spirits company and the industrial investment group. The reference guide *The Executive Grapevine* had been used by the government service organisation and one of the anonymous respondents; the latter had also responded to mail-shots from headhunters seeking business.

Overall, search firms were chosen by trial and error and informal contacts, often without much knowledge of their reputations and specialisms. The Select Directory at the end of this book seeks to make this choice more systematic and to reduce, at least partially, the inevitable element of risk.

THE CANDIDATE'S POINT OF VIEW

The candidate survey differed from the client survey in three respects: first, the rate of response was slightly lower, despite the fact that it was carefully based on the *Financial Times* listings of movements of executives and on firms where much headhunting was known to have taken place; second, the views of headhunters were more negative; and third, none would mention the names of specific search firms or venture opinions on them in particular.

Some of the less professional search firms have been known to treat candidates shoddily, and even the leading firms would admit that a few of the candidates they had encountered would be justified in feeling hard-done-by. The headhunting process itself inevitably leaves in its wake a number of disgruntled executives and would-be executives. For every successful candidate there are bound to be at least two who were pipped at the post, who jumped the final fence only to find that the client had chosen one of their fellow front-runners: and these were the ones who – by and large – responded to the survey rather than the successful ones. Although this is hardly the headhunter's fault, the candidate will naturally feel annoyance or even anger that his or her expectations have been raised and then dashed, often without much explanation.

The failed short-list candidates are surrounded by increasing circles of other disappointed souls: to continue our horseracing imagery, the front-runners are followed by the minor placings, those who met the headhunter and talked at length about the opportunity, who were among the top ten, but not the top three or four. Beyond them are the also-rans, other disaffected characters, who were on the receiving end of tempting, exciting, ego-boosting telephone calls which were never subsequently followed up, from headhunters of whom they never heard anything again. Even further out, with less reason for antagonism towards search consultants but still known to bear malice, are the hopefuls who never appeared on the race card at all, who sent in their CVs and waited in vain for a response.

Many candidates all down the line think of headhunters as privileged individuals able to hand out plum jobs willy-nilly to those in their favour; at the same time – somewhat contradictorily – they regard them as dodgy, cowboy characters who have arrived at their coveted positions in life after having failed at everything else they have attempted.

One particular candidate responding to the survey went to a great deal of trouble to commit his decidedly anti-headhunting views to paper. Working in the very competitive insurance industry, principally at Lloyd's, he had been approached four times by four different headhunting firms, only one of whose names he remembered (one of the smaller UK-based consultancies). He argued that because Lloyd's, as a market place, had its own effective communications network by word of mouth for anyone seeking a change of job or a company looking for a specialist, any use of headhunters was immediately suspicious. A company seeking to recruit in this specialty area would, if they used a search consultant, immediately reveal themselves as not having the right contacts in the market. Headhunters have no place in such an environment, he suggested.

This candidate and others also in a similar position saw search consultants as a tool of ignorant companies seeking insider-knowledge; and he thinks they are no better than their employers. He feels that there is no way that an external agency can obtain the feel of a market place like Lloyd's. Another criticism generally expressed was that headhunters, having approached a candidate and then been turned down, did not hesitate to make the most of the contact they had made despite the rejection and go on to ask, 'Well, can you recommend someone who would be interested?' One particular candidate's reaction was amazement at their nerve, and he would always immediately refuse 'to do the headhunters' job for them'.

Although they usually listen to what headhunters have to sell, many candidates were irritated by the questions they were asked. 'Would you be interested in moving jobs? Are you happy? Does your present job offer you sufficient challenge? Would you like greater fulfilment in your job?' One candidate considered that headhunters would waste a lot less time if they immediately admitted which company they were acting for. 'I know they need to protect their client's confidentiality but there are certainly many companies I would not consider working for and that ought to be got out of the way early on.' After all, in view of the calibre of candidates they approach, they should be able to expect them to keep their confidence if asked. Many candidates showed little appreciation of the problems from the headhunter's point of view.

It is easy for many candidates such as one of those quoted above to criticise headhunters: they feel they have no need for them, because of the nature of the internal communications network at Lloyd's and because recent changes in the City and the resulting increased need for various financial specialists appear to have had no impact on Lloyd's insurance jobs. The candidate quoted above – along with many clients – values stability in business and considers that once a company (presumably in the Lloyd's insurance market) has established a successful formula, it then strives hard to keep the status quo. He thinks this is more important than a high turnover of staff, despite the fresh minds and attitudes this may encourage.

Much of this and several other candidates' arguments are not convincing because their remarks reveal contradictory opinions and a lack of principles. Many candidates would think nothing of taking advantage of headhunters by accepting a free overseas trip and free entertainment such as drinks, lunch or dinner, whilst having no intention whatsoever of changing jobs. Finally, despite all the pejorative remarks and many statements along the lines of 'I personally do not think very highly of headhunters', most accept fully that the headhunting business in Britain is here to stay.

Other respondents to the candidate survey were less negative. One, for example, had been approached by four or five recognised firms without result but, significantly, had made more progress with an intermediary. He described his experience thus:

> There are two types of approach falling into two separate categories. Those who give the impression that they are fishing for information; they may be looking for a recommendation for somebody else who may be suitable to approach. Or they may give the impression that they are not quite sure if you are the right candidate, i.e. they have not done their homework. The most professional approach which I had was in fact via an intermediary who was acting on behalf of an existing customer of the company who employed me and whose objective was to sound out general interest without disturbing the importance of on-going business relationships. Although detailed discussions did take place and were finally unsuccessful, this careful approach managed to maintain an on-going business relationship . . . The general approach which they make is extremely varied, from being quite clandestine to being rather pushy. I think the more senior one becomes, the more serious any headhunting approach becomes. The manner with which one deals with any such approach may well have an important bearing on an opportunity at some later date.

In contrast to the respondent quoted earlier, this candidate saw headhunting as 'an important way of progressing, particularly for individuals who work for smaller companies or in very specialised fields'. He was above the idea of taking advantage of headhunters through accepting free lunches and trips without intending to move: 'Time is one's most valuable commodity.'

Many headhunters themselves accept that some candidates are justified in considering that they have had a raw deal. As we suggested, this applies even to the largest and most prestigious search firms. One leading search consultant described how he had once mistakenly presented the wrong candidate for a job. The client concerned wanted both a finance director and a managing director; the headhunter had found a good candidate with an accountancy background to be MD, before deciding that the same man would be better in the finance director position. Unfortunately, the headhunter forgot to inform the candidate, so the meeting between the candidate and the client collapsed in misunderstanding. The candidate thought he was going for an interview to be MD when the client thought he was to meet the proposed finance director. But in this instance, the client was more offended than the candidate, and stormed out of the meeting, leaving the candidate puzzled but generally philosophical and according to the headhunter, 'he was quite amused and delightful about it.'

Most headhunters argue that the candidates who criticise them do so because they, the candidates, have been unsuccessful. It is sour grapes, they say, because the candidates no doubt sent in many copies of their CV without response; fell by the wayside in competition with better candidates; failed to convince the would-be employer that they were right for the job; or were just plain unlucky and not in the right place at the right time. Headhunters' favourite candidates, often those who have subsequently become users of search in their own right, are the winners.

(Part of the survey of client usage of executive search appeared in *Euromoney* in September 1988.)

QUESTIONNAIRE

1. May I quote you or your company or do you prefer total anonymity?

2. Do you use headhunters regularly or on specific occasions only?

3. Which departments in your firm frequently require executives? Do you ever ask headhunters to recruit a whole team?

4. What is the salary range of executives recruited?

5. Are candidates selected generally appropriate given their level of salary and the expenses incurred?

6. Do you use international or UK search firms, or does this depend on your particular requirements at the time? What are the advantages of using a large over a small firm?

7. Which search firms have you used over the past five years? Do you have any comments on their performance?

8. How did you find out about these firms in the first place?

9. What are the advantages of using executive search companies over employing your own recruiting facilities? Do you find them more expensive?

10. Do you employ any defence mechanisms to protect your firm against poaching by other firms via headhunters?

11. Have there been any breaches of confidentiality or illegal use of information by search firms you have employed in the past?

12. Have any headhunters joined your firm to fill in a position they were initially asked to search for?

13. How did the Big Bang and the recent Crash affect your recruiting?

Thank you very much for your co-operation.

RESULTS FROM 30 COMPANIES

1. Request for Anonymity:
   Yes 11
   No 19
2. Use of Headhunters:
   Regularly 14
   Specific occasions only 9
   Very rarely 6
3. Departments of companies with greatest usage of search (can be more than one):
   Financial 11
   For entire teams 0
   Marketing 6
   Information technology 2
   New sectors 6
   No specific department 15
4. Salary range recruited (only lower limit noted):
   Above £30 000 5
   Above £35 000 7
   Above £40 000 8
   Above £50 000 3
   A separate decision is taken in each case 7
5. Candidates presented by headhunters:
   Generally appropriate 24
   Not always appropriate 6
6. Use of international and national search firms:

    Mostly international firms 13
    Mostly national firms 4
    Combination of both 13
7. Use of particular named search firms:
    Confidential information 11
    One or two named firms 2
    One or two unnamed firms 1
    Three or four named firms 3
    Three or four unnamed firms 4
    Several named firms 5
    Several unnamed firms 4
8. Source of information on search firms (often more than one):
    Direct approach from search firm 8
    Advertisement by search firm 2
    Recommendation from a previous user 8
    Direct experience of a senior executive 8
    Years of personal contacts 11
    The Executive Grapevine 2
9. Advantages of using executive search (often more than one):
    They have wider range of contacts 7
    They save time 6
    They provide an external view, knowledge of the market 11
    Ensuring complete confidentiality 5
    Able to concentrate on one search at a time 1
    Avoiding maintaining own recruiting department 1
    Can be used jointly with in-house recruiting 7
    Senior executives do not read advertisements 5
    Senior executives prefer approach from an intermediary 11
9A. Cost of using executive search compared with in-house recruiting:
    Search more expensive, and too expensive 14
    Search more expensive, but worth it 8
    Search less expensive 1
    Works out about the same 7
10. Defence mechanisms against loss of executives through headhunters:
    Exclusion clauses in contracts 7
    Good conditions of employment 11
    None used 5
    None possible 7
11. Confidentiality of search firms used (often more than one):
    Adequate 17
    Not completely trusted 7
    No way of knowing 11
12. Search consultants joining companies who hired them for search:
    Not in our case 28
    Has happened 2
13. Impact of Big Bang on recruiting:
    More recruiting 14
    Less recruiting 0
    No difference 16
13A. Impact of Crash on recruiting:
    More recruiting 0
    Less recruiting 12
    No difference 18

4

The Headhunting Process

GENERAL INTRODUCTION

To cut through the mystique surrounding the search process, we need a systematic examination of every stage of how an assignment is handled, to see how the headhunting process itself actually works.

This begins with the first contact between the headhunter and the client – or would-be client – at the briefing stage, at which the whole problem of the position to be filled is first raised. How should the client prepare for this meeting, and what questions will a headhunter ask? In very many cases, at this stage the headhunter will be competing against rival search firms for the job. The presentation will therefore be concerned not merely with the client's recruitment problem, but why the client should choose that particular consultant and search firm. Sometimes the client will decide then and there, immediately after the shoot-out or competitive pitch for the assignment at his or her office; on other occasions, especially in the case of a subsidiary or branch of a large multinational, each search firm pitching for the assignment will subsequently write letters to the client discussing the appointment and describing their own particular credentials for the task: four such letters, from four competing search firms, are analysed below. How should the client choose between them? Once a headhunter has been engaged, what initial enquiries should then be made before the search begins?

Back at the search firm's offices, what happens when the assignment is turned over to the research department? Which methods are used to narrow down the field of candidates? Each firm has a slightly different approach to the research phase, both in the variety of sources – formal and informal – and in the role the researcher plays in the assignment as a whole. What are the quickest and most effective research techniques? What is the nature of the relationship between the researcher and the consultant? Who makes the telephone calls?

What happens when the would-be candidates are interviewed by the headhunter? What should both be looking for? How does the search consultant set about fleshing out the bones of a CV when he or she meets the subject face to face? How does the headhunter use information from the interview to report back to the client? And what might a candidate expect when faced with psychometric testing? How frequently do clients, and search firms, insist on it? What is its value in the selection process?

The final decision on which candidate to appoint rests with the client, but on the basis of what sort of information, and how much time with the candidates? What part does the headhunter play in the final negotiations? What happens afterwards: should the search consultant keep in touch with both the successful candidate and (presumably) satisfied client? What happens if it all goes wrong and the company subsequently feels unhappy with the new appointee, or the expertly headhunted individual is just as expertly headhunted by someone else soon afterwards, or decides that he or she does not actually like the new position after all? What form of guarantees do headhunters make, and what is their after-sales service like?

HOW IT WORKS, BY RODDY GOW OF RUSSELL REYNOLDS

An overview of the process, by way of general introduction and from the point of view of both client and consultant becomes clear from the following discussion, which took place at Broadcasting House in London and was broadcast on BBC Radio Scotland in November, 1987, between Roddy Gow, Managing Director of Russell Reynolds' London office, and Alasdair Macfarland, the Personnel Director of a leading Scottish whisky company.

So what first happens when a company has a senior vacancy to fill? At what stage would a headhunter be called in? Gow suggested not immediately, unless the company is one which has used executive search in the past. By the time he is asked to start work, two events may have taken place. First, an executive may have left unexpectedly, and an attempt to find an internal replacement has failed; or, second, adequate thought has not been given to the question of succession, and an important director is rapidly approaching retirement, whilst the executive assumed to accept promotion to this position has other plans. Generally, but not always, there is a high degree of urgency involved and Macfarland agreed that this would be likely to increase once the company has tried and failed to handle the problem itself.

Does the client then inform the search firm about the nature of the requirement, or do the two meet to discuss the problem? Gow, who would always take one of his colleagues to the client briefing with him to ensure continuity if for any reason he was unable to carry on with the search, would expect to discuss the circumstances surrounding the requirement with the client and the successful candidate's future colleague in some detail, and what was needed would be decided together before defining the actual position to be filled. The questions Gow would particularly ask would first concern how confidential the search process was to be. Then he would need to know the nature of the management and corporate structure of the company and how the new executive was to fit into that structure; how senior the position to be filled is, what the reporting lines and the key responsibilities of the individual to be recruited are, and what qualifications are needed.

This information would enable Gow to draw up what he likes to call a two-dimensional specification: details of the position which can be agreed in writing. Of more interest from his point of view, however, is the third dimension, which cannot so easily be put into words: what sort of executive fits this company? What important criteria does the particular company have that is unique to that company and reflects the personality of its leaders and culture? What solution might be acceptable, and what proposals would it absolutely refuse to consider? For example, would they or would they not employ a woman? To what level of responsibility could the person they are looking for ultimately aspire or, in other words, what is the upward potential of the job? Is there anyone in the company already who feels that he or she is in line for the job, and will he be disappointed if an outsider is appointed instead? Who is going to be involved with managing the search project from the client end, and who is going to be on the jury to choose between the candidates at the short-list stage?

The successful candidate does not by any means always come from outside the company. Macfarland argued that before moving to the stage of appointing a search firm, the personnel director should have already exhausted the possibilities within the company; in view of the ultimate cost of involvement with a headhunter, sensibly the company should have already carried out the process of checking its own people thoroughly. Macfarland sees the role of the headhunter as coming in then, and penetrating beneath the surface of the problem. This is a much greater task than seeking an executive to fill the post from outside, for the headhunter may well discover that there is someone inside the company who is ideally suited and whom the client has not noticed. Gow suggests that this can easily happen in the case of a large company with diversified subsidiaries, a large global trading company or any major business with overseas operations. It has often been known for an individual somewhere to be overlooked, who subsequently turns out to be the ideal person for the position to be filled.

Sometimes, after the client briefing, the headhunter and client together find that there is not actually a job to be filled after all. At the briefing stage, often before the headhunter has agreed to undertake the assignment and before the client has officially appointed him or her, they may both agree that there is no need for outside search at all. In this case what the client actually requires is reassurance that internal executives measure up well against the competition that may exist in the market place generally, and that in reality the headhunter has been called on to supply a second opinion. Macfarland had not employed headhunters for such a purpose, but was aware that others had done so. Gow admits that he would never wish to start work on an assignment unless he could be sure that there was 'a desire to hire' on the part of the client.

Once the specification of the type of executive required had been agreed, how would the headhunter approach the task of pin-pointing the individual? Would he or she already have a mental picture of the list of people he or she might approach, or be starting from scratch? Before beginning work on the search, Gow would ask to visit the place where the executive to be appointed would work and, if the company were involved in manufacturing, to have seen at least some of the factories and workshops. If possible – if the search were not too confidential – Gow would ask to meet the colleagues with whom the new executive would work, to understand how he or she would fit into the organisation, even to the extent of seeing the chair and desk which would be occupied. Macfarland agreed that this was essential for the headhunter to grasp fully all the dimensions of the problem.

Gow maintains that only very rarely has he had to start a search from scratch. If the position is a general management appointment, it is very likely that he or his firm, Russell Reynolds, will have direct experience of working in the same industry. Having been involved in executive search for over fifteen years in London, Russell Reynolds have completed literally thousands of senior management assignments, so there would already be an extensive residue of contacts in their data base. Gow and his colleagues have inevitably come to know, in the course of their work, a number of very senior directors and also a number of less senior but highly knowledgeable executives with whom they may talk about a search project on a confidential basis, and pick their brains as sources of information.

The headhunter would also expect to discuss with clients those companies they see as in the same business as themselves and the executives within them whom they most admire. Macfarland agreed that most clients have a view of who their competition is, and this helps the headhunter to focus on the field of candidates in which to look and where he or she is likely to find them.

But does this mean that headhunting is to some extent poaching? In that when an executive is moved, he or she is inevitably denuding one place to add to another, the charge of poaching is valid: it is a fact of life in headhunting. In Gow's view, for an executive to be poached may be seen as a back-handed compliment to a company; it reflects the organisation's success in training and management development. There are strict rules about poaching in headhunting, especially relating to previous and existing clients. Poaching from one's clients, argues Gow, is akin to a little boy building a tower of bricks and trying to remove bricks from underneath while at the same time putting them on the top. An executive whom Gow had recruited would not subsequently be contacted for another opportunity. This code of conduct – practised by the leading firms but not necessarily strictly adhered to by all – naturally limits the number of clients in one sector of any search firm. Paradoxically, too many clients can sometimes be bad for business in the executive search world.

In eyeing up the client company's competition so that he or she can find suitable candidates for the job, how does the consultant go about making the initial approach? Gow insists that the headhunter has to know as much as possible about the executive before calling him or her. Telephone calls to candidates from search consultants can, of course, vary enormously in quality, from headhunters who do their research properly to those who know nothing at all about the person they are calling and end up causing considerable embarrassment. Senior staff in top companies are used to receiving calls from headhunters, and soon realise whether or not the consultant has really done the necessary homework and found out much about them before telephoning.

One of the headhunter's greatest problems is that the people whom he or she is ringing up are, by definition – otherwise he or should not be ringing them up in the first place – successful, hard-working and busy, invariably too busy to look through newspapers for job advertisements and never having much time for long telephone conversations. So the search consultant has to put across, as the representative or ambassador of the client, in a short period of time during the first brief telephone call exactly what the problem is and who is needed to solve it. The headhunter has to impart this information in such a way that it is going to attract the attention of the individual and arouse his or her curiosity enough to set up an initial meeting. No headhunter can adequately interview important potential candidates over the telephone, so most calls are made with the view of setting up a meeting somewhere, often at the headhunter's office.

The headhunter's problems in making such telephone calls – especially to candidates working in financial institutions – are compounded by the fact that many telephone conversations received by these concerns are taped as a matter of policy. Several finance houses keep records of the conversations held across their telephone lines. If a search consultant is telephoning the treasurer of a bank, for example, and the call was taped and heard by the latter's superior, this would cause great problems for the consultant's client, probably another bank trying to headhunt that treasurer; so, in these cases, the headhunter has to try to interest the candidate in the position with the minimum of information, and ask that the conversation be renewed later, possibly when the latter is at home later that evening. This problem of the recording of incoming telephone calls is not, of course, encountered across the board in British business, but it emphasises the discretion with which a headhunter must always work. Discretion is one of the most vital attributes of a successful search consultant: every day, people are going to impart many confidential items of information, things about themselves which should never be repeated without their express permission.

When the headhunter does finally come up with someone who seems to be the ideal person for the job, inevitably the client – left to make the final decision – does not always agree; but in Macfarland's experience, in the majority of cases, if the headhunter has done his or her homework and has worked closely with the client all along, the problem will be satisafctorily resolved and the position filled. In any case, it is not a question of the client either accepting or rejecting one candidate. It is the headhunter's job to present, in a timely fashion, a group of candidates – four, five, six, or even seven or eight – after having weeded out very many more deemed unsuitable. Those who never reached this stage could well have been highly competent on technical and professional grounds, but not suitable in terms of the totality of the problem.

The final, most suitable candidates are presented to the client first by report and then physically by interview, in a sufficiently short period of time such that when the client sees the fifth candidate, he or she can still remember what the first was like. The headhunter can help the client manage the interviewing process by acting as an intermediary in the delicate salary negotiations and by carrying out extensive reference checking on the chosen candidate before the person is actually hired.

Could this solution have been achieved by advertising, especially in view of the high charges imposed by most headhunting firms? Macfarland argues that advertising can be just as expensive: advertisements go to the world, and that is why one pays so much for them. But the client only wants one executive in the end, and the odds are that the person has not even seen the advertisement, let alone applied for the post. Advertising offers no guarantee of success and, for appointments paying at least £40 000, Macfarland prefers to invest, channelling everything towards the one ideal person, via a search firm. If, and this is increasingly the case, top jobs are not advertised, does this encourage an elitism in business into which it is very hard for up-and-coming executives to break? Both Gow and Macfarland agree that this is to some extent true, but welcome such elitism. After all, they argue, here we are discussing executives who are going to have a tremendous influence on all aspects of the business they enter, so they must be among the elite and a member of the elite tailored for the specific job in mind.

Gow accepts that the personnel director or other executive responsible for the search is putting his or her reputation on the line just as much as the headhunter. In seeking to fill an especially crucial position, in 'looking for someone who can make things happen, to be a lamp around which moths will fly', as Gow puts it, the client and the consultant both have a great deal at stake. And what is the success rate? Gow points to his firm's level of repeat business of 80%, a considerable achievement in the world of British industry and finance, where memories are short on success and long on failure. Macfarland accepts that, more often than not, headhunters have performed satisfactorily for him, and they do have an important place in business practice.

THE BRIEF

In outlining the first stages of a typical executive search programme, Miles Broadbent, Chief Executive of leading British search firm Norman Broadbent, was asked here to consider the process from the client's point of view.

When the new client (C) first telephones the headhunter, C may indicate simply the title of the position which needs to be filled. C will then ask the headhunter to visit him or her at the client's premises or, for reasons of confidentiality, may request a meeting in the headhunter's office. At this very early stage, the consultant should ask C to prepare for the initial meeting. The headhunter will ask C to come to the meeting with an organisation chart, indicating where the job fits and to whom the person will report. The consultant should also ask C to prepare an initial job specification, and also to give some thought to the type of person C wants to hire, and the parameters of the compensation package which the company is prepared to offer. It is a good discipline for C to have to write at least something down on paper before the first meeting with the headhunter.

When the first meeting takes place, the headhunter will want to know something about the history and culture of the organisation, and also what happened to create the vacancy which is to be filled. Is the previous job holder retiring; did he or she leave; or was he or she fired? If it was not a simple question of retirement, then the consultant needs to know why the previous incumbent went, because this is one of the early questions which potential candidates will ask of the headhunter. The headhunter will then want to know C's views on the preferred age of the person, who will do the interviewing of the final candidates, what sort of qualifications the candidates need to have, and what sort of job experience would be most desirable. The consultant also needs to know any organisations which are off-limits for the search, and C should also establish from the headhunter which companies are off-limits to the search firm.

The briefing to the consultant should be carried out by the immediate superior of the person to be hired. He or she is the ultimate decision-maker, and the only one who really knows what qualities and what type of person are needed. It is often useful to have the Personnel director or head of human resources at this same first initial meeting, because in many cases the chairman or chief executive does not find it easy to express or verbalise a description of the culture of the organisation. Furthermore, according to Miles Broadbent, most chairmen never seem to know much about the details of the normal fringe benefits which the company offers to senior executives.

The headhunter should leave this initial meeting with a clear under-standing of why C wishes to recruit somebody to fill the job, and what sort of person is needed to be the ideal candidate. When the consultant returns to the firm's office, the next task is to prepare a draft of the job specification which describes C's organisation, the responsibilities and reporting structure of the job to be filled, the qualifications, age and so on of the ideal candidate, and a clear indication of the principal features of the compensation package which will be offered, i.e. whether in addition to salary there is a bonus and/or stock options.

The headhunter now submits to C a letter – four examples of which are discussed next – which sets out the proposed methodology of the search, the fees which will be charged, and the draft specification. The consultant should very clearly request that C carefully read the job specification and amend it or correct it as necessary. This is vital to ensure that C is clear at the outset out the sort of person he or she wants to hire, and the headhunter has a shared understanding of the detailed objectives of the search. The more difficult and less effective clients do not bother to read the job specification properly and thus can cause themselves and the headhunter considerable pain later in the search. The best clients read the job specification very carefully and make precise and detailed corrections and amendments in order to make sure that the job specification is drawn clearly and succinctly.

Finally, before starting the search, but when confirmation that the headhunter has won the assignment has been received, a visit to C's principal office or location is absolutely vital. In some cases secrecy prevents the headhunter from making this visit – such as when a replacement for an existing executive is being sought, whilst the present incumbent is still installed – but, when at all possible, the headhunter should seek to spend at least a day visiting the plant and offices of his new client, and meeting as many as possible of the key directors and senior management of the organisation. Only in this way will the consultant develop a feel for the culture and environment into which the new recruit will be injected. The headhunter will also gain from this visit a picture and understanding of C. This is not only valuable in pin-pointing likely candidates, but also enables the consultant to speak with much more authority to potential candidates about his or her client. There is nothing worse than a headhunter who seems to know very little about the client for whom the search is being undertaken. On the other hand, there is nothing more impressive than a headhunter who is able to answer any questions that potential candidates care to throw.

A competitive pitch for an assignment

It has become increasingly common practice – in fact, verging on the norm – for a client to approach not just one but a range of headhunting firms, encompassing both the large international businesses and smaller, home-grown outfits. Many clients will stage a shoot-out or competitive pitch for each individual assignment as the need arises. Thereby the user of search can directly compare the different solutions offered, approaches and scale of charges. What manner of presentation can be expected? What are the criteria for choosing between the firms?

Four letters, from four different search firms, have been obtained in order to make a comparison between the various initial briefs prepared by the competing headhunters immediately after the shoot-out. These first briefs set out in writing each headhunter's understanding of the field of operations and market position of the client company, the job specification and profile of the ideal candidate, and why they in particular should be selected for the assignment. The example here goes back to July 1987, when a division of a leading food storage container manufacturer required a new Management Information Systems (MIS) Director to help set up a new office in Switzerland. As the subsidiary of a larger corporation, the decision regarding which search firm to appoint was not taken on the spot but was referred back to head office: hence the letters were needed to support each firm's pitch.

Senior executives of the client company met consultants from the Geneva office of Russell Reynolds, the Paris office of Korn/Ferry, the Geneva office of John Stork and the Geneva office of Carre Orban. The pitch for this assignment thus included the largest fee-earner in Britain, the largest headhunting company worldwide, and two well-respected British firms, both with a range of overseas offices.

All four firms wrote to the client immediately after their initial meetings, all confidently hoping to be engaged and all arguing the case as to why they should be chosen.

Russell Reynolds

Their approaches varied very considerably. First, Russell Reynolds set out its understanding of the client's requirement with a short job specification, including the expected salary. It had never worked for this particular company before, so Russell Reynolds explained at great length exactly how it would conduct the search, starting with further meetings with the client, the preparation of a more detailed job specification, the nature of the research it would carry out, and how it would arrive at a short list. It was made clear that comprehensive reference checks on candidates would only be compiled when they reached the short-list stage, and then only on those in whom the client expressed a strong interest. This seems to be common practice among headhunters, although apparently dangerous and risky: it would be highly embarrassing if all the candidates presented were subsequently revealed as unsuitable or not to be recommended. It is highly necessary, however, as taking references can, of course, reveal the fact that an executive is being considered for a position, thereby breaking the confidentiality of the search.

It is no surprise that headhunting firms use letters prepared to a formula to pitch for assignments, which they adapt to each case and personalise where appropriate. Lack of care here suggests a failure to attend to detail and, at worst, may be offensive to the client. In this instance, Russell Reynolds was guilty of referring in its brief to this client of 'the opportunity at your bank'. Tighter quality controls imposed since have rendered such a mistake unlikely to recur.

Russell Reynolds offered a particularly speedy service, promising to present the first candidates after five or six weeks from mid-August 1987, once the assignment had begun. A fee was quoted of one-third of the first year's cash compensation, including salary and bonus, which would be estimated in advance and charged in three interim retainers, with SF60 000 seen as a working minimum based on the successful candidate's salary of SF150 000 to SF200 000. To cover themselves against one of the worst headhunting eventualities, Russell Reynolds stated that if an invoice for expenses sent to the client was outstanding for not longer than 30 days they would suspend work on the assignment immediately. It was then promised that if the assignment was not completed within the stipulated three months, Russell Reynolds would carry on searching for another three months charging out-of-pocket expenses only.

This guarantee was followed by a brief statement of the qualifications of the Russell Reynolds consultants who would conduct the search, drawing attention to their particular suitability to work on this assignment. The services of three consultants were offered, all having worked in the client's areas, with appropriate language and technical qualifications, and a variety of financial and systems organisation experience; but – notably – none had had much to do with a large manufacturer, such as the client, in this instance.

Russell Reynolds' pitch concluded with a one-page first draft specification of its understanding of the client's activities, the position to be filled and its interpretation of the ideal candidate for the job. Usefully, the consultant hoping to lead the search then identified what he already saw as the main problem areas and possible future pitfalls of the assignment. He warned that Switzerland was not regarded as in the forefront of MIS development; that Swiss-born managers with the necessary technical competence and experience would be thin on the ground and thus hard to find, and possibly even harder to extract from their present jobs; that there would be a need to define more closely the details of the new set-up in Switzerland, and thus the new MIS director's task; and that the clients might find themselves having to pay a considerably higher initial salary than they were anticipating.

Thus, Russell Reynolds covered themselves in advance for any future difficulties and showed that they had already given thought to solving the overall problem. In six clear pages they had set out a fair pitch for the job. Unfortunately, in assuming no prior knowledge of the headhunting process on the part of the client, the tone of the brief tended to err on the side of over-confidence and even a hint of condescension.

Korn/Ferry

Korn/Ferry's pitch was twice as long as Russell Reynolds'. The outline of the client's requirement, covering more than two pages, was full of very basic information about the client company, for them to confirm Korn/ Ferry's understanding of their activities; it is questionable if this was really necessary. It was not always clear whether or not Korn/Ferry was merely repeating what they were told, or if it had already made some preliminary investigations. For example, Korn/Ferry confidently stated in its brief that 'since nobody within the existing organisation had the stature for the job, you have decided to recruit someone from the outside'. Had Korn/Ferry already looked at – and rejected – any possible internal candidates? The client already had an MIS team in each of their sales subsidiaries, so was Korn/Ferry wise to discount this source at such an early stage, even if the client was doubtful?

Korn/Ferry's outline of the client's requirement was followed by an entire page solely concerned with the singing of its own praises, which was not in any way tailored to the particular assignment in hand. Each consultant selected for the job was pictured and described in great detail in an appendix at the end of the brief, without pointing out his or her suitability for the task in hand. Korn/Ferry's two-page summary of 'How We Conduct Assignments' again bore no relation to the client whatsoever and, like Russell Reynolds, proposed carrying out reference-checking only after candidates had been presented and selected as strong possibilities by the client, and not before.

The fee quoted by Korn/Ferry was the same as Russell Reynolds – 33⅓% plus expenses – but it had in mind a lower minimum fee for the appointment, of SF55 000 rather than SF60 000, based on a salary of SF165 000, although excluding expenses which could equal another 20%. Korn/Ferry did not commit itself to how long it thought the assignment would take, but it did offer a guarantee that 'if for any reason during the trial period, which should not exceed six months, you decide to terminate the candidate [!] we would restart the search assignment free of charge except for additional expense items which would then be incurred'. To a much greater extent than Russell Reynolds' proposal, Korn/Ferry's letter was a standardised response to this opportunity with minimum specification details. Of its total of twelve pages, this brief dedicated just over one page only to the specific assignment, and there was no initial outline of the possible future problems of the search.

John Stork

John Stork's brief 3½-page proposal – in contrast with Korn/Ferry's and Russell Reynolds' – is refreshingly free of standardised padding, without an unnecessary word. A 'Project Note', summarising the meeting with the client, is clearly set out point by point, not lumped together in long, indigestible paragraphs which deter, rather than encourage, the reader. John Stork's summary is easily the most perceptive of the successful candidate's future duties, which it considers both within a general framework of the long-term plans of the company and in terms of those which are to have first priority.

Like Russell Reynolds, John Stork warned the client that they would need to offer a higher salary to attract really good candidates. As a next step, it was proposed to submit an 'Appointment Analysis' describing the ramifications of the position to be filled, designed for the consumption of short-listed candidates.

Unlike Russell Reynolds or Korn/Ferry, John Stork consultants do not charge fees as a proportion of the successful candidate's salary, but suggest a fee based on expected time and difficulty. In this case it is much the same as the others – SF55 000 – but John Stork quote lower additional expenses of 12%, although it warns that these might be doubled in such a fully international assignment as this. John Stork did not, at this stage, promise to complete the job as quickly as Russell Reynolds, but did predict that a short list would be ready in six to eight weeks. Unlike its competitors, John Stork gave a practical idea of the work involved, pointing out that it would expect to talk to at least 80 people in connection with the assignment, as potential candidates and/ or sources, meeting at least fifteen of them.

There is no mention in John Stork's proposal of which of its consultants would undertake the assignment, and there is nothing about their methods or track record. Instead – but we have no evidence of this – they could have sent, or left at the meeting, the firm's official brochure, but that available at the time would not appear to be particularly informative.

Carré Orban

Carré Orban's proposal is as long as Korn/Ferry's, and as usual begins with a summary of its understanding of the problem. Compared with the large American-based headhunting firms, Carré Orban gives the impression of being over-eager, almost desperate for the work. There are constant references to 'the great importance of the assignment', the 'frank and comprehensive briefing' it was given that 'would enable us to start this most important assignment immediately upon confirmation'. The writers give the impression that they see this as an exceptionally top-ranking, prestigious opportunity, more so than much of their usual work, which may include a good deal of lower-level searches; Russell Reynolds and Korn/Ferry, on the other hand, have a more blasé attitude: they deal with assignments at this level all the time.

Even so, Carré Orban appears from its brief to be the most professional of the four tenderers for the job. It is exceptional among its competitors here in making a declaration that 'all matters discussed in this context will naturally be treated in strictest confidence': this first headhunting commandment should be clearly stated as a matter of course in all first briefs. In the light of the priority obviously attached to confidentiality, Carré Orban assigns a code reference to each assignment undertaken; thus if documentation relating to search fell into the wrong hands, it would be difficult to identify.

Carré Orban's summary of the client's problem is precise and to the point. In three pages, with two useful organisational charts, the consultants clearly identified the position to be filled. Unlike their competitors, they clearly stated the type of computer hardware with which the successful candidate would have to work, clearly a crucial aspect of the job. Carré Orban's profile of the ideal candidate, of over two pages, is more detailed than its rivals' and is the only one to analyse the necessary personal traits of the successful candidate, in the context of both the geographical circumstances of the job and of the corporate culture of the client company.

Also, unlike the other pitches, Carré Orban had established that the client did not specify any other companies as being 'no-touch' as hunting grounds for candidates. But what about the companies who were already clients of Carré Orban, and thus off-limits in this search? This is a particularly pertinent question to ask of Korn/Ferry and Russell Reynolds, both well known for the large number of multinationals on their books. Not one of the four briefs suggest that this question – potentially most embarrassing from the headhunters' point of view – was asked at all, suggesting perhaps that the client was not at this time an especially experienced user of search. Of course, this matter could have been agreed verbally at the shoot-out and none of the headhunters felt that it needed restating in the brief.

Carré Orban then set out its philosophy and methods, which compared well with Korn/Ferry's in being much more detailed and specific. It also included an insistence on certain undertakings by the client, especially in terms of not employing another search firm for the same assignment at the same time; clients distrusting search companies have been known to do this.

Carré Orban saw this assignment as possibly taking longer than the other search firms had estimated, expecting the research to take at least two months, with a short list ready by the third month. Again quoting a fee based on the salary offered, of approximately SF60 000, it was suggested that expenses would total another 18–20%. The consultants committed themselves to completing the search within three months, without extra fee charges if it took longer, and agreed to replace the candidate free of fees if he or she left the position within six months of taking it up.

There is nothing in Carré Orban's proposal about the credentials of the consultants to undertake the job, but their names were appended. Presumably further details were supplied at the shoot-out, but it would have strengthened Carré Orban's case if these have been reiterated in the brief.

The shoot-out letters: how to choose?

Much may be deduced by simply comparing how the different firms sign off their proposals. It reveals the nature of the relationship they thought they had established with the client, and the basis they hope it will maintain in the future. Russell Reynolds used a formal 'yours sincerely'; Korn/Ferry were slightly over the top with 'best and warmest regards'; John Stork used an uncommitted 'yours'; and Carré Orban signed off with a rather ingratiating and obsequious 'kindest personal regards'.

So, what should the client employing the headhunter look for in the initial brief? On what grounds should the choice be made? Frequently, the successful search consultant is simply the one with whom the client feels most comfortable as, after all, they will have to be able to work together closely. But a lot of money is at stake here, and the winning firm should clearly be highly professional, experienced and willing to put its cards on the table. As far as the user of search is concerned, the headhunting firm should:

1. present a brief and clear understanding of the problem, and state when the work could begin;
2. set out the search firm's methods and approach in a precise, competent, relevant manner, and clients should be wary of potentially dangerous short-cuts;
3. have taken some time and trouble with the proposal, and indicated that the firm was willing to become very closely involved with the client's problem, as opposed merely to setting its headhunting wheels in motion with a standardised, ready-made solution;
4. set out a time scale for the search programme. Too brief an estimate looks suspicious: has the headhunter really understood the problem?;
5. provide a clear and perceptive profile of the ideal candidate. Are any specific search and recruiting problems envisaged at this stage?;
6. make a clear statement of the firm's charges. Is this based on one-third of the successful candidate's salary, or is it a professional fee? This can have a bearing on the attitude of the headhunter to the search, as it suggests it is in the consultant's interest that the appointee is paid as much as possible, when this can hardly be to the client's advantage. The client will normally want to keep the search budget as low as possible, or is the importance of the assignment such that this consideration is relatively insignificant? Is there any kind of guarantee, in the event of dissatisfaction on the part of the client, that the search would be continued for expenses only after a certain period had elapsed?;
7. estimate the total cost of the search and placement overall, including expenses. Some headhunters have been known almost to double their total bill with expenses charges. The client should expect an estimate of these, and insist on prior approval being sought for all large individual expense items, such as intercontinental flights and lengthy overseas phone calls;
8. describe in detail the credentials of the headhunting consultants who will take on the job. If the client wants the man or woman present at the shoot-out to take on the assignment, then this should be insisted upon at the outset, otherwise it could very

well be handled by a less experienced and less able lower-ranking associate with more time at his or her disposal. Clients should be wary of firms where the MD does the selling and the other consultants, kept in the background, do the work. Have the consultants poised to take on the assignment had the necessary experience to understand the ramifications of the position to be filled, by having worked in a similar company, having carried out a closely-related function, and having helped solve many other search assignments of a similar nature? Does the consultant possess the technical and linguistic ability to take on the specific assignment? Certain consultants have gained a reputation for expertise in specific areas; the client should seek the views of personnel and executive colleagues in his or her own and other firms, especially when taking on a new headhunting firm for the first time;

9. reiterate the importance of confidentiality and be willing to commit themselves to it absolutely;

10. ask the client what companies the search firm should not use as hunting grounds from the client's point of view, and the consultant should give a clear idea which companies are off-limits to the headhunting firm. Should the headhunter reveal the names of existing clients in this regard? Would this break their confidentiality agreements?

Finally, if the client, after the shoot-out, feels that a close enough relationship had been developed with a particular headhunter to justify the latter signing off a brief with the words 'warmest personal regards', then they should consider engaging that firm. If not, they would do well to be wary. It is better to be businesslike than over-chummy until a real *modus operandi* has been established and the search is showing good progress or has been successfully completed.

RESEARCH

In the overall strategy to draw up a short list of candidates for the client, the research element is arguably most important of all. Most assignments spend more time in the hands of a headhunter's research department than any other stage of the headhunting process, except perhaps during the successful candidate working out his or her notice; and if the client is not happy with the short list, then it is back to the drawing board and the assignment will be turned over to the researcher again. Before consultants can begin work on screening and sifting through the first trawl of potential candidates to get to the initial long short list, they are entirely dependent on the researcher's input.

Yet, despite all these considerations, the research aspect of search is the one most shrouded in mystery from the client's point of view. Most users of search, however experienced and knowledgeable, know almost nothing about what happens at the research stage and the skills needed for this job. It has indeed proved difficult here to obtain a clear picture of exactly what happens when the assignment 'goes to the research department'.

It might also be suggested that many senior headhunting consultants themselves have but a sketchy idea of what goes on at this point. David Kay, of GKR, writing in *The Executive Grapevine* under the title 'Analysis of a Search' does not pay much attention to the role of research, at least in this particular article. Many headhunters' researchers complain that their consultant bosses do not understand their jobs, and as a result they lack encouragement and adequate technical support.

The aim of this sub-section was initially to present a clear picture of the basic essentials of headhunting research, but the findings suggest that it is much more complex, sophisticated and of greater importance to the search process than a cursory knowledge of the business would indicate, and cannot be easily distilled. Instead of presenting a synthesis of various headhunting research methods, individual researchers have been asked to speak out. Their experiences show, first, that the differing attitudes to research by headhunting firms is one of the principal differences between them, and research capability is a useful criteria of their professionalism; and second, that headhunting research is immensely skilled and hard work and, once they realise what is involved, most clients are more appreciative of what they get for their money. Increasingly efficient research systems and methods are helping to make headhunting more cost-effective for lower-level searches, so good researchers are thus encouraging further growth of the headhunting industry as a whole.

After considering the common attitudes to research from the point of view of the senior consultants, we will examine the role of this aspect of the headhunting process from the point of view of a specialist freelance researcher, arguably one of the most experienced and well-known in the business. She reveals the existence of a very large demand for quality research, and the fact that fewer and fewer companies are prepared to undertake in-house search work, mainly on the basis of the research work involved. Before examining case-histories of individual researchers to amplify these findings and discover how headhunting research works in practice, we will briefly investigate what happens at the meetings of the Executive Research Association.

Headhunting research: myths and reality

To what extent is new research undertaken for each particular headhunting assignment, and how reliant is the researcher on the existing candidate and source documentation already available from the search firm's data bank, amassed from previous assignments, coded and stored?

Possibly the most widespread – and certainly the most inaccurate – myth of the headhunting business is that headhunters' candidates all spring magically from their data banks, and thus clients prefer to go to the largest and most long-established search firms because these have the most extensive files. There is some evidence in our survey of clients' use of headhunters, summarised in Chapter 3, that many users of search think that this is wholly or at least partly the case. Representations and descriptions of search in the media have encouraged belief in this myth; for example, probably unintentionally but most unfortunately, the impression that candidates' names merely popped out of a computer came over strongly in a BBC 'Money Programme' documentary about headhunting in which Stephen Rowlinson of Korn/Ferry undertook an assignment to find a new director of satellite communications for Robert Maxwell. This is perhaps inevitable when fourteen hours of filming are reduced to 20 minutes of final footage. In reality – and this is the main point of this chapter – only a tiny minority of successful candidates are found in this way, although data banks have a recognised value for identifying sources which might lead to candidates.

Headhunters traditionally have played their cards close to their chests and revealed little about what happens during a search. David Kay, in the article referred to above, suggests that because clients are paying for a service, they have a right to know at any time what is being done for the fee they are paying. This is especially true of the research process, which takes up so many costly man- (or, more usually, woman-) hours.

The client will normally expect the headhunters' research staff to prepare a list of companies in which potential candidates are likely to be found and to establish who is doing the relevant jobs (or has done them previously) in those companies and, as far as possible, how good they are. As soon as the researcher comes up with approximately 40 to 60 names seen as strong possibilities – and, in 80% of search firms, the researcher will have already made initial telephone contact – then the consultant can get to work on talking to them and building up a comprehensive and well-informed list of potential candidates, interviewing the most promising and producing a short list of the best.

At which point does the researcher come into the story: at some stage of the client briefing, such as visiting some part of the client company's operations, or only when the assignment comes back to the search firm's office? At which point does the researcher hand the assignment back over to the consultant: when a bare list of names to try has been compiled, or when a list of people already contacted, initially briefed and preliminarily reference-checked has been drawn up?

This question of the role of researchers varies enormously between search firms. For instance, Heidrick and Struggles frequently and apparently successfully appoints new consultants out of the ranks of their most able and experienced researchers to ESE, their 'younger executive' search business; whilst British-based John Stork maintains that 'once a researcher, always a researcher' and that research and consultancy skills are totally separate and never the twain shall meet. In some headhunter's offices, research is seen as the backbone of the business, and researchers are deliberately involved in all aspects of the search; in others, they are little more than filing-clerks, and are paid and treated accordingly.

David Kay suggests that if a client is not sure whether or not the search firm has done a thorough job, he should ask to go through their working papers with them, to make sure they have done a comprehensive and truly wide-ranging search. Kay considers that a client is justified in wanting to know to whom the researchers and/or consultants have spoken, to see if all possible avenues have been explored or if the search firm has just run their eyes over their files to see if they can get their short list from their own data base. Kay recommends that a client should ask the consultant how each name on the short list emerged in the first place: was it from the data bank or from fresh research?

Research from the inside: Mychelle Hunter

Mychelle Hunter – who founded her own headhunting research company, Breckenridge Research Ltd, and who is arguably one of the leading authorities on headhunting research in Britain and Europe – strongly supports the view that the majority of appointments made by search are, and should be, the result of original, creative research. This assertion dominates her outlook. Hunter is trying to establish the very highest standards of headhunting research; as such, her criteria of research methods and skills are of great value to the user of search in assessing how good the research input of an executive search firm can be. She advises search firms proud of their research facility to use their researchers and their product as advertisements for business; clients should judge consultancies partly by the quality of their researchers, and from the consultant's point of view this means making an effort to involve the researcher in the briefings and client visits. This also helps overcome the primary problem which Hunter has encountered among researchers: a lack of self-confidence and feeling of non-involvement in the overall project.

Clients are getting their money's worth from a headhunter only if the research department has done as good and thorough a job as the consultant, and done the job before the consultant gets to grips with it. Inadequate and inexpert research is worse than spoiling the ship for a ha'p'orth of tar; it would be akin to sending that ship to ports of call without knowing what cargoes might be found there, what their quality was like and whether or not there was any demand for them.

Hunter has been involved in headhunting for ten years, since setting up the research function for PA's new headhunting unit in 1978, having been appointed to consultancy level at the age of 37. A globe-trotting American, she had previously worked with management consultants in San Francisco and in Monte Carlo, before joining the *Financial Times* Information Service. The establishment of her own company followed her stint with PA in 1984, with the initial goal of offering contract research to headhunting firms when they were overloaded and their own research staff could not cope with all the assignments coming in.

Hunter quickly discovered, after notifying only twelve people in London about her new business, that this research overload facility was in such demand that she was unable to handle the volume of work; rather than expanding her own operations at this stage, she decided to offer a training course for researchers for the executive search firms. As a result, she has trained a very large proportion of London researchers and many in Europe. Although this has brought an improvement in headhunting research standards by at least ensuring a systematic, disciplined and thorough approach rather than an unstructured, learning-on-the-job, random attitude to research work – at least among those she has trained – Hunter feels that the value of the researcher's input is seriously undervalued, by consultants and clients alike.

Researchers in the USA are much less prone to being treated as the Cinderellas of the headhunting world, and the quality of their work, and contribution to the success of each assignment, is recognised accordingly. The directors of research of the top American executive search firms are as well known by name in the executive recruitment profession as the leading consultants. In New York, the stage has been reached whereby many headhunting researchers are themselves being headhunted, by companies who admire and want their skills. The quality and professionalism of headhunting in Britain, especially in terms of what the client is getting for their money, depends on exacting research, and this will soon be as recognised and appreciated as on the other side of the Atlantic. Hunter sees the role of the executive search researcher as similar to the criminal investigator or to the great detectives of literature: Sherlock Holmes, Inspector Maigret, Hercule Poirot. They observed, analysed, made deductions and identified the criminal. They possessed acute powers of observation, and they had an obsessive curiosity; less of a skill than a gift, they had a well-developed sense of intuition. Research is thus, she argues, a highly creative and disciplined process of investigation. It is the hunt down the path for clues; some are informative, others deceptive. Each clue must be examined, evaluated and accepted or rejected. Every clue is worthy of examination. This, of course, applies to every type of research, scientific, medical or commercial.

The manner in which Hunter handles the headhunting research process at Breckenridge Research Ltd would come as a great surprise to many clients and consultants, especially those who expect the most modern and most professional service to be accompanied by expensive and sophisticated electronic and technical computing gadgetry, with extensive written files and records all carefully cross-referenced and indexed. Headhunters' research departments, according to popular myth, are mostly giant repositiories of thousands of CVs, and vary only according to the space-age nature of how they are stored and accessed. Yet in Breckenridge Research there are no computers or electronic retrieval systems, and not a CV in sight. Hunter questions how much she would find use for such a system, as she argues that most of her assignments do not repeat themselves exactly, either in industry or function, and she feels that it is unlikely that any of the candidates' CVs she might keep would be of value to future assignments.

Hunter recognises that the coding of candidates – a job which occupies much of the time of many headhunters' researchers – is a highly-skilled activity which requires an excellent knowledge of industries and functions. But she argues that an intelligent and creative person would soon become bored with the coding work and would gain no job satisfaction at all; meanwhile, a less intelligent person would not do the job properly. Finally, whatever is put in the system has to be updated, maintained and nourished, requiring time and money. So why have such a system at all? At PA, Hunter did use such systems and did find excellent candidates. But, she insists, the majority of appointments resulted from original research.

Basic research techniques do not vary enormously, and are very much the same throughout the world, although certain directories and other publications may differ; what does vary significantly is the attitude to it, and thus its quality. It is important to emphasise the nature of research as creative, intelligent and investigative, supported by – inevitably – substantially repetitive techniques and considerable drudgery. Anyone considering the role of headhunters' researcher must understand the drawbacks, yet at the same time be motivated by learning about new products and new industries. Otherwise headhunting research is allowed to become overwhelmingly tedious, a situation inviting shoddy work.

What qualities should consultants – and clients, if they have a chance to meet one – look for in a researcher? The best researchers are tenacious, highly attentive to detail, able to work on their own initiative, imaginative, enquiring, investigative and broad in their thinking with strong analytical skills. Those firms who tend to confine their researchers strictly to the back room would welcome the introverted, as in these circumstances headhunting research would not be particularly gregarious; but at the same time the researcher needs a pleasing voice and excellent telephone manner, and must really enjoy telephone work. A headhunting researcher who has not left his or her office all day and received no visitors could still have talked to 60 or as many as 80 people during that time, all faceless voices whose owners he or she may never meet. Having said that, it would be wrong to say that the research job is about people; instead it is about structures, how people fit into an organisational structure, and the structure of companies within the industry into which the researcher is looking.

Headhunting research needs, above all, great reserves of patience and toleration of frustration, combined with a strong drive to finish the task in hand. In a small consultancy, it would be better to hire as researcher a person with industrial or commercial experience. It would be very difficult for a university or college-leaver to work alone without the back-up of an experienced researcher. A person lacking in research and/ or industry experience would be better off working in a larger research department, otherwise he or she might feel completely lost and isolated, particularly if the consultant was impatient or out most of the time.

All researchers should have spent some time in industry, not only to be more effective at their research, but also because few really good researchers will want to go on being researchers forever. It would be unlikely for a researcher, however experienced in the headhunting process, to become a successful consultant without substantial commercial or industrial experience, unless they could make up for this with a remarkable flair for the marketing and selling of business to clients and positions to candidates. Increasingly, however, many researchers are achieving the transition to consultant, especially through obtaining more relevant qualifications, such as an MBA. At least 25% of researchers aim ultimately to become headhunting consultants; the others seek to run research departments, enter other areas of research or simply stay where they are. Particularly enlightened search firms have been known to support their researchers financially in their studies, by paying fees and allowing time off work.

Not all researchers will inevitably leave headhunting research if they leave their search firm: some may go freelance or part-time. This is particularly attractive to married women, and also appeals strongly to search firms. For a small consultancy, using freelances can be the most effective solution to their research problem, avoiding the burden of employee overheads, especially when work is slack. They can also dispense with the problem of training. Freelancing is one way in which researchers can increase their earnings for basically the same job – in addition to providing themselves with greater variety to help offset tedium – because they can charge much higher fees than are comparable with a full-time researcher in regular employment. Freelancing can boost a researcher's morale, especially those who justifiably feel that their work is the most difficult aspect of headhunting yet receives the least financial reward. Such feelings of resentment are constantly being exacerbated by reports of the mega-salaries of top consultants, especially those based on a share of the income from assignments, into which the researcher will frequently have put more hard graft than the head-hunter, and often as much creative thought and imagination.

Mychelle Hunter's view of the role of the researcher, in an article in *The Times* of October 1984, when her company was first launched, is as valid now as it was then:

> If the researcher can subtly make the transition from a supplier of information to an originator of new questions and new solutions through research, someone, somewhere, will take notice. If the researcher's solutions display suggestions that are not only the obvious but the subtle, and that a less overt and even opposite avenue has been trod, then the originality shown may begin to be recognised and these skills applied to other areas.
>
> Rather than transferring printed matter from one piece of paper to another, the researcher will look beyond the apparent into what awaits discovery. The researcher then may become indispensable and good research work might even become a marketable product for the company.

How to learn headhunting research

The course, 'Conducting Executive Search Assignments' taught at Breckenridge Research Ltd, aims to introduce personnel and recruitment managers and executives to the techniques which will allow them to conduct their own executive searches for key staff, and gives a clear picture of the research aspect of a typical assignment. It presents a simulated recruitment project, with instruction and exercises to lead students through the steps involved in identifying candidates and filling the job, emphasis being placed on the development of analytical and research skills.

The researcher must learn how to analyse the position to be filled. Where does the candidate fit into the company structure? In which industries might the candidate be found? The target companies to be searched must then be selected, by a thorough evaluation of their products, market, turnover and other criteria, and then their structure and relevant departments analysed.

This entails the use of a wide range of published information, including directories, trade journals and libraries. Increasingly, on-line information accessed by computer is used by many research departments. Although Hunter does not necessarily use this facility in her own company, she discusses the matter at length in the course. Much use is also made of news-cuttings reporting on company and industry-wide performance.

The researcher must then find and make use of contacts in relevant industries. This means utilising the existing in-house information sources within their own company, such as employees who may have contacts within the target companies. At this point the researcher must make cold calls to find the relevant candidates within the target companies, and evaluate and interview the most promising. The researcher/personnel manager's job ends with the appointment, or the turning over of the final candidate to the appointing executive. Finally, the information culled from this assignment may be stored within a candidate retrieval system, which the researcher should know how to develop.

The recognition within the research world of this course is such that it attracts more than a hundred students a year, costing £1500 for three days. The course is accompanied by a solid and detailed training manual, which emphasises that dealing with organisational structures is the main task of the researcher. These research and analytical skills can be transferable to a wide range of industrial and commercial concerns, and researchers should see their abilities as being marketable among a range of clients.

Within the course, not only must researchers understand the network of job titles within an organisation and their reporting lines, but they must also be able to cope with more mundane problems, such as trying to get beyond a company's switchboard to the person to whom they need to talk. It would amaze and appal many executives to know that a disturbing number of company switchboard operators, many of whom have occupied their positions for upwards of 20 years, have but a vague idea of the official job titles of the company's executives and managers; they may know them by their first names and greet them every morning, but the statement that Bill is Director of Corporate Human Resource Development, Industrial Relations and Special Projects would frequently produce a blank stare.

Many chief executives must be entirely ignorant of the impression given of their company by their switchboard staff, and the difficulty involved in speaking to certain staff whose titles are quoted but not their names. Hunter described a personal experience of telephoning a major construction company to enquire whether or not they had ever built hospitals. She was passed between fifteen different people before someone told her, 'I don't know', and rang off. The ignorance of many switchboard operators is exceeded only by a disturbing number of secretaries who have no idea of the qualifications of their bosses. Coping with such frustration is an integral part of the course.

As in all research, the best tactic is always to move from the known to the unknown. So the course begins with an introduction to all the general directories, trade journals, information produced by professional associations and published reference tools available, and how to set up an effective reference library. Then it turns to more specific sources relating to particular businesses: individual company annual reports, company magazines and newsletters, and other in-house corporate documentation. How widely available are company organisational charts, and how useful are they? How may they be reconstructed from piecemeal snippets of information?

'Obtaining the candidate' is the most difficult problem of the whole business of headhunting research, and it is at this point that many of the personnel/recruitment managers/directors realise the amount of sheer hard work and tenacity involved in getting through to people. Few in-house personnel staff have a really accurate idea of how time-consuming, demanding and complex headhunting research can be.

As a result, the course actually defeats its own object. It aims to inspire those attending to adopt an attitude of determination to rise to the challenge of headhunting work, and to work towards the goal of their company being able to take over all its in-house recruiting requirements, no matter how senior, without the need for employing external consultants. However, in practice, the course reveals to personnel managers and directors the value of the research input which external consultants can provide, and the vast majority immediately decide that they would far rather pay for this work to be done for them than do it themselves.

During the four years in which the course has been offered, it has become clear that the issues of time, convenience, complexity and sheer hassle are the deciding factors: money, in comparison, does not enter into it. The majority of companies who decide to train staff to take over headhunting work – which, in-house, means mostly headhunting research work – by sending them on short courses such as Breckenridge's, quickly change their minds when they realise what is involved. The prospect of simply being supplied with a short list, especially from headhunters with whom they are familiar and who are familiar with them, becomes infinitely more appealing than wading through business directories and individual company documentation, grappling with different and often baffling corporate structures, battling with ignorant switchboard operators and surly secretaries or having to try time and time again to get through to the ever-elusive candidate.

Thus, by promoting the value of the input of the researcher, Mychelle Hunter has done much to encourage an increased acceptance and widespread use of search, by so effectively convincing clients of what they are getting for their money that they would not contemplate the alternative of handling recruitment themselves. The realisation of the cost-effectiveness of external consultants for headhunting research is also helping fuel the trend towards the use of search for lower-level appointments, either by calling on the lower-level search facilities offered as a separate service by many of the top headhunting firms, or by employing smaller search firms who generally work at this level. The elements of hard, long-sustained and complex work – the main features of headhunting research – form, in practice, one of the most convincing arguments for using search which a headhunter can put forward to a doubtful client.

When a search consultant talks about how he or she can understand the client's corporate culture and problems of direction from an external objective; match the client company with similar organisations from which candidates may emerge; compare complex corporate structures in looking for comparable job descriptions; act as intermediary in approaching candidates; advise on salaries and conditions; perceive the quality of a client's executives in the context of the market place as a whole; and commit themselves to solving the problem and presenting a good short list of excellent candidates – in demonstrating all the services which the search firm can offer, consultants are promoting the work of their research departments as much as, if not more than, their own input into the problem. In this context, the headhunter is the front man, who negotiates with the client and again with the final candidates, who does not necessarily undertake much of the work in between. How else can top consultants handle as many as twelve or even fifteen assignments at any one time?

The Executive Research Association

Any investigation of the research aspect of the headhunting business would be incomplete without reference to the Executive Research Association. Formed in June 1986, it meets six times a year at the New Cavendish Club in Great Cumberland Place, and acts as a forum for headhunting researchers from a wide range of firms, both British and international. It is frowned on by several MDs of headhunting firms who see it as an insidious and conspiratorial organisation, in which disgruntled researchers complain about their employers and leak their 'secrets' to other firms via their similarly disillusioned and mutinous fellows. On these grounds, executive search bosses have been known to discourage or even ban their research staff from attending Executive Research Association meetings, which has served to render attractive a gathering which might otherwise have appeared dull.

In reality, the meetings are scenes of lively and intelligent debate, generally concerned with how headhunting researchers can improve their skills at their job (of considerable value to their employers) and how they can improve their own prospects (perhaps less in their employers' interests). Usually featuring one or more speakers, the meetings are organised and managed by the Association's co-founder, Daphne Silvester, previously a consultant in selection with the management consultancy division of leading City accountants Coopers & Lybrand, and now freelance.

Although now apparently on the other side of the fence, Silvester has a continuing interest in headhunting research, which took up much of her life before she crossed the great consultant/researcher divide and gained her present position. From working in recruitment for Shell she moved into the research and information department of a merchant bank. Her first venture into search was with the American headhunting firm of Keirnan & Co., from which she moved on to become research manager for GKR. From there she joined Tyzack, gaining entry into the partnership after a year.

Yet for all her headhunting research work, Silvester eventually became frustrated as carefully nurtured candidates were taken over by the consultants in the final stages. As the consultants for whom she worked expanded their business, she willingly took on an increasingly heavy and proportionally greater workload, reaching the stage where she was responsible for perhaps 75% of the work on many assignments. Occasionally she tackled a complete assignment from start to finish, generally lower-level ones not seen as cost-effective and worthwhile for hard-pressed consultants; but most of the time she was caught in the middle. Silvester's attainment of her present position is one answer to the eternal question of 'Is there life after research?' By working as a consultant in selection, she is able to do a whole job and have the satisfaction of actually placing people and feeling that she is making an impact.

Guest speaker: Hilary Sears

A more ambitious solution to the potential cul-de-sac of headhunting research was suggested in an inspiring and practical address given during a meeting of the Executive Research Association by Hilary B. Sears. She was, until recently, a principal of Carré, Orban & Partners, a highly respected smaller firm with strong representation in Europe. Sears is keen to promote the idea of researchers working towards the goal of consultancy, and suggests how this might be done. From a background in advertising, Sears herself sought to improve her prospects by investing £7000 and a year of her life in obtaining a Cranfield MBA, during which time she chose the executive search business as a special topic of study. Her appointment as a consultant at Carré Orban followed soon afterwards.

Sears argues that researchers can become consultants by having obtained a degree, spent three or four years in the business world, and gained three or four years' experience in research; but they can progress much more quickly with an MBA, taking advantage of the kudos and insight which that can give. Alternatively, researchers can climb the tree by way of other branches: by showing exceptional commitment to their work; by having a strong mentor, a senior consultant in their firm or preferably the MD; or by developing an important specialisation. Either way, they must be prepared for very hard work and sustained effort. An ambitious and interested researcher will know what additional training and skills are needed to make the transition, such as interviewing and report-writing, and will seek out opportunities to develop these. For example, researchers can handle interviews of 'walk-ins' – would-be candidates who walk in off the streets – in the case of those search firms who are prepared to give their researchers' time in this way.

The most difficult skill to learn for the researcher on the path to becoming a consultant is business development. Consultants in some search firms, including one of the market leaders, are presented with targets of new business to bring in, and are subjected to considerable pressure on this front. Any researcher hoping to make the grade at such firms must be prepared for this.

However, on the whole researchers can have better prospects with the larger, international headhunting firms because – as Mvchelle Hunter would agree – they tend to recognise researchers as an essential part of the headhunting team, and the most able and senior of them enjoy a status almost comparable with that of the consultants. These firms expect researchers to ask for opportunities, realising that, like consultants, they may well move to a rival search firm if they are dissatisfied. Research departments in American executive search firms are frequently separate profit centres, and their directors are powerful, prestigious and well-paid. Already some headhunters in Britain openly recognise the importance of their research managers, and have their photographs and details published in brochures along with those of the consultants, often as a response to the interest expressed by clients.

If a researcher is generally happy in research work, then Sears recommends them to join a firm sympathetic to researchers; if they want to make the grade as consultants, then above all they must learn, and develop a flair for, the creation of new business. Meeting clients on briefings and client visits certainly helps, and about half of the 60 or so researchers present at this particular Executive Research Association meeting had been involved in such client contact, but acknowledged that such opportunites had happened very recently. This trend has produced a need for more confident and assertive researchers, a race apart from the back-room introverted types. Many of the researchers at the meeting certainly looked the part too, in smart suits and outfits comparable with the most upwardly-mobile executives.

Even the least ambitious researchers were clearly *au fait* with the business world, enough to tell the difference between a product manager and a production manager, for example, and had already passed the stage of regarding chief executives with awe. The most able, intelligent and committed, who had developed a sophisticated and detailed knowledge of many sectors of industry and commerce, still found it difficult to break into consulting, however. Many felt that their attempts to become consultants were being blocked by the trend, over the last two or three years, for gamekeepers to become poachers: for businessmen to be taken on as new consultants by those search firms who are expanding in size and wanting to develop certain industry specialisms and/or have been unsuccessful in tempting enough good consultants away from other search firms. The ranks of researchers need to be more generally recognised as a source of consultants, and trained and encouraged accordingly to respond to the requirements of search firms in the future.

If researchers wish to improve their status and earning power but do not aspire to becoming fully-fledged headhunters, then their research skills can be just as effectively transferred elsewhere, such as in sales, marketing and advertising. A confident headhunting researcher, with experience of meeting clients and use of sophisticated information technology, has highly marketable skills. By encouraging belief in the value and importance of headhunting research – to consultants, users of search, British industry and commerce as a whole and, most of all, those within the ranks of researchers who may sometimes lack confidence and motivation – the Executive Research Association may be seen as a force for good rather than evil in the British headhunting business.

Finally, what is it really like being a researcher on the job, and what attracts people to the work, and what is the nature of their backgrounds? Alison Burnside of Korn/Ferry, Mike Goldstone of Heidrick and Struggles, and Robert Birkett of Merton Associates all have their own different views and experiences.

Alison Burnside of Korn/Ferry

Alison Burnside of Korn/Ferry is not part of a traditional research department, as may be found at Russell Reynolds and GKR; instead, she is answerable directly and exclusively to just one individual director, responsible for both his PA and research work at the same time. This has enabled her to enter headhunting research with a mixed degree in humanities and a postgraduate business secretarial course. Unsure of her ultimate goal whilst at college, Burnside tried a variety of jobs – as a secretary, then a PA in different sectors of the Thyssen Bornemisza Group – before answering an advertisement and joining Korn/Ferry in April 1987. She now finds headhunting research attractive enough to aspire towards a research-only job and away from PA work; she is not sure about wanting to become a consultant.

A typical assignment – from Burnside's point of view – begins when her director explains what happened at his first meeting with the client, when he was invited to take on the project. Occasionally, Burnside has been invited to client briefings, and stresses that this would be more frequent if she was in a research-only job. Her director when interviewed was Chris Denham, who headhunted Dorothy Palmer-Fry from Shell into Trebor, as described in case study II, and who specialised in hi-tech and fast-moving consumer goods sector (FMCG) work, so Burnside has had experience of researching a range of industries.

Both would then put together a research plan, identifying the types of companies from which it is hoped candidates will emerge. Next, Burnside starts work in the Korn/Ferry library, first of all scanning the headhunting researcher's bible, *Kompass*. Here she can look up products and services to give company names, and then consult the company index for names of directors and managers. All this is not quite as easy as it sounds, however; very frequently these listings are out of date or incomplete. Other sources are those published by the American firm Dunn & Bradstreet, and specialist guides and volumes of *Who's Who*, such as those concerned with hi-tech and computing. If the assignment is in a completely new area, Burnside will consult the *Directory of Directories* and order the appropriate reference book.

Burnside's task is to find the names of candidates and sources; if they are senior, high-ranking people, such as MDs, with salaries around the £60 000 mark, she passes their names on to her director. Otherwise, for less lofty positions, she will handle the initial calls herself and set up meetings with her director if appropriate. In her telephone contacts, her professional standards are expected to be entirely equal to those of the consultants, whatever the seniority of the potential candidate or source.

In addition to using the resources of the library, Burnside will do a computer run on the people in 'the system', Korn/Ferry's data bank. A basic IBM system accessible from desk-top terminals in front of the researchers, it is managed by a specialist data-processor who logs in the CVs of ex-candidates and sources. This is a good place in which to check names; for example, if Burnside sees the name of a rising star of the computing industry in the pages of *Computer Weekly*, she can check to see if there are fuller personal and career details in the system before trying the more difficult route of telephoning around for information. The system is conveniently cross-referenced so that all executives within a certain salary band can be accessed; or they can be classified by qualifications, function, industry sector and so on. If a likely candidate is tracked down in the system, Burnside can add to this information from the files of past assignments. Some researchers and consultants use the system more than others; but the majority believe that most of the candidates will come from original research, despite the endless cold calls which this entails, feeling that many people in the system will be irrelevant unless it is a sector where a great deal of work has already been done. Burnside estimates that on a typical assignment she may use 20 or more names from the system, but mainly as sources rather than as candidates.

The number of sources and candidates approached during a search inevitably depends on its duration. Most consultants hope to see an assignment opened and closed in three months altogether, but some searches are exceptionally long, as in the case of the Trebor job. Another determining factor is the confidentiality of the search. Trying to obtain information and drum up candidate interest in a position without giving anything away is very difficult. If not enough information about the client is revealed, no one is interested; if too much, the candidate or source will guess who is looking and the client's cover will be blown.

As soon as she has collected about half-a-dozen names, unless they are particularly senior, Burnside will begin telephoning, carefully logging every call to keep a record of all persons approached in this particular search. In many cases, several phone calls will have to be made to each candidate or source, especially if they are constantly travelling. When she finally gets through, the normal procedure is for Burnside to introduce herself, her director and the firm, and to ask if she has chosen a convenient time to call. This is the cue for the closing of office doors or – especially in open-plan offices with colleagues eavesdropping all the time – the exchanging of home telephone numbers.

Avoiding telephone conversations discussing search assignments in the offices of candidates and sources is particularly necessary in the case of headhunting in the financial services sector, where – as Roddy Gow of Russell Reynolds described in the introduction to this chapter – many telephone calls received or made (especially in dealing rooms) are taped. In these instances, the researcher has somehow to convey their message to the would-be candidate or source, without giving the game away to someone else listening to the tape, and without indicating that he or she is phoning on behalf of a search firm or a particular client. Experienced and oft-headhunted executives usually guess what the call is all about, but nervous and brand-new researchers often find it daunting to have to think on their feet, and use their ingenuity and resourcefulness to bypass such problems.

Nervousness at having to make cold calls decreases proportionally with the amount of experience a researcher has notched up, and the amount of preparation that has been done on each candidate or source. Sometimes it is possible for a researcher easily to screen out unsuitable candidates over the telephone, but Burnside feels that it is not necessarily a good idea to exclude people who give a poor initial impression over the wires. They could have just fallen out with their colleagues or a superior, and feel angry and snap at the hopeful researcher; on the other hand, an executive who is telephoned when he or she has just rowed with the boss might be in just the mood to consider moving to another job. Because of the uncertainty, Burnside will always obtain a CV before making the decision on whether or not a person should be interviewed or not.

As in the case of the number of calls per assignment, the number of candidates interviewed before the short-list stage will also vary according to the difficulty of the assignment and the amount of time it has taken. In a typical assignment, Burnside estimates that at least fifteen, maybe twenty, candidates will be invited for interview, generally at Korn/Ferry's office. She is occasionally asked to be present at the interviews and, as in the case of her attendance at client briefings, feels that this would happen more often if she were working in research-only work.

In the case of candidates who have made it to the short list and are to be presented to the client, Burnside helps her director to write up a report on each, based on their CV and interview. These reports tend to be of about eight to ten pages each, without photographs but with physical descriptions, and always include details of the candidate's current salary. Within her PA function, Burnside then types them up on the word processor and sends them off, usually in groups of three at a time for the client to compare, and then arranges times for the client and candidates to meet. When this takes place at Korn/Ferry's offices, Burnside finds herself in another time-honoured PA role: making the tea or coffee, although her director has been known occasionally to do the same.

Her work can sometimes be potentially upsetting, especially when making cold calls to potential sources. One irate executive barked, 'Why should I tell you anything? Are you going to pay me? Who do you think you are anyway?'; this is fair enough, she thought, especially as senior businessmen want to keep their good people and the last thing they want to do is to give their names to someone who might tempt them away.

Mike Goldstone of Heidrick and Struggles

Mike Goldstone of Heidrick and Struggles, unlike the other two examples of researchers quoted here, intended all along to use research as a stepping-stone to consultancy, an attitude encouraged by his employers, who recruited him partly for his potential in this direction. However, he crossed the great headhunting divide much more quickly than either party expected: in just eighteen months. He is now part of the firm's search affiliate handling the recruitment of younger executives – ESE Consultants – and has been joined by a colleague who has similarly crossed from research. At the same time, he has completed his MBA.

Goldstone came with a background in research, but of an entirely different nature: after university, he spent five years as a political analyst with the Ministry of Defence. This was more formal academic research, but it gave him the chance to develop a nose for discovery and for pursuing hunches, and he began to be more and more attracted to the idea of commercially-orientated investigation. He considered doing an MBA then, but felt the need for some industrial/commercial experience first.

Headhunting research, for Goldstone, gave the immediate opportunity to develop his research skills in business, and provided him with an instant window on the commercial world. For the future, it suggested all sorts of possibilities, including headhunting consultancy itself. He felt at the time that this was the ideal solution for someone without much knowledge of industry and without a precise career goal; he could gain experience as a headhunting researcher for a couple of years, perhaps headhunt an interesting job for himself, and then try for an MBA. He was very much aware of the shortage of highly qualified businessmen in Britain, quoting the regrettable fact that only 3% of them have high professional qualifications, and that MBA graduates are coming out at a rate of only 2000 a year, when at least 6000–8000 are needed. His employers encouraged him to study fc. his MBA whilst working as a researcher, paying the fees and allowing him time off.

Work as a researcher for Heidrick and Struggles brought Goldstone the close industry and commerce contact that he had hoped, yet this would not necessarily have been the case had he joined other search firms. He was brought in on each assignment at the client briefing stage, helping determine the job specification, and discussing with the client the target companies. Each assignment then entered the research stage for about a month. Goldstone quickly appreciated the differences between academic and commercial research: the latter presented a double agenda of having to cover the ground, but with speed as the added dimension. The trick was to make effective short cuts, to find the nuggets without panning the whole stream. Goldstone found much greater scope for developing lateral thinking in headhunting research than in his previous work; he enjoys the subtle sideways approach which can turn up the unexpected. His attitude to research is perhaps more academic, sophisticated and creative than Burnside's, especially because he has more autonomy and responsibility, and is not distracted by PA and secretarial work. His experience emphasises the variations in the research function within different headhunting firms, and suggest that a really ambitious and able researcher, helped by sympathetic consultants and an encouraging MD, can develop the potential of the job. As in so many related business areas, a job like this is what you make it.

When he worked as a researcher, Goldstone took on all the preliminary telephoning work, identifying and talking to all the sources and candidates, of whatever seniority. It was his work, just as much as the consultant's, to sell the position and the client company to the candidates, and to convince them of Heidrick and Struggles' professionalism. This was the difficult part; far easier and more familiar was the work on source books and the on-line information from the computer.

Goldstone estimates that he, and fellow researchers at Heidrick and Struggles, are able to build up two-thirds of the basic information for each assignment from previous searches and sources, i.e. from the data bank; the remaining third comes from reference books and cold-calling. As a researcher, he became closely involved with all the candidates and sources, and was encouraged to take a good deal of trouble to understand the corporate culture of each client company fully.

He is critical of search firms who restrict their researchers to 'the librarianship phase', who deal with reference books and switchboards and who are not allowed much contact with clients or candidates. This renders research a sterile activity, and will only frustrate the researcher who really ought to be investigating the client company culture with a view to making the position attractive to the candidate, and delivering to the consultant a range of candidates already primed and interested.

Goldstone places much emphasis on the crucial role of really thorough background research, combined with an overall understanding of the client company culture, quoting the example of a typical search for the director of marketing for an FMCG company. The clients were looking for someone young, aged 35–40. Problem number one was therefore how to tell candidates' ages on the telephone, which meant that cold-calling had to be backed by a tremendous amount of detailed research, and that very many potential sources were initially identified and approached, and their advice sought, to build up a picture of each potential candidate. Being committed to appearing as professional and knowledgeable as possible from the outset, Goldstone had to be satisfied that he had a shrewd idea of the potential candidate's age and background – in terms of qualifications and adaptability to the company culture – before he made any direct approaches.

Extensive prior knowledge of would-be candidates is much more effective in massaging their egos than anything a researcher or consultant can say without background information. This is absolutely essential in making overtures to candidates in especially senior positions, who have probably experienced frequent contact with headhunters and who are therefore in a position to judge their relative merits. Candidates' criteria is based very much on the amount of research a headhunter has done and how much he or she has found out about them.

Believing that fitting a candidate to a position depends 50% on their ability and 50% on their style, Goldstone considers it crazy for a search firm not to allow researchers a first-hand opportunity to interpret that style for themselves and identify its features in discussion with the client. Dependence purely on the consultant's view of, for instance, a factor which accounts for at least half of the overall requirements of the position to be filled can lead to important misinterpretation and certainly wastes time.

A cardinal error in headhunting research, maintains Goldstone, is to telephone as many people as possible who might remotely be able to suggest candidates, or who might conceivably be suitable for the position themselves. This gives a poor impression to potential candidates and sources – who may, of course, be users of search themselves one day even if they are not already – and suggests that the homework has not been done properly. Goldstone believes that really detailed, thorough research – which he calls 'cross-vectoring' – means that most people he first comes across through research can be eliminated without having to speak to them.

As a general rule, the older and more senior the candidate, the easier cross-vectoring becomes. Young executives in their late 20s and early 30s are inevitably far more difficult to identify than those who have had time to make a greater impact. The chiefs are always much more obvious than the Indians.

Goldstone, in looking for sources of information, makes the distinction between those who are the peers and those who are the suppliers or buyers. One can take the example of the search for a top buyer for a major department store. The researcher can identify and approach other store buyers and use them as sources if they are not interested or appropriate for the position; or the researcher can approach the buyers' main commercial contacts, the sales directors of, say, Yves St Laurent. The outsiders can usually provide a far richer picture of each potential candidate and will know more of them. So the researcher should approach the buyers or sellers of business, not just the pool of potential candidates; the fund managers are better judges of stockbrokers than other stockbrokers or small investors.

Another image which Goldstone used in his headhunting research, and which he offers as a final piece of advice to fellow researchers, is that if you knock on the front door and get turned away, do not feel you are stuck. You must climb in through the kitchen window: purely hypothetically, of course. Research should be seen as a challenge, and a good researcher must be absolutely determined to crack each problem, using all the initiative and imagination at his or her disposal.

Robert Birkett of Merton

Robert Birkett of Merton Associates is a third type of headhunting researcher. If Burnside may be categorised as a researcher/PA and Goldstone a research executive or research consultant, then Birkett is a researcher manager. He works in close contact with members of both these categories, serves to co-ordinate their work within the search firm as a whole and provides comprehensive desk research using computerised and manual resources to support researchers and partners. In particular, he is able to summon on-line information to prepare industry reports, which is useful for search assignments and business development, as well as for Merton's other activities in management consultancy, mergers and divestments, and for the international network of search firms – Transearch – which Merton heads. This arrangement works well for a smaller, British-based consultancy; larger, international search firms – handling a greater number of assignments – tend to separate data and on-line supervision from research management.

Birkett is interested in the back-room element of research, rather than pushing for more client contact and eventual consultancy work. He sees headhunting research as part of the wider field of commercial and industrial research generally. From university he joined Lucas, first as a Staff Job Analyst and then as a Market Research Analyst, where he developed an interest in, and considerable knowledge of, data base construction and reporting techniques to meet marketing needs. He is of the opinion, in common with Merton's founder, Michael Silverman, that a company may be seen as a market place and an executive as a product.

Birkett argues that on-line information is now so extensive that, used selectively and intelligently, it can save time and ensure greater accuracy in headhunting research; above all, it can provide information which is as up to date as possible, in an industry where basic background facts relating to both candidates and clients are in a state of constant flux. Immediate on-line research checks can help the headhunter, when negotiating with clients and candidates, to make a positive impression of market awareness and up-to-the-minute knowledge, instead of committing a disastrous *faux pas*. There is all the difference in the world between touting for search business with a company about to take over another and clearly on the look-out for a new management team, and approaching a firm which has just been acquired and in no position to hire or fire anyone.

Birkett's role, seen as an important part of the firm's approach, is to provide a 'tailored research service' to each of Merton's twelve partners, who between them cover 36 market specialisms. They have gained a reputation for specialist search expertise in the property world – which accounts for over a quarter of its total business – and partners working in this sector have their own separate research executives. Another particularly important sector is FMCG and retail companies; the consultant specialising in this has his own research PA. The management consultancy side of the business needs a different but related sort of research, such as in the preparation of job evaluation and manpower planning studies, and market research and salary surveys. Birkett provides administrative support to the international search work in which Transearch is involved. He also helps with background research for business development in all these areas.

Birkett's dual goal is to provide the resources to complete assignments both to time and within a tightly controlled budget. Smaller, British-based firms without the financial resources of the big international executive search businesses are able to compete – as we saw in the client survey – because they have to control expenses closely in order to survive potential cash-flow disasters, savings they can pass on to their clients. Birkett shows that a small search firm can provide a cheaper, but just as effective and accurate, research-based service as a very large, international firm.

In outlining search assignment research needs, Birkett includes the identification of company turnover, products, location and reputation, together with job and person specifications and overall market trends. On an average of twice a week, he will assist a consultant in drawing up a 'plan of action' on a search assignment, which follows the discussion of the brief between the consultant and the client after a shoot-out, when the assignment has been won. Birkett will help decide the time scale, the target companies and the job specification, which will be based on research of the client company's recent history and activities. Birkett often also prepares an anonymous summary of the appointment – to enlighten 'possibles' concerning the nature of the job and the corporate culture to be expected – for use in the search programme.

These research requirements are met by a combination of sources. On the one hand is the in-house library and the internal data base, and on the other hand are out-housed libraries such as those of business schools and professional associations, and on-line databases.

The in-house library which Birkett has developed includes an extensive manual filing system of cuttings from newspapers and the specialist press relating to the business sectors in which the firm's consultants are interested. He and his small team provide a 'current awareness service' to each director, including obtaining the latest company reports and accounts. The latest media packs are acquired from magazines to support any assignment where advertising as well as search is necessary, as in the public sector, and comparative advertising cost sheets and readership statistics *vis-à-vis* particular sectors are compiled.

Initial directory and printed source research – which does not vary significantly between search firms of any size and background – is followed by work on the internal data base, which includes candidates from short lists, CVs sent in speculatively, and previous assignment files, now totalling over 20 000 individuals. Birkett supervises the task of keeping this up to date, undertaken by four support staff. He tries constantly to improve the coding systems to make the data bases more effective for the firm's changing needs. At the end of every assignment, coders are brought in to prepare the details for computerisation; this work is undertaken by two very experienced retired senior managers, who provide the expertise to correctly apply codes and highlight the most important areas of candidate experience for rapid, precise market-orientated inputting. One of the problems often encountered in going over from a manual to a computerised system of record-keeping is a loss of detail, a problem to which Birkett and his colleagues appear to have found a solution.

The internal data bases are constantly being refined so that candidates or referral sources are easily available. The information is stored on a networked minicomputer which can be accessed by all Merton personnel.

Out-housed libraries are also utilised when necessary, such as those of the London Business School, the City Business Library, the British Institute of Management, the Institute of Marketing and the Market Research Society. Birkett makes a point of being professionally affiliated to as many of these bodies as possible, including the Institute of Information Science. It all helps provide contacts and keeps him up to date with the latest sources of information, such as on-line databases.

Birkett points out that many hundreds of data bases are available on-line, and this does not have to be through very fancy, ultra-sophisticated equipment. Most leading search firms, including Merton, have their own computers but, with a basic Amstrad or any other home personal computer/word processor (PCW) with a modem and British Telecom packet switch stream system, a researcher can gain on-line access for about £600. Then the data bases become instantly available, and can produce information for about £75 an hour in the case of Textline, for example. Birkett has investigated nearly a hundred on-line data bases since he began using them two years ago, but he considers that a researcher who has mastered ten is doing well and probably has all the information to hand that he or she needs. The most popular on-line host services loaded with separate specialist data bases are Textline, Datastar, Dialog and Pergamon Infoline, whose host computers are based respectively in the UK, Switzerland, the USA and the UK. Many data bases are on-line versions of manual publications such as *Key British Enterprises* and *Who Owns Whom*.

Birkett emphasises that the great advantages of having the material on-line are rapid cross-referencing, saving several days of laborious manual research; speed; and currency of information. Merton's researchers can produce an edited on-line print-out which can serve as a report as it stands, within 30 minutes of receiving a request from a consultant. Once this level of facility and familiarity with on-line searches has been achieved, this source – despite its relatively high capital and running costs compared with manual systems – is clearly cost-effective.

An on-line search on a company – its people, activities, financial performance and culture – can be invaluable for a new business presentation, and can form the basis of a study to be supplemented with desk research in-house and out-house into company annual reports, stockbrokers' appraisals, Extel cards, McCarthy cards, searches at Companies' House and personal contacts from the in-house data base. Effective business development depends very much upon being better informed than the competition.

Material such as salary data is not available on-line, but Birkett has built up the internal data base to complement the on-line information, helpful in Merton's management consultancy practice. For instance, Birkett has been involved in the firm's salary survey assignments on behalf of clients in a number of industries, especially in the food and retail sector, including one of the largest supermarket chains in Britain. He used the in-house data bases available to construct a wide-ranging set of comparative salary data, augmented by manually-available published sources.

Birkett's – and Merton's partners' – interest in the computer is by no means confined to its facility for gaining access to information; they believe that it can only be useful if it generates the type of information that enhances the quality and speed of a search which the cross-referencing of all types of computerised data permits. He closely watches progress in both hardware and software, liaising with specialist consultants to ensure that he is aware of the latest developments, and that he is exploiting Merton's computer resources to maximum efficiency. Apart from actually programming the computer itself, Birkett offers, within a reasonable budget, a wide-ranging, fully comprehensive and electronically sophisticated executive search research service.

INTERVIEWING

Interviewing is a tool used frequently and by almost anyone in many aspects of everyday life, yet it is rarely understood as a scientific and systematic process. In the headhunting context, it begins ideally in the previous part of the headhunting process, at the research stage. Thorough background research on the candidate's suitability for the job is vital to establish the headhunter's credibility in the interview itself because the candidate, who has been approached and invited to interview by the headhunter, is at first in the stronger position within the relationship.

When candidates become convinced of the headhunter's knowledge and appreciation of their skills and achievements, and also become attracted to the significance and possibilities of the opportunity being presented to them, then the imbalance in the relationship disappears. At this key stage, the headhunter takes charge. The client employing the headhunter appreciates that the client can be in a weak position *vis-à-vis* the candidate, as the candidate can know much about the client firm at this stage, but a client recruiting via advertising can know only what the candidate choses to tell. Employing a headhunter enables the client to avoid this weak position from the start.

When does a candidate become a candidate? A working definition could be the point when the approached person expresses a committed interest in the offered position, when he or she agrees to meet the client and when it becomes clear that if offered the job, he or she will take it.

One problem in this context can emerge in discussions with the client who, despite employing a headhunter actively to search for someone, insists on calling the candidate an 'applicant'. One particular headhunted candidate, on being asked by a tactless and unthinking client why he had applied for the job, replied that he had not, and promptly walked out.

At the beginning of an interview between a potential candidate and a headhunter, the former needs to establish how competent the latter, and the search firm as a whole, is. It can happen, of course, that a candidate will pursue an attractive opportunity whilst disliking and distrusting the headhunter. This can certainly make life difficult for the headhunter in establishing a picture of the personality of the candidate.

It is frequently true that the more senior the executive, the more difficult it can be to build up this picture, especially if he or she has moved jobs comparatively rarely and not recently, and is not used to unfolding details about his or her previous life. It is, of course, unwise to rely upon what people say about themselves in terms of their track record. Especially in the case of executives in the financial services sector, there is often a considerable discrepancy between what a candidate will say he or she has achieved, and the perception of that person's colleagues. Thus informal referencing is a crucial part of pre-interview homework; and not just talking to people suggested by the candidate. It is not unusual for a good headhunter, in the course of an assignment, to collect nine formal references about one candidate.

Gathering several formal references is particularly important when some are less than favourable than others. In one instance, a search for a marketing director turned up a candidate who appeared ideal until one source gave a reference that was totally at odds with the previous three. Tracking down why the fourth reference was so out of character took another nine enquiries before it was revealed that the candidate had embarked on an affair with a secretary which had subsequently thrown his professional behaviour into doubt. The number of references sought is a good guide to the thoroughness and professional standards of a headhunter.

In another case, in a search for a Board director of a top international company, the client turned down all fifteen candidates presented by the headhunter, and instead became interested in an executive who had been turned up by another search firm working on a lower-level assignment elsewhere in the company. This candidate was known to the first headhunter who, despite having been forced to abandon the assignment, decided to check him out. Three referees gave unfavourable references, which pointed to specific reasons why the candidate had been sacked from previous jobs, including one where a questionable transaction had caused his company to pay a heavy fine. It was not clear whether or not the candidate had been alone in this or had been drawn in by the line manager directly in charge of that particular department, but the first headhunter was so disturbed that he passed on his findings to the client. In this case, the client refused to believe the warnings and was satisfied by the candidate's assurances. The first headhunter would never have recommended the appointment, but by this stage the assignment had been taken out of his hands.

A good headhunter is especially on the lookout for reasons why a candidate left a previous job. For a financial position particularly, the need for unquestioned integrity is paramount: being fired on a morality is more significant than being fired on a competency issue in this case. Good headhunters take many references, and take notice of them.

In trying to interest the potential candidate in a position, the headhunter is not always at liberty to reveal the client's name. But trying to sell an anonymous job is hard work, and undesirable for the headhunter, akin to working with an arm tied behind one's back, and clients are encouraged to be open when possible. It is clearly unfair to potential candidates to expect them to accept this unequal exchange of information. It can lead to a client losing good candidates, as many of the latter will immediately turn down an opportunity put forward without the client's name. It has happened that when clients have subsequently changed their minds and allowed their names to be revealed – under pressure from the headhunter – candidates who had initially refused to consider the job had expressed real interest when contacted again and provided with fuller details.

Fortunately, nine out of ten clients in Britain allow their names to be revealed, if not initially then at least by the point when the candidate is interviewed by the headhunter. Some candidates take instant objection to a particular company and do not allow the headhunting process to continue any further once they know these details; grounds for instant rejection range from association with a particular product, such as cigarettes or certain pharmaceuticals tested on animals, a bad name for performance or unethical behaviour, or the fact that the company seeking the executive is on the executive's company's hit list, unknown to the headhunter.

Where are interviews between potential candidates and headhunters held? More often than not, the first meeting will take place in the head-hunter's office, which has the advantage of being neutral territory. Sub-sequently, it may also be seen as the best setting – for the same reason – for at least the first meeting between the client and the candidate. In the case of particularly important, senior candidates with very tight schedules, then the headhunter comes to them. Such a candidate could well be a client in the future. Otherwise, an initial discussion, a getting-to-know-you, could take place without papers in a club or pub, but this is more likely to happen later, after details have been worked out.

The procedure at these interviews usually centres around going through the potential candidate's CV. The format of CV most welcome to the headhunter is one where all the dates of job changes are clearly stated. Again, very senior executives can be a problem here: those who have moved rarely, or only internally, may find themselves without a CV at all. They may, on the other hand, appear in *Who's Who*. A leading headhunter recently remarked that a surprising number of their senior candidates appeared listed in some detail in this source.

Conscientious and professional headhunters will not take on face value the details with which they are presented, but check their authenticity, even down to the university degree. The leading head-hunters all regard themselves as sticklers for detail in this regard, especially after discoveries of cases of candidates with several CVs, each with different dates and jobs. One candidate in particular claimed to have gained a first-class degree from Cambridge. Verifying this revealed that not only had the candidate lied about the degree, but also that he had not studied at Cambridge at all, and moreover his entire career as outlined in his CV was a fabrication. Headhunters have been known to bring in the Fraud Squad if a client has made a serious and expensive mistake because of this; but this should never be necessary if head-hunters do enough reference checking, and are perceptive during interviews where body language can provide revealing clues.

A conscientious headhunter will not hesitate to drop a potential candidate if they discover inaccuracies and untruths in a CV, even if they are apparently unimportant, because if a person is prepared to lie about such details as the class of their degree, they could well be lying about other aspects of their CV and, more significantly, could continue lying in their new job. Unfortunately, the emergence of firms specialis-ing in helping people prepare impressive CVs may have encouraged the production of less than completely accurate examples.

Headhunters need to be aware of the personal side of the candidate's life, however painful or embarrassing this might be to either or both parties, because this can have an important bearing on the candidate's motives for taking a new job. For example, an increased salary is especially attractive to a candidate paying out large sums in alimony, school fees and/or a large mortgage or bank loan. There is, of course, nothing wrong with moving to a new job for more money, but this should not cloud a candidate's judgement in making a strategic change in the context of his or her career pattern as a whole.

A female candidate with young children may be attracted to a company offering flexible working hours and the possibility of working reduced hours during domestic crises. For example, in case study II, when a female candidate – who was subsequently successful in the appointment – was first approached to consider leaving multinational giant Shell to join medium-sized British confectionery manufacturer Trebor, she was interested in the advantage presented by the flexibility of working at the latter, as Shell does not employ part-time staff at all.

A candidate without such constraints will have different priorities, and may be attracted to move primarily on the grounds of needing greater – or just different – challenges at work. This kind of motivation can be especially critical in seeking to fill a really demanding and revolutionary new role in a company needing a shake-up. Thus the headhunter is particularly alert to a candidate's attitude to future salary. Candidates especially interested in the possibility of enhanced financial rewards will also want to know about stock options, bonuses and perks such as company cars, education and health provisions, and offers of low-interest loans.

How the headhunter presents candidates to clients has a critical bearing on the outcome of the assignment, especially as there have been many instances of clients immediately wishing to appoint the first candidate they meet, because they like what they see, and often because they are anxious to fill the position quickly. A good headhunter will discuss a range of candidates equally with the client, and will present them as close to one another as possible for the client to judge and make a speedy decision.

The headhunter will prime the candidate about the client before they meet, but they expect good and keen candidates to do their own homework on a company through their own sources. However, a professional headhunter should be able to answer enough questions which the candidate might raise about the client for the latter to be able to judge whether or not this would be a good move. The headhunter should not only supply published brochures and reports and accounts of the client company for the candidate to take away, to discuss with their partner and friends but should also describe the client's corporate culture and management style, and real details of exactly where the candidate will sit at work, aspects of their daily routine and, in particular, exactly who he or she will have to report to. This is all vital information for the candidate, and also a way in which candidates can check out the headhunter's and search firm's competence and the professionalism of their approach.

A serious candidate will be concerned to know exactly what it will be like to work for the client. Defining the appropriate business culture, and how this fits into the candidate's previous experience, is crucial. Companies attach greater or lesser importance to moulding the personalities and behaviour of their employees; those with especially strong cultures, such as Procter & Gamble, Unilever and Shell, rarely use headhunters at all, as we have seen. But a comparable problem does occur in headhunting Civil Service appointments, now increasingly common, which impose constraints unlike those required by private sector business. Recruiting in privatised industries can also throw up complex corporate culture problems.

Sometimes a headhunter will be brought into an organisation with a strong corporate culture which has not recruited outside before, just to check that their people are as good as anyone outside. One large British food manufacturer – which may be seen as having overpromoted and then subsequently fired a number of internal staff – recently called in a headhunter to review its staff generally, and made a number of outside appointments. Headhunters who work on the basis of a fee for work done, rather than on a proportion of the successful candidate's salary, are happy to undertake such work. On the understanding that it is better to go for the devil you know, a client may prefer an internal candidate against one from outside, but knowing that they have been compared within the field of talent available by a headhunter who knows the market well will satisfy clients that they have the best.

In analysing the candidate's attitude to business culture and interpersonal relationships at work, the headhunter needs to gather opinions of those the candidate worked with. How good was he or she at working with other people, either senior or junior? One particular candidate considered by a leading headhunting firm appeared to be very able but to have clashed with fellow employees. He had moved at least every three to four years, particularly to overseas jobs and back to the UK, in which he was apparently successful, but there was no obvious explanation for the move in each case. Reference checking revealed that this candidate was weak at sustaining long, productive relationships with fellow executives in one particular situation, and had found his niche as a 'project man'. Although he had not previously defined it as such, the candidate realised that his strength lay in solving immediate corporate problems without tackling the necessary subsequent rebuilding work. Ability to work amicably with others is always an asset, but it is more important in some contexts than others. Professional hatchet-men are more effective if they do not get too close to their fellow executives. A good headhunter will analyse the pattern of a candidate's career and utilise their strengths rather than weaknesses.

The headhunter, when briefing the client about candidates, needs to know as much about the candidate as possible. One of the most unpleasant parts of a headhunter's work can be having subsequently to drop a candidate whom he had previously encouraged because final reference checking revealed significant flaws.

It is not a headhunter's job to act as God in making a judgement about a candidate. The sole concern should be making a dispassionate match between a candidate and the specification. When a headhunter is working for a client who has never used search before, then the positive aspects of a candidate would be emphasised; but with a sophisticated client, a headhunter might explore a candidate's weaknesses as well as strengths.

This will be summarised in the candidate reports – which should be succinct rather than lengthy – explaining the reasons why each candidate has been put forward. These generally start by analysing and interpreting the candidate's CV. Many headhunters will also be sure to warn the client of any oddities in physical appearance to prevent the client making a snap false judgement on someone who is exceptionally short, wears luminous green socks, speaks with a strong Scottish accent or whatever.

Once the client has met the candidate, then other methods of evaluation may be employed, including psychometric testing.

Postscript: a note on psychometric testing

The use of psychometric resting is becoming more and more common; that it was employed in two out of the three case studies quoted in Chapter 5 is significant and possibly representative of searches generally. Geoffrey Golzen, writing in *The Sunday Times* in September 1987, advocates its still wider use, to 'steer square pegs away from round holes'. Those coming into contact with testing techniques – consultants, clients, and, of course, candidates – have generally been impressed.

However, some of the leading headhunters from the major international search firms consider that it is unrealistic and even offensive to require a very senior executive to spend anything from 45 minutes to a whole day of his or her valuable time being tested in this way; such executives may feel that the client should be able to make such an important decision without resorting to a form of hocus-pocus, and if the client really wants them then why should they be subjected to such an exercise?

Many search consultants working immediately below this level would disagree. Ian Ashworth & Associates are enthusiastic users of psychometric testing, and so are AGC Consultants, who boast Sir Michael Edwardes among their clients. AGC's Michael Leigh argues that tests 'have been shown to provide a pretty accurate profile of the subject's values, interests and attitudes', but they are most effective as a part of a wider process. 'You can test a solicitor for his or her capacity in abstract reasoning, or a finance person for numeracy, but you can't establish whether they'd make a good accountant or solicitor from that alone,' Leigh explains. 'You need a whole battery of tests to establish, for instance, how well they interact with others, because that's also part of the picture.'

Some employers have also spoken out in favour of psychometric testing. Hugh Eyles of Coutts & Co. argues that:

the answers can give you some indication of how realistic someone's aspirations might be, as well as where to direct the search. For instance, a lot of candidates want to run their own business, but success depends on personality, judgment and perseverance as much as anything else. These are qualities you can test for.

Yet if psychometric testing is more appropriate to lower-level searches –
where there are more people to choose from and their attributes are
more similar – its cost is a deterrent and more difficult to justify in
searches earning lower fees, of which it would represent a substantial
proportion. A full psychometric test programme can cost over £1000 and
take up a whole day. Leigh of AGC is not put off: 'It costs a hell of a lot to
recruit and train a manager. Though psychometric testing on its own is
no substitute for a face-to-face interview, the two together have been
shown to be an effective selection tool and an accurate way of predicting
performance.'

Reed Employment has shown a sensitive initiative in joining with the
Vocational Guidance Association to produce a simple self-administering
personality test, designed for temporary staff which could be applied to
the search business, and might be more acceptable to consultants,
clients and candidates alike. Shorter and less expensive tests are making
headway, with three-hour exercises which can be taken at home
becoming popular. The tests most commonly used by executive search
and selection consultants are Cattell 16 PF, OPQ, LIFO, Myers-Briggs,
PAPI and PPA. The Reed/VGA test is loosely based on Cattell.

Typical among the 184 multiple-choice questions asked in the Cattell
16 PF Test would be this: 'In music, I enjoy: (a) military band marches;
(b) violin solos; (c) uncertain'. This seems very straightforward; how
easy is it to fake one's answers to appear much more high-powered and
attractive to employers than one really is? Leigh explains that 'tests are
devised with inbuilt lie-detectors, and you can see when answers simply
don't tally. And a trained psychologist can tell when someone emerges
as simply too good to be true.'

Another question is whether one can train oneself to perform well in
tests by studying books on how to test one's IQ. IQ has in fact very little
to do with psychometric testing; a high IQ does not necessarily indicate
one's ability to survive and flourish in the real world. Leigh comments
that 'working your way through a book of tests may enable you to
perform better in the sort of questions you'd be good at answering
anyway, but if you're weak in abstract reasoning, it won't improve your
performance, except maybe in making you less nervous'. Occupational
psychologists do take nervousness into account when evaluating results. They also look at the way questions have been dealt with as well
as the actual answers. Of vital interest is the question of whether the
candidate is slow but thorough, quick but careless, plodding but
accurate, or fast but slipshod.

The latest development in psychometric testing is a currently fashion-
able technique know as biodata, or scored biographical data. Leigh
describes it essentially as 'just a sophisticated way of looking at CVs for a
career pattern. The idea is that if you were a sixer in the Cubs, a prefect

and so forth, you'd be likely to have leadership qualities.' Biodata is a preselection device, obtainable from a questionnaire in a multiple-choice format, looking for two categories of information. First, it analyses input variables, i.e. the effects on an individual by parents, teachers and close friends; second, it examines prior behaviour, or an individual's experiences which might have a bearing on future behaviour, either because one is a reflection of the other, or because there is behavioural consistency between the two.

Biodata has yet to make a significant impact on selection techniques. In a survey by PA Personnel Services in 1987, half their sample of companies used psychometric testing of some kind, but only 6% employed biodata in the selection of junior and senior managers and graduates. It has made few inroads into search firms, either. Biodata is hardly suitable for executive search or lower-level selection assignments; because it is so time-consuming and expensive to develop, costing in the region of £25 000 to establish the necessary large sample for validity, it is much more appropriate in large organisations. It is therefore confined to such companies and, within these, the lower-grade, high-volume end of the job spectrum. Yet it has shown remarkable levels of accuracy and validity when related to subsequent job performance, and a simpler and less expensive form of biodata could find wide acceptability.

Selection tests generally have been used widely in personnel departments of large companies for several years. Basically, two types of test are used: tests of capacity, and tests of attitude or behaviour. The former is concerned with general intelligence and reasoning, and includes tests to assess special aptitudes; the latter includes personality and interest tests. A survey of major employers of 1976 showed that 72% used tests of some kind, but these organisations all had over 2000 employees. Tests were not seen as a practical proposition to small firms, who lacked adequate financial and administrative resources, and in any case recruited a relatively small number of applicants. Some organisations, irrespective of size, were attached to the interview principle and respected the opinion of their personnel director and his managers without the need for additional testing.

Donald Hudd: assessment psychologist

The growth of executive search has produced a need for simple and flexible testing techniques which can be employed either at the request of a particular client – as in the case of Trebor in Case Study II, or on behalf of a search firm that strongly advocates their use, such as MSL in Case Study III. Donald Hudd, who provided the tests which were taken as part of the selection process for the position with Notts County Council, is typical of a growing number of 'human resource management consultants'. How does he see the value of his skills within the context of the headhunting process? What is it like for a candidate to undergo his tests? What sort of insight can he provide for the client?

Hudd works with Castleton Partners, a team of consultants who operate from quietly professional, almost homely offices near Baker Street underground station. He holds as MSc in psychology, another master's degree in applied psychology, and is an associate of The British Psychological Society. He has worked for over seven years in this field, and considers the occupational and corporate aspects most stimulating and difficult. It takes at least two years, Hudd estimates, to begin to understand the workings of organisations and how people fit into them.

Hudd's psychometric assessment work is divided between companies and headhunting firms in a ratio of 80:20; much of the former is internal analysis of existing staff, but in many cases it is also in connection with a headhunting assignment, where Hudd is engaged and paid by the client rather than the search firm. The results belong to the person paying the fees. According to Hudd few search firms, and few clients, have the internal resources to use and evaluate tests effectively on their own.

In the headhunting process, Hudd's role varies from merely assessing the results of a small number of tests at a distance without meeting the candidate, to involvement in many aspects of the client briefing and selection process. Sometimes he will assess one candidate for a job; occasionally a dozen. He has been called in to assess the potential of a secretary for promotion to a management post; and he has scrutinised a whole Board of directors for their willingness and ability to adapt to major corporate restructuring, and identified gaps in the team needing new Board members.

Hudd was asked to describe his involvement in a typical headhunting assignment. First of all Hudd would expect, in consultation with the search consultant and with the client, to be briefed about the company itself. Was it profitable or unprofitable? Was it in a mature and stable market place for its products or services? Were there any major competitive threats or prospects of an unfriendly bid, or not? All this has a bearing on the nature of the work environment: is commercial concern motivated by production quality and control and tight margins; or is corporate survival based on innovation, or acquisition; or is the principal need to mend fences with City pension funds? Is the company looking for a person who will squeeze things, or a visionary? Do they want a hit-man, a high-profile corporate image-builder, a buyer of acquisitions, or someone to maintain the status quo? Once he has established the data at this level on what sort of candidate is needed, Hudd turns to an examination of less tangible issues.

Hudd needs to feel he understands the corporate culture in order to define further the qualities most required by the candidate; and not only the corporate culture the way the chairman or MD describes it. He likes to know – for instance – the age profile and make-up of the Board, how long and how well they have worked together, if the company is public or private, if the shares are owned by a few pension funds or many small individuals, if the management infrastructure is stable, if there are industrial relations problems, and if they have been recruiting clones or a wide spread of different types of manager.

In the past, some clients have expected Hudd to carry out his assessment work based on a brief job description sent in the post. Unless he knows the company well, this is inadequate for him to do his job properly. Other clients have not told him the whole story, as in the case of a group chief executive who was looking for assessment as a source of ammunition against a rival, and who wanted a new director merely to back up his position against another director, and force the latter to resign; the existence of this motive eventually filtered through to Hudd, who would not have taken on the assignment if he had known this from the outset.

In one particular case Hudd noted that a Board of directors was disunited, operating by acrimony and the creating of fiefdoms. It needed an executive with strong team-building qualities. After briefings and an analysis of the corporate problems, Hudd carried out an assessment of each member of the Board, as well as candidates for the job; the successful candidate – a woman who was especially able to empathise with them as individuals and work at establishing harmony between them – was considerably assisted in her task ahead by Hudd's assessments.

What do these assessments look like? Hudd quoted the example of assessments he had carried out on three candidates for the post of director of organisation development in a major public sector body in the London area. The report was based on the results of a series of psychometric tests, referred to by Hudd as 'a battery of instruments' which lasted a whole day, including a three- to four-hour interview with Hudd himself. The five-page reports, each of which took over half a day to compile, summarised the main findings, with the first page listing the main strengths and limitations, all closely geared to the known requirements of the job. The report then described the degree of 'know-how' of the job already possessed by the candidate, their managerial skill – including planning, delegation and control – intellectual efficiency, judgement, decision-making ability, skill in building relationships and influencing the ability of others, their general approach to work and key personal characteristics. Hudd did not recommend any of them. From the tests, he argued, none had the qualities and abilities in sufficient measure to do the job. After subsequent interviews, the organisation in question agreed.

Sometimes Hudd will administer, score the tests and analyse the results on the spot, such as when he accompanies MSL consultants on their assignments, staying throughout the 2½-day interview process which MSL favours. Hudd's ordeal is almost as onerous as the candidates' because, in order to analyse all the test results in time to help with the final selection, he meets the candidates at the beginning of the process, sees them through the tests, then spends all night summarising the findings and writing the reports. Hudd has a strong commitment to refining and improving his service, and is clearly fascinated by the personal insights the tests can reveal.

Some indication of a candidate's experiences of psychometric testing are given in Ann Crichton's story (case study III in Chapter 5). She took her tests at home, completing them in three hours. The tests were of the kind that are not strictly timed, and were concerned with evaluating the interpersonal skills, managerial style and work approach needed in the job.

Hudd described the various tests currently in use, and warned that the ones he uses are not publicly available. They are kept confidential and under lock and key, and he would allow only a very cursory examination of them. The intelligence test papers appear to be a bewildering mass of coloured objects, numbers, words and shapes, and Hudd could hardly be expected to reveal trade secrets on their interpretation. His final candidate reports seem to bear no relation to the test papers themselves, but he is at least 85% correct in his analysis and observation. This can be very useful to candidates. Hudd has found that the individual debriefing he holds with them afterwards can, if they were successful in gaining the appointment, increase their insight into how to handle the new job; if they were not selected, Hudd explains why. He also uses assessment in other ways. If an executive is not performing effectively in a job, Hudd provides a career review service which enables a person to take stock of their job and identify and act positively on performance blockages. Additionally he can offer the counselling needed to explore alternative career opportunities.

Relatively few executives, in Hudd's experience, have taken umbrage at the thought of being subjected to psychometric testing. The head-hunter who is presenting them is more likely to be alarmed, lest it be discovered that the match suggested is not as close as he or she had hoped.

The range of tests on offer is increasing all the time, and with them the training courses needed for their interpretation. But they are not necessarily always very useful. For example, a commonly available test, now widely franchised and heavily sold, has an equivalent public domain software version costing only £15. Through over-exposure and easy access, the test may have relatively little value. As a test it is only

1a. Gerry Roche, 'King of Manhattan Headhunters', now Chairman, Heidrick and Struggles, who has put more CEOs and Presidents into US companies than any other single search consultant.

1b. Dr John Viney, Managing Partner of Heidrick and Struggles since 1985.

2. Nigel Dyckhoff *(left)*, Senior Director of Spencer Stuart worldwide; David Kimbell, Chairman of Spencer Stuart worldwide and UK Managing Director; and Kit Power, Chairman of Spencer Stuart in the UK.

3b. Julia Budd, previously with Bain, who joined Egon Zehnder in 1987.

3a. John Grumbar, Managing Partner, Egon Zehnder, London.

4. Stephen Rowlinson, London Managing Director of Korn/Ferry, who had previously spent seven years in general management consultancy with McKinsey.

5. Roddy Gow, Managing Director of Russell Reynolds in London, who leads the highest-earning search business in Britain.

6. Bert Young, Chairman of Alexander Hughes, established in London in 1964.

7. Hamish Kidd of Clive and Stokes *(left)* with original founders Clive *(centre)* and Stokes.

8b. John Stork, who set up his own search firm in London in 1973.

8a. Michael Silverman, who founded Merton Associates in 1976.

9. Nigel Humphreys of Tyzack, who helped lead the firm's corporate revolution in 1981, when it turned from high-level advertising to executive search.

10. David Norman, formerly with Russell Reynolds, who set up on his own in 1982 before founding Norman Broadbent in 1983.

11. Miles Broadbent, Chief Executive of Norman Broadbent, which he founded jointly with David Norman in 1983.

12. Stephen Bampfylde *(left)* and Anthony Saxton, founders of Saxton Bampfylde in 1986.

13. Mark Weedon, previously Managing Director of Egon Zehnder in London (now with Heidrick and Struggles) who carried out the search for BAA.

14. Ann Crichton, Nottinghamshire's new Director of Economic Development, appointed in the early summer of 1988, shown here with Paddy Tipping *(bearded)*, the Chairman of the Economic Development Committee, and Cllr Stewart Pattinson, Opposition Spokesman for Economic Development.

15. J.P.P. (John) Smith, who found Ann Crichton for Notts County Council in Case Study III, was Director of Public Appointments with MSL for three years. In July 1988 he set up his own company, Succession Planning Associates.

16. Jonathon Baines of Baines Gwinner, a leading specialist City headhunting firm, founded in 1986.

useful in revealing a candidate's individual social confidence, a quality which is usually quite apparent in interviews. Tests must be predictive, and they must be interpreted according to certain specified norms and a defined universe. They should also meet the professional standards of The British Psychological Society.

The top end of the market for assessment testing, which employs consultants such as Hudd, sees this service as a kind of insurance policy, an added dimension to their appraisal of senior staff. To them, an in-depth, independent assessment costing around £800 per candidate is comparatively inexpensive, in relation to business profitability resulting from choosing effective executives.

Hudd's view of the search industry, in his contacts with headhunters over the last seven years, is generally favourable, but he differentiates between the firms that go fishing rather than trawling for candidates. The latter, less selective and less able to pin-point good candidates accurately, are sometimes worried about Hudd's findings, and want to see the reports before their delivery to the client. Few clients, on the other hand, will object to the headhunter insisting on testing, as long as they can be convinced that it is worth the money. Hudd always tells them that although his services might appear expensive, they should think of the downside consequences on their business if they make the wrong appointment.

THE CLIENT DECIDES

Miles Broadbent of Norman Broadbent was asked to describe the final stages of the headhunting process, focusing on the relationship between the search consultant and the client. He maintains that if the executive search firm presents a short list of more than six to eight people, then the headhunter has not done enough sifting to reduce the universe of candidates to a manageable number. Broadbent thinks, although the client may not agree, that the ideal search has only one candidate. In practice, clients not unreasonably want to be sure that the search firm has earned its fee and really covered the market. Clients are therefore extremely unlikely to be satisfied if they see less than four candidates on the short list. He considers that clients are not able to develop a good feel for who is available in the market place unless they see three or four people.

Broadbent often tells clients that, after being in the headhunting business for so many years, he can sometimes put his finger directly on the candidate who best fits their requirements. In several cases he claims to have told the client at the initial briefing meeting he knows the ideal person for them. In one case, where he was working for a company in a particular sector of the retail market, it became clear that they had previously conducted searches with two other headhunting firms and also run an advertisement, but what they had not done was to aim high enough. Broadbent has found that sometimes the clients and search firm often fail simply because they have not gone to the top in the industry. In this particular case, Broadbent asked his retail client whether they had gone for Mr X, who was MD of the largest company in their sector. They told him that they had not, because they were convinced that they would not be able to reach him and recruit him. Broadbent insisted that they must make the attempt, and ultimately they did hire this very man. That is perhaps indicative of the way executive search should be conducted, and gives an impression of the excitement which the headhunter derives from satisfying the client in a better way than perhaps the client expected.

Most clients of search firms are constantly seeking a better solution than the first suggested by the headhunter. If the first candidate presented is very good, then it creates hopes that an even better person can be found. Although Broadbent says he enjoys demanding clients, because they stretch his capacity and are enthusiastic about finding a good solution, it has to be realised that 'the better is the enemy of the good'. A client should seek to hire the best person for the job, but if a good candidate is identified early in the search, then the client should be persuaded to move quickly to hire him or her. The disadvantages of not closing in quickly on good candidates are that either they will lose enthusiasm or interest in the new opportunity, or they will be attracted by some other competitive opportunity which may be placed before them. Once the search has started, it is the task of the headhunter to ensure that the client pursues the candidates with vigour. It is by a combination of effort on the part of the headhunter and client that a successful search is concluded. If the headhunter is slow to put forward candidates, or if the client is unavailable and unable or unwilling to make enough time to interview candidates who have been presented, then the search is doomed to failure. The exercise requires speed, energy and enthusiasm on both sides.

A search should normally be concluded in about 90 days. This does not mean to say that the search cannot be done more quickly. The fastest search Broadbent has achieved took only sixteen days. Equally, searches have taken very much longer than 90 days, but a client should certainly be disappointed if he or she is not close to a solution after three months.

In the case of Broadbent's famous sixteen-day search, the client came to the conclusion that it had been too easy, and the firm did not deserve its fee. Broadbent had to explain that clients come to his firm in a similar way that one goes to a lawyer or an accountant. It is not a question of being paid for how long the job takes, but it is being paid for one's knowledge of the industry, and contacts with people within the industry who might be susceptible to a move. Far from being disappointed about the search being done quickly, the client should be very pleased. After all, one of the main reasons for employing a search consultant is to save the client's management time. If the search is done very quickly, the client has thus used the minimum management time, and made the maximum saving by going to the headhunter who knows his market.

In Broadbent's view the successful candidate who survives all the stages of the headhunting process – including selection by the client – has to meet three major broad criteria. These three criteria have different weight of importance. About 20% is the candidate's level of intellectual ability, normally indicated by his or her qualifications, such as having qualified as a chartered accountant – ideally winning a prize or a place – and having a good degree, regardless of the subject of the degree. Another 20% of the candidate's important attributes are the jobs done which are relevant to the particular client's needs, and this does not simply mean that the candidate was the Sales Director or the Finance Director or the MD. What matters most is what was achieved within those jobs, such as how sales and profits were increased. But the most important factor in the success of a candidate is the chemistry or fit with the client and the culture of the client company. In comparison with the qualification and achievements this attribute accounts for 60% of the requirement of the successful candidate. It is also obviously the most difficult and challenging part for the headhunter to fit. This is where a good knowledge of the client and the jigsaw of the corporate culture comes in handy, and where repeat business enables the headhunter to do a better job. A good and on-going relationship with a headhunter is something that the client should also aim for, for the same reasons.

If the headhunter is recruiting a chief executive for a company which needs a turnaround, then the new chief executive must be tough and prepared to take hard decisions. On the other hand, if the new chief executive is going to be in charge of a group of 'prima donna' types, then he or she should be very sensitive and subtle. If the chief executive is going to be in charge of an international business, then he must be prepared to travel, with a supportive spouse who will be used to frequent absences.

Repeat business is, as mentioned above, valuable for both the headhunter and the client. If a headhunter is working for an organisation for the first time, then he or she needs to spend quite a lot of time becoming familiar with the culture and meeting as many relevant senior executives as possible. When it comes to doing the second search for the same organisation, then the headhunter can move much more quickly, and with much more confidence, because he or she has already gained experience of the organisation. In particular it is very helpful where the headhunter has recruited the chairman or chief executive, and is now called upon to recruit the finance director, marketing director or divisional managing director. In this case the headhunter can tell a candidate about the company, and also a great deal, based on direct and recent experience, about the background and style of the chairman and chief executive for whom he or she will be working. The attitudes of chief executives, and often also their family background and domestic circumstances, all have an impact on their behaviour, and the kind of person with whom they would be comfortable. If the chief executives spend weekends with their families in the country, and then come to London and effectively work from 9 a.m. Monday morning to 5 p.m. on Friday, staying in a flat in London during the week, and not returning home until Friday, they will probably be workaholics, who will expect immediate subordinates to devote Monday to Friday entirely to business. This is not comfortable for a candidate who attaches greater importance to family needs, but it is a style of working which exists, has to be recognised and is often very effective. Not everybody may approve of it, but a candidate should certainly be willing to fit in with that style, if he or she is going to take a job with an organisation which has a chief executive who believes in it.

Although there are significant advantages to a company in using the same headhunter for all their senior searches, clients often use more than one search firm, in the same way that they use more than one supplier for goods. It has the effect of keeping the search firm on its toes, and also may broaden the scope of candidates who are presented to the client company. It rather depends on the number of searches which the company commissions during any one year as to whether it makes sense to use one search firm or more than one. It also depends on the level of assignments and the functional areas of specialty.

The question of repeat business leads directly to the question of the follow-up of successful candidates. Broadbent has found it a rewarding exercise, both in an intellectual and pecuniary sense. He believes that a headhunter should follow up the successful candidate – and the client company – at six months and twelve months after the new candidate starts work. The six-month follow-up can be a telephone call to both sides, but the twelve-month follow-up should probably be a face-to-face meeting to review progress. Candidates certainly appreciate an on-going interest by the headhunter, and the headhunter can often be helpful both to the client and candidate in letting each other know how they feel about the way things are going. Although many companies have formal assessment and evaluation systems, they often seem to forget to evaluate and assess their most senior colleagues. Broadbent has often heard candidates say to him 'It is nice to know that [the client] does think I am doing a good job.'

The follow-up process can be of benefit to the headhunter, as it often results in further business for the search firm. The candidate who takes the new job, and then never hears from the headhunter again, may well give future assignments on behalf of the new company to other consultants whom he or she believes might be more interested. The candidate who thinks the headhunter cares is very likely to give the same headhunter more business when it occurs. Even the follow-up meeting itself jogs the candidates' memory as to who helped them get the job, and it therefore inclines candidates towards giving further business to the same headhunter.

It is a good idea for the headhunter to telephone or write to the candidate on the first day he or she joins. First of all, the new candidate does not often receive many telephone calls or letters on the first day, and second, Broadbent has known occasions when the candidate arrived at the company only to find that there was no office or desk, or in one case they appeared to have forgotten about him, and the job he had been offered had been given to somebody else.

The follow-up also gives tremendous vicarious satisfaction to the headhunter. Broadbent has frequently been called in to find a new chief executive for a business which was ailing or in trouble, and has been pleased to note the impact the new chief executive can have on a company, and the subsequent transformation of the company from a sickbed case to a strong and healthy leader in its industry. There is also no reason why, once the appointment of the new chief executive has been made public, the headhunter should not invest money in that company, and share the gain which accrues to all shareholders on the appointment of an effective chief executive. Broadbent sees this as the ultimate test of the headhunter's confidence in the candidate recommended.

The examples of successful headhunted chief executives in the UK are numerous. Broadbent derived particular pleasure from helping David Norman and the Russell Reynolds team to place Colin Marshall, now Sir Colin in his appointment as Chief Executive of British Airways. Mike Gifford – another appointment – has been equally successful as Chief Executive of the Rank Organisation, which was certainly very much on the sick list when he took over in 1983. Another search produced David Jones, who took over Grattan Warehouses just before it appeared to be going bankrupt, and he multiplied the share price eleven times by the time that Next bought Grattan in 1986. There are many examples of smaller companies where a new chief executive has transformed the situation. John Hudson has been tremendously successful as Chief Executive of a medium-sized Midlands company called Wagon Industrial Holdings plc. Adrian Parsons has had what the *Investor's Chronicle* described as a 'miraculous effect' on Silkolene plc since he took over in

1986. There is of course the odd situation which has not worked out but, on the whole, if the headhunter's job on checking references is thorough, then there is no reason why the headhunter should not score a success rate of at least 90% in appointments.

Postscript: understanding business cultures

In discussing how the headhunting process works, frequent mention has been made of the vital need for the consultant and the researcher both to understand fully the subtle nuances of the corporate culture of the client company. Without this understanding, a search is doomed from the start. The requirement that a candidate should fit into, and be comfortable with, the corporate image, persona, atmosphere and vibes is seen to be as important as technical skills and academic qualifications. For every position to be filled, there are usually plenty of people who would be able to do it; the crucial question, and the one that is often the strongest criterion in the client's final choice, is will that candidate be at home in the company culture?

Yet actually pin-pointing the precise nature of a particular business culture is very difficult. Experienced headhunters and researchers can and do successfully match candidates and cultures of like with like, but they would be hard-pressed to put the matter into words, and explain why an individual was perfect for that company.

The following analysis of seven basic theoretical business cultures has been adapted from an article originally written for *Harpers & Queen*. It is an attempt – inevitably subjective and open to dispute – to define the indefinable, always recognising that every company is intrinsically different. But no analysis of headhunting in Britain would be complete without an appraisal of its customers from the consultants' point of view. Every client is seen as broadly falling within one of these categories, and every potential candidate too.

These categories do not include the financial sector or service companies, which have their own sub-cultures, but concentrate on corporate giants, the blue-chip companies, especially the largest employers and most steady earners which are seen as particularly attractive clients to search firms because of their potential and capacity for repeat business. Also, they may be seen as the rocks of the economy, washed over but not submerged by stock market ebbs and flows. In blue-chip companies, a successful executive is one who has come to terms with understanding and working within a subtle but powerful corporate culture – acknowledging, appreciating and developing that culture – and thereby eventually able to become one of its chief manipulators.

As long as there have been companies, there has been company culture. Look, for example, at Britain's much-loved historic railways: Sir

John Betjeman wrote that 'the individuality of great railway companies was expressed in styles of architecture, typography and liveries of engines and carriages, even down to the knives and forks and crockery used in the refreshment rooms and dining cars'.

The different railway lines were basically offering an identical service, but they needed to project a specific image, to which all their diverse employees conformed, immediately identifiable far from base and attractive in a unique way. Betjeman saw the Great Western as fast, unfussy and elitist, reflecting Brunel's personal style; the Midland was grand, heavy Gothic, built more for comfort than speed; and the Great Northern was workmanlike and homely.

Company culture is unshaken by economic upturns and downturns, and can even survive nationalisation. Thus the Great Western's services, now the sleek high-speed trains out of Paddington, are still the most punctual and efficient; and St Pancras is still more imposing than its basic and practical neighbour, King's Cross. The oldest railway retainers, and even some of the most enthusiastically company-conscious young managers, still cherish a distinct corporate persona handed down from a bygone age.

Anthony Sampson saw just the same in *The Seven Sisters*. The seven protagonists of the world oil industry all have identical opportunities and limitations in international oil markets, but all have identifiably different outlooks. Texaco is known for financial caution and secrecy; Mobil is loquacious, extrovert and publicity-seeking; BP is solid and patriotic; Exxon is flashy and full of rhetoric as the king of the oil barons; Shell, only marginally second, is pompous and superior; Gulf, as one of the oldest, was seen as having a self-contained, family-firm image before being swallowed up by tough and ruthless California-based Chevron. The operators of these companies are all oil men, but this is like saying all trees are green. They are recognisably members of quite different organisations, and can be spotted at long range like breeds of horses or makes of cars.

The seven blue-chip business cultures

Company cultures are determined by one or more of six variables: their products, their style of service, the personality of the founder/chairman/ chief executive, how long they have been established, how close they are to the everyday consumer and how they promote their own image. Perceptions of these cultures vary between past and present employees, journalists, PR men and, of course, headhunters. Each category tries to sum up the personality, aspirations and style of the management of a company, which to a greater or lesser extent permeates down to the grass roots to form each company's guiding philosophy. There is not

necessarily any significance about their order below; none is seen as a
'better' or 'worse' company to work for, just different.

Business Culture A
The typical business culture A company could be described as cheap and
cheerful, attracting down-to-earth and unpretentious personalities.
These companies are known for selling mass-appeal everyday goods
close to the consumer in a bright and breezy way. Many of the
companies in this sector date back to the last century and the inter-war
years, have diversified widely and suffered varying fortunes. The
management include many who have worked their way up from the
shop floor. Some are growing out of business culture A into business
culture D – see below – often by headhunting public-school people for a
more upmarket management style. But changing corporate culture is
never easy.

Business Culture B
Business culture B companies are paternalistic and conservative, with
a working environment to suit the conventional and old-fashioned at
heart. With nineteenth-century origins and strong family ownership,
they are tasteful and discreet with unashamedly middle-class leanings.
They have refused to diversify as much as their rivals within business
culture A, and they enjoy a generally higher reputation, whilst at the
same time being conscious of their difficulties in appealing to young
people, both as consumers and managers.

   Companies within business culture B have an elitist attitude to
selecting trainees, and look after those they choose. They are good,
steady firms but they are not necessarily wildly exciting to work for, and
sometimes their risk-averse, time-serving environments fail to attract
the quality of people they need. They are not seen to be as prestigious
and progressive as the companies in business culture C, but have the
same strict set of corporate rules and, in many cases, lack of opportunity
for initiative.

Business Culture C
Working for a business culture C company is like joining the best club in
the world. Less of a job and more of a way of life, these companies take
over their people's existence completely and mould them into their very
rigid and powerful cultures. Their strong company ethic makes them
clannish and discourages mobility, so they are companies for those who
feel a need to belong; they are social systems on their own, and a shiver
goes down the backs of many when they even think of working
'outside'. These companies are big business empires, and have developed into conglomerates after years of commercial imperialism,
to take on the appearance of having become almost timeless. Their

hand-picked staff appreciate the honour of their calling, rejecting the entreaties of headhunters: these are the most difficult companies from which to tempt executives to leave, and they rarely call on headhunters' services themselves. Their employees are the most readily identifiable of all these cultures, most easily spotted by headhunters and all who watch the corporate business scene. They develop into certain types, and react according to type.

Business Culture D
These companies are basically new wine in old bottles, a blend of the old and the new. They attract those with an occasional taste for adventure but a need for an aura of stability. They have old roots, but unlike their competitors within business culture B, they have undergone more change, diversification and shake-up. A typical business culture D company has had injections of new blood and new acquisitions, but has become a mixed bag, sometimes with an uncertain culture and future. The training offered generally lacks the quality of companies of business cultures B or C, and working for them has necessarily more risks attached; thus they include the most high-paying companies.

Members of business culture D can be showy without substance. Staff come and go faster in business culture D than almost any of the other categories. Many have been accused of never having enough time to train a manager, and they are quickly intolerant of those who do not perform. But they do have movement between departments within a carefully-constructed system of horizontal integration, unlike their rivals in business culture B.

Business Culture E
A typical company of this category is the latest thing on the corporate scene, breaking new barriers, go-getting into the newest markets and products. These companies are not among the largest employers and, together with business cultures F and G, may be seen as more on the fringes of corporate life. Business culture E companies have a novel approach to entrepreneurship: they are into mass-selling, but not like the business culture A companies. Their goods and services are younger and newer and more hi-tech, and they project a more upmarket and sophisticated image which is nonetheless still showy and noisy, reflected in the personalities of their top management. These companies generally are looking for people with flair and energy, and are not too worried about their backgrounds.

Most business culture E companies are involved in services rather than manufacturing, and thus strictly speaking are not real blue-chip companies: their lack of a large capital base – and thus weight of interfering shareholders – enables them to be more innovative. They can grow very fast, and some could be business culture C companies of the future, with commitment to their products, high quality and discipline. The success of the smaller companies within business culture E can be hard to sustain for long; they may be booming today but may go bust tomorrow.

Business Culture F
These companies are *la créme de la créme*, the most prestigious of all. But again, in terms of employing numbers of executives and staff, they are not necessarily important and rarely enter the headhunter's domain. They have often been the first in the field in their business, and are certainly among the best. At least they consider themselves to be the best, and they price their goods accordingly. These companies are proud and obsessed by quality, in what they do and the people who work for them. Many have powerful family backing, giving the corporate name real respectability, but they have more style and class, and are more successful and high-earning than the companies of business culture B.

Almost by definition there are not many of them. Additions to this category could come from the most prestigious of the business culture C companies; and as in business culture C companies, those in this category tend to stay put, resisting headhunters' entreaties. They are justified in doing so: unlike companies in business cultures E and G, these firms look to the future and are prepared to invest in the necessary R & D and corporate planning. People will still be working for these companies 200 years from now, when firms in business cultures E and G will be long forgotten. However, some business culture F companies are almost institutions and, as such, are in danger of not being taken seriously in a strongly-competitive environment.

Business Culture G
The type of company in this category is tough, ruthless and aggressive; a fighter. Attracting people who can easily shrug off accusations of grabbing, asset-stripping and corporate raiding, these companies are controversial and unpredictable. They have often grown at the expense of their less determined rivals. Many top headhunters would not necessarily welcome assignments for companies they view in this category; in any case, they often have their own extensive networks of contacts.

These companies are known for hands-on management and the dominant personality of their man at the helm. This gives them much of their leverage. Business leaders in this category are single-minded and to the point. They play catch as catch can with business rivals without batting an eyelid. The image of these companies suggests armies of manipulators in darkened rooms, buying and selling and all strictly undercover. Many have amassed large personal fortunes. The most outstanding are seen as archetypal acquisitors, well-known predators beloved of shareholders but not necessarily so popular with employees.

(An extended revision of this study of business cultures – with examples – was originally commissioned by *Harpers & Queen* magazine; this extract appears with their permission.)

5

Three Headhunting Case Studies

CASE STUDY I: BAA PLC APPOINTS A NEW CHIEF EXECUTIVE

BAA plc, formerly the British Airports Authority, owns and operates seven major UK airports, including Heathrow and Gatwick: these are two of the busiest airports in the world, both handling more aircraft than New York's JFK. The seven airports of BAA together handle 75% of all passenger traffic and 85% of air cargo in the UK. With 7000 employees, BAA has achieved a turnover of some £400 million, and a consistent growth record in profitability. This search dates back to late 1986 when the need for an outside executive search for a new chief executive at BAA arose for two main reasons.

First, the forthcoming privatisation of BAA meant that, in order to make the share more attractive to investors, additional unregulated income would be required from new ventures and diversification. This would be additional to aircraft landing fees and concessions, and other major parts of BAA's income which would continue to be regulated by the Government to a formula of 3% less than inflation. Also the organisation would have to show it had achieved maximum efficiency in its existing core business. Both requirements called for private sector entrepreneurial discipline not available within what had until recently been a semi-governmental organisation. The mere appointment of a 'big name' businessman, it was thought, could increase the privatisation price and thereby add to the Government's coffers. Second, the Chairman and CEO, Sir Norman Payne – the trained engineer who gave the nation Gatwick Airport in its present form, and who to most was BAA – had reached his early 60s and, while retaining the Chairmanship, wanted over a 2–3 year period to reduce his massive workload by splitting his role. Meanwhile there was an MD running the actual airports, but this individual was already a long-time BAA man who was not considered appropriate as chief executive in the new privatised era.

A three-man executive search selection committee was formed consisting of Sir Norman Payne, the Deputy Secretary in charge of Aviation at the Department of Transport and Professor John Heath of the London Business School, a former BAA non-executive director. Four of the leading international search firms were invited to a shoot-out during late

158

October and early November 1986 to meet the committee and to present proposals as to how they would handle the search.

In mid-November, after several further meetings, this Committee decided to ask Mark Weedon – then London manager – and his colleagues at Egon Zehnder to undertake the search. (Weedon subsequently left Egon Zehnder, and joined Heidrick and Struggles in January 1989.) As a first step, a 'long list' of potential target candidates – unapproached at this stage – was to be prepared, and interviews were to be held with a vast number of directors, all of whom had to have their say. These included the three non-executive directors; Teddy Boyd, BAA's Deputy Chairman, representing the four Scottish airports; Sidney Weighell, the former General Secretary of the National Union of Railwaymen, representing the Union voice; and Hugh Ashton, a director of Hanson Trust and formerly a senior director at BAA's merchant bank, Schroders, representing the City voice. Interviews were also to be held with the Department of Transport, with two current Corporate Finance Directors at Schroders, with a County Bank director who represented the Government, and with four BAA senior executives, the Group Finance Director, the Head of BAA's Service Company (both of whom applied for the job, and were interviewed by Egon Zehnder as internal candidates) and the MDs of the Heathrow and Gatwick companies.

The initial specification called for an experienced general manager, aged late 30s to mid-40s with some slight flexibility allowed at the upper end, who should ideally have had experience of the leisure sector in areas such as transport, hotels, tourism and property. It was recognised that it would also be highly desirable if candidates had had some experience of working with the government or in a similarly regulated environment. Experience of successful employee relations was also important, and candidates' careers had to show a consistent progression in responsibilities and clear evidence of achievement. A degree or equivalent was preferred, but business experience and achievements were seen as more important than academic qualifications, and languages would be regarded as a bonus rather than being essential. In personal terms, the ideal candidate should be internationally minded, results-orientated, entrepreneurial and well organised. He or she would have to be a self-starter, able to motivate and lead a team. The ability to negotiate convincingly at top level, a strong profit orientation and a flair for detecting and realising market opportunities were all important, as well as numeracy, articulateness, and literacy.

The compensation was suggested at around the £80 000 level, with an absolute ceiling of £90 000, to which could be added stock options after privatisation. Normal bonuses and benefits such as a car, good index-linked pension scheme and life and health insurances in accordance with the importance of the position would be included. Egon Zehnder, unlike many of its competitors, charges a fixed fee rather than the more usual one-third of the first year salary and bonus, and its fee was agreed at £9000 per month for a three-month period plus out of pocket expenses which were unlikely to exceed 10–15%.

The consultant responsible for the search, Mark Weedon, launched the research phase of the search while concurrently undertaking the many interviews: with the non-executive directors, the Department of Transport, the merchant bankers, and the four internal BAA staff. Egon Zehnder's research department then investigated the initial target companies to find existing or previous senior executives at transportation companies (such as P&O, Ocean Transport and Trading, National Freight Company, Christian Salvesen), travel companies (such as Thomson Holidays), hotel companies (such as Trust House Forte, Grand Metropolitan, Lex), and other leisure sector companies (such as Granada Group, Hertz and Avis). Other individuals were found by Egon Zehnder, all potentially relevant from their current or former roles. These included a former airline head running the English Tourist Board, various former divisional directors of the National Enterprise Board, and both present and former senior executives at other semi-government organisations or nationalised industries. An amusing episode occurred at the first committee briefing meeting, when Egon Zehnder asked about the issue of robbing Peter to pay Paul. Were semi-government-owned companies, particularly in the transport area, such as British Airways, London Transport and the National Bus Company, to be regarded as off-limits from the viewpoint of BAA or the Department? Sir Norman Payne roared with laughter and passed the question straight to an uncomfortable Deputy Secretary saying 'There you are, there's a straight question, how about a straight answer?' While this issue was initially referred back to the Department, the straight answer eventually came back suggesting that it depended on which precise individual and organisation was involved but, in principle, there were to be no blanket off-limits companies.

The search proper then began, the initial long list having been cleared and a few names eliminated, and approaches began in earnest. In general terms, the position was found to be attractive and high profile, but the compensation was seen as not particularly attractive for someone who was already a chief executive/MD of a significant company, particularly since the bonus potential was relatively low, and there could be a problem in buying out the stock options which many of the potential candidates already had with their current companies. Nevertheless, in this first phase, over 50 potential candidates were approached, fifteen were interviewed (some declining to pursue the opportunity after interview, some being screened out by Egon Zehnder), and four were presented to the client as actual candidates (in addition to Egon Zehnder's written appraisals of the two internal BAA candidates).

These four candidates were, first, the former chairman and chief executive of a major cruise shipping line which included hotels, who had previously run a group of companies which included a leisure centre, a shopping centre and various other service businesses (who, interestingly and unbeknown to Egon Zehnder, had previously been offered a non-executive directorship at BAA, but had declined when his Group Chairman refused permission). The second was the former head of international operations for a major car-rental company, who was currently in a senior position in the City. The third was the Chairman and CEO of a public company involved in the hotels and casinos business. The fourth, a Divisional Director of a public company who had formerly been a divisional director of the National Enterprise Board, had previously worked in retailing.

The procedure with these four candidates was the same in each case: they would meet Sir Norman Payne for about an hour and then, a few days later, they would spend a further hour with Sir Norman and the non-executive directors of the Board, supplemented by the Secretary at the Department of Transport. On both occasions an Egon Zehnder consultant was also to be present, an unusual but important feature of this particular firm's consulting approach: this was seen as especially important in subsequent reviews of the relative merits of each candidate. The two internal BAA candidates, one of whom was already an Executive Director, also met Sir Norman and the non-executive directors.

The result of these meetings, which took place during the second half of January and throughout February 1987, was that two candidates were retained by the Board. These were the first two described above: one with the cruise line, and one from international car rental. The two internal candidates, with the other two outsiders, had been eliminated. Formal references were then taken up which, in one case, represented something of a problem since his former Group Chairman cast some doubt on his abilities.

However, the Secretary at the Department of Transport at this point voiced the opinion that the search had perhaps been too narrowly based. It had been focused, as was agreed, on the transport and leisure sectors but it was felt the age range had been perhaps a little young and should be extended to early 50s. The compensation could also be increased to a maximum of £100 000 and, if necessary, BAA should be prepared to consider buying out part of the stock option benefits forgone by any of the new candidates found in a new search. Since there was a further three or four weeks before a decision had to be made, and the name of the successful candidate inserted into the Pathfinder prospectus for the privatisation, it was agreed that Egon Zehnder would broaden the search in the hope that an even bigger name could be attracted to help put a higher price on the shares. Egon Zehnder sought, and was given, a further month's fee for this significant change in the specification.

In the second round which occurred in the last three weeks of March and the first week of April 1987, a further 25 potential candidates were approached, six were interviewed and three were presented to the client. A further sensitive episode occurred at this point, when it was discovered that two of those approached were both Divisional Directors of Hanson Trust, one of whose Main Board Directors was one of the non-executive directors at BAA who had been interviewed earlier by the search consultant; this required very careful and confidential kid-gloves treatment.

In the event the three new candidates were, first, one of the Divisional Directors of Hanson Trust; second, the Chief Executive of a major public company in international service business; and third, the 50-year-old Chairman and Chief Executive of a shipping and harbour company who had just resigned following a take-over. The front runner from the previous round was also included in a further meeting with the Board non-executive directors, since it had been agreed that he was a perfectly acceptable candidate whom Sir Norman Payne would have been happy to have appointed, and it would be unfair for him to have been left out. After Sir Norman had seen the three new candidates, the Board met on the afternoon of 13 April 1987, to decide between these four candidates.

Their choice was Jeremy Marshall, Divisional Director of Hanson Trust. He had been involved in the acquisition of Imperial Group, undertaking the divestment of their Courage Breweries to the Australian group, Elders. He was now running Imperial Foods; this had included some hotels and these he had subsequently sold. As Marshall put it, on welcoming his new appointment and particularly since Divisional Directors of Hanson Trust are rarely appointed to the Main Board, 'it is time to move up from the Engine Room to the Bridge.' Subject to references, and a final interview with the Transport Minister John Moore, Jeremy Marshall was to be offered the position of Chief Executive of BAA plc, his name inserted in the Pathfinder prospectus for the privatisation in May after which he would participate in some roadshows, and would start on a full-time basis at BAA in mid-June 1987.

Despite some last minute hesitation with negotiations on timing and on the compensation package, Jeremy Marshall was duly offered and accepted the position in late April and started work at BAA plc in mid-June. Thus, an executive search exercise launched by the search firm in mid-November 1986, resulted in a hiring decision five months later, and the successful candidate starting work seven months later, a time scale not unusual at this level.

In many respects, this was a relatively standard executive search exercise to find the Chief Executive of a medium-to large-sized public company, but it did have some interesting features. First, it was out of the ordinary, with the Government having quite an influence on the appointment, as well as the usual Chairman and Board; second, there was a relatively tight schedule, which was met by the search consultant despite being asked to relaunch the search with a broader specification and even tighter timeframe for the second round; third, the search consultant interviewed separately a rather larger number of non-executive directors, merchant bankers and even internal staff than is normally the case for such an appointment – and there was an inevitable measure of variation in the perceived ideal profile – but, in the event, these initial meetings did prove helpful in focusing the search, despite the extra time taken; and fourth, there were some sensitive points in the course of the search, such as the issue of robbing Peter to pay Paul, where one public sector potential candidate was actually vetoed by the Department of Transport who said that they would prefer to see him remain where he was.

A further problem was the difficult reference-taking process in the case of one candidate, one of whose referees was well known to the Department and Minister, and who clearly did not wish to see that candidate appointed. And finally, the fact that the successful candidate came from the same company as one of the non-executive directors required extreme confidentiality so as not to compromise that candidate should he not have been appointed.

CASE STUDY II: TREBOR'S NEW MANAGER OF HUMAN RESOURCE DEVELOPMENT

The remaining two case study examples quoted here are women. Such a choice might appear difficult to justify when successful women candidates account for but 5% or 10% of the total, yet it may be suggested that headhunting can oil the wheels of women's entry into the higher echelons of business. Headhunters will put forward women candidates alongside men – obviously only if they are equally qualified and suitable technically and professionally – whereas women are very often entirely overlooked in more traditional, old-fashioned recruiting based on the not-what-you-know-but-who-you-know principle. Both the successful women candidates quoted here are also interesting examples of creative and imaginative headhunting.

In case study II, Dorothy Palmer-Fry was headhunted by ex-Korn/ Ferry consultant Chris Denham, in competition with six male candidates. Her new employers saw her as the most promising and suitable candidate, whilst she has found a new and satisfying niche where she would never have thought of looking.

The search began when the client company, Woodford Green-based confectionery manufacturer Trebor, approached Korn/Ferry. Denham was chosen from among Korn/Ferry's ten consultants because of his experience both in personnel and with FMCG companies, as Trebor wanted a personnel executive to rank among the top dozen managers of the group, on a salary of around £40 000. Denham had worked for eight years in personnel with Unilever, and in his three years' headhunting with Korn/Ferry much of his work was in FMCGs, very much Trebor's sector. (Denham left Korn/Ferry in early 1989).

This search turned out to be particularly tough and long drawn-out. The usual time-span quoted by the majority of headhunters on accepting an assignment is three months: relatively few assignments, from the first contact between the headhunter and the client, to the moment when the successful candidate starts work, are completed more quickly than this. Six months is not unusual, but between Denham's first visit to Woodford Green in November 1986 and when Palmer-Fry took up her post in September 1987, ten months elapsed.

In his first client visit, Denham met the head of personnel at Trebor, to whom the successful candidate would have to report. Jennifer Haigh had worked her way up to the Board by the age of 37, having worked for a spell as a factory general manager. She and Denham discussed the job specification for about three hours, after which Denham drew up a brief of about ten pages, proposing exactly how he would conduct the search. They were to meet again, on neutral territory, at a restaurant near Korn/Ferry's office in St James's Square.

Denham and his PA/researcher – who has contributed to the section of this study examining the role of research within the headhunting process – then faced scores of hours telephoning potential sources and candidates. First, professors of business schools in Britain, Europe and the USA were approached for names of human resource managers they knew, had perhaps trained, and particularly recommended. Second, Denham turned to his old personnel contacts at Unilever, and the heads of development and training at other major employers also well-regarded for their in-house training facilities, like BAT, ICI and Procter & Gamble. Third, Korn/Ferry's data bank – of over 15 000 names – was checked. This principally comprises names of sources who have suggested candidates, all those who have appeared on short lists, those who have been successfully placed and those who have submitted particularly impressive CVs. Korn/Ferry receive hundreds of 'write-ins' per week in total. Relatively few – about 5% – actually lead to a job, but they are always welcomed in theory and many such applicants at least get a useful interview out of it.

Denham and his PA/researcher identified at least 80 contacts involving over 300 telephone calls for this particular assignment, and were able to produce a first short list of candidates in January 1987. Personnel is a much smaller field than, say, marketing or finance, and candidates with the personnel skills who could fit into the corporate culture at Trebor, and wanted to move, were thin on the ground. Unfortunately those that Denham did find fell below the high expectations of Jennifer Haigh and the Trebor Board. This temporary hiatus in the search process sent Haigh and Denham back to the drawing board. One problem was that Trebor's image did not appear sufficiently glamorous to attract the best people, so Denham went to great lengths to promote Trebor as an enlightened, progressive, dynamic company with lots of opportunities. Denham identified two more candidates in late February, but again according to Haigh they did not fit the bill.

It was as late as April 1987 when Denham first presented Dorothy Palmer-Fry to Trebor. He had come across her through a combination of research and contacts. From her work at Shell, Denham had first heard Palmer-Fry's name in his initial trawl for sources; he had also met her informally at a social function near his home. Denham agrees that headhunters are never really off-duty: any gathering of people may include potential sources, candidates or clients.

At the beginning of the search, Palmer-Fry was reasonably contented with the prospect of staying at Shell; but by April 1987 when Denham – now finding the search an uphill struggle – called her again, she was interested. Denham effectively and convincingly sold Trebor to her, although she admitted great initial reluctance to consider working for a medium-size British manufacturing company after thirteen years with one of the leading oil multinationals. She was impressed by how much Denham knew not only about Trebor, but also about herself. Palmer-Fry made her own investigations on the side and all of Denham's information stood up to cross-checking.

Palmer-Fry had worked as Shell's Chief Nursing Adviser worldwide for seven years, then moved to graduate training and finally to career planning for petroleum engineers, involving several North Sea oil rig visits. Then opportunities began to contract, with the promotion of nationals at overseas offices, and the expansion of Shell into Arab and Moslem areas, where women could hardly expect to make much progress.

Palmer-Fry had already observed this development when Denham contacted her. Practical and ambitious, she has always worked; despite having three children she had never taken time off besides the statutory four months minimum leave. One of the reasons why Palmer-Fry was prepared to consider leaving Shell was because they never allow part-time work. She had already been short-listed for a position with a London health authority which did offer this concession.

Palmer-Fry had been on the receiving end of headhunters' telephone calls twice before, but she had not previously shown much interest in their offers. But when Denham called for the second time, she agreed to a meeting at Korn/Ferry, which lasted nearly three hours; Denham soon realised that she was one of the most credible of all his candidates, as well as being the only woman he presented in person. At 43 she had the experience, and enough strength and stability of character to do the rounds of Trebor's confectionery manufacturing units and to discuss personnel problems with tough foremen and win their respect and confidence. They discussed her experience, personality, aspirations, values, and her perceived strengths and limitations.

She had known little about Trebor before so Denham briefed her about their diversification into many foods besides confectionery; their hundreds of lines including Sharp's toffee and Maynard's Wine Gums; the group distribution facility which is the second largest carrier in the UK; their wholesale company and their sophisticated computer systems. Palmer-Fry was very interested, but faced the problems of moving from a rich multinational with 220 000 employees worldwide to a 3200-strong British manufacturer.

Denham warned her that she would inevitably suffer culture-shock, but she was attracted by the greater degree of involvement and personal influence which the smaller business promised. She admitted that she would never have developed an interest in Trebor if it had not been for Denham's influence.

At Trebor, she had two lengthy interviews, with Haigh and with the MD, and was then subjected to psychological testing. For a whole afternoon, an outside consultant employed by Trebor minutely examined her verbal and non-verbal gestures and mannerisms during conversation to judge her character and skills. This form of analysis, used by Trebor for seventeen years, is by no means widespread in Britain, and is certainly more popular in the USA. It posed no problem for Palmer-Fry, and Trebor were more than impressed with her 10 out of 10 for dynamism, ability to handle several problems simultaneously, her pragmatism and her high capacity for work.

On her behalf, Denham negotiated her salary package, on the grounds that this might have put Palmer-Fry into a confrontation situation unhelpful for her future relationship with Trebor. They had discussed all this at length, at a second meeting after Trebor made their offer. The assignment drew to a close satisfactorily for all parties but, in case of an unforeseen problem, Denham drew attention to Korn/Ferry's guarantee to the client that they will replace free of charge a candidate who leaves within six months. Trebor had been particularly demanding, as Denham felt that any of the seven candidates could have effectively taken the position.

(An account of this case study first appeared in *Cosmopolitan* magazine, April 1988.)

CASE STUDY III: A DIRECTOR OF ECONOMIC DEVELOPMENT FOR NOTTINGHAMSHIRE COUNTY COUNCIL

If Labour-controlled Nottinghamshire County Council had been told in late 1987, when they began their search for a new Director of Economic Development, that in April 1988 they would be offering the job to an American woman who ran her own PR consulting firm and lived in Brighton, they would not have believed it possible. Yet, after they had tried and failed to fill the position by advertising, and appointed John Smith (formerly of MSL and now running his own company, Succession Planning Associates) to the assignment, this was precisely what happened.

It was to be a search marked by several strange twists and coincidences. Notts County Council did not directly approach John Smith, but vice versa. Smith, working on a similar but unrelated assignment – he was then director of MSL's public sector appointments division – came across a candidate who had replied to Notts County Council's advertisement but had not been appointed. Indeed, no one had. Smith promptly telephoned the executive in charge of the search from the Council's end and offered his services.

In Smith's experience, Labour-controlled councils are relatively infrequent users of search; Conservative-dominated councils, by comparison – perhaps because more of the councillors are likely to be businessmen who have already come into contact with headhunters and other consultants – were much more likely to look to search in preference to handling their own recruiting problems. However, Smith knew that Notts had used headhunters once or twice in the past few years, and guessed that they were now likely to be receptive to the idea again. As a result of his call, Smith was invited to join consultants from Korn/Ferry and Norman Broadbent and travelled up to Nottingham to take part in a shoot-out for the assignment. As a result of Smith's experience in public sector work, he landed the job and began work in January 1988.

Smith's approach to the search was a combination of executive search and advertising. In public sector appointments, where advertising is statutory, all headhunting firms working in this area are bound to announce each vacancy in the press. The local government journals publishing this information carry advertisements bearing such names as Korn/Ferry, as well as search and selection firms who deal in lower-level assignments. MSL operates in a range of sectors, but their work in high-level public appointments justifies their inclusion here.

Smith was ultimately to produce a short list of seven candidates for the post. Of the four finalists who made it through to the final round of interviews, two had been found by advertising, one by search, and one – Ann Crichton, the successful candidate – had been discovered through a mixture of advertising, search and sheer accident.

Smith and Crichton both live in the Brighton area and regularly commute to London, occasionally even sharing the same train compartment; they had also come across each other socially in the town, where her husband-to-be is Robin Beechey, Chief Executive of East Sussex County Council. On a Sunday in early February 1988, they met whilst checking train times on Brighton Station, and Crichton mentioned that she had seen the advertisement for the Notts position. She expressed real interest in the job, but said she had not considered applying; she thought that they would hardly want an American, and did not realise that her qualifications were quite so appropriate. Yet as she discussed her career with Smith, her suitability became more and more apparent.

Crichton's work at that time, running her own company – because it was concerned with the PR and marketing of international business expansion developments – fitted in well with Notts County Council's need for a wide-perspective, private-sector approach to its economic development problems. Her previous experience in the USA was also relevant: latterly she had run a Federal government agency helping to create jobs, but she had been Mayor of the city of Decatur in her native Georgia and had worked extensively in local economic development. She thus understood the problems of an economically disadvantaged region which suffered from unemployment and lack of investment. Her responsibilities with the US Department of Commerce had led to her appointment as a Regional Director of Economic Development under President Carter. In the private sector, she had worked with public officials on behalf of Peat Marwick Mitchell, running their government and economic development practice. Through Robin Beechey, she had become knowledgeable about local government in Britain, and felt strongly committed to this country. With him she had attended various conferences and meetings, including an Association of County Councils conference at Nottingham.

Crichton had not been headhunted to any of her previous positions, but was familiar with search through her time with Peat Marwick Mitchell, who have their own executive search division. She was thus happy to discuss the position more formally with Smith in his London office. Smith forwarded her CV and a paper she had written at his request outlining her achievements in the field of economic development; she promptly joined the short list.

Before she attended the extensive three-day interview programme which Smith had devised for the seven short-listed candidates in

Nottingham, Crichton paid a visit to the city and locality. At the city library, she consulted the Nottinghamshire Structure Plan, minutes of previous meetings of the Economic Development Committee and the Council's annual reports, homework which would stand her in good stead for the rigours to come. It is unlikely that other candidates had gone to such trouble.

In describing the actual interview process, Crichton was keen to emphasise that although Notts is a Labour-controlled council, the selection decision was strongly bi-partisan, with involvement from the Conservative councillors. She was impressed by their sound business approach and sensitivity to local problems – especially unemployment – which over-rode any issue of party politics.

The first ordeal was to meet the other candidates – all men – over coffee, together with the Chief Executive's deputy and a group of other chief officers. Smith, who had organised the structure of the interviewing process in consultation with the councillors (a procedure he had outlined at the shoot-out), and who was present to assess the short-listed candidates throughout the final selection process, was on hand to introduce people and encourage circulation when many on both sides inevitably felt slightly awkward. After the Deputy Chief Executive had made a short introductory presentation of the economic activities of Notts County generally, all the candidates, Smith and several chief officers with responsibilites for economic development piled into a coach for a tour of the inner city and certain industrial developments. Crichton's reactions to these sights were that although there were many problems and the job would be quite a challenge, measurable progress had been achieved and the Council was doing a number of creative things, such as using their superannuation fund for local economic investment, with some notable success.

Their final stop was at Plessey's large regional office. In a joint venture with the Council, Plessey had undertaken the renovation of a local building to provide space for small start-up companies. Here the candidates met ten key people from the local business community, including the President of the Chamber of Commerce. This was not just for the benefit of candidates; these businessmen were to supply feedback later to the councillors.

Back at County Hall, the candidates faced a series of team interviews. The nine elected members of the Council involved in the selection were divided into three groups of three, and each panel saw each candidate for fifteen minutes, representing the first formal interview. Three candidates were then weeded out and the contest was between four finalists. Then – and this is common practice on Smith's public sector assignments – the candidates were put in a room, and told to set out on paper in the space of an hour how they saw the economic problems of the area. These were then typed, and the candidates asked to proof them for typing errors only, before they were passed to the elected members. The candidates then attended a reception to meet again in an informal setting the elected members and a mixture of other interested parties. As before, the atmosphere was above all bi-partisan, co-operative and friendly.

The next morning, the formal 45-minute decisive interviews began. Having analysed the competition, Crichton felt that she was in with a good chance and actually enjoyed her interview, the third in the series. The nine elected members, Smith, the Deputy Chief Executive and a personnel officer, congregated around the large Boardroom table. Crichton was then asked to speak to her paper, written the day before, which the elected members had since read and appraised. She was requested to summarise her ideas in five minutes, without being able to refer to the paper; the interviewers were thus able to see at first hand if she could think on her feet. The Chairman asked her a question, and then each of the elected members, in turn, asked her one other question each. Crichton, feeling that they all knew a great deal about her, felt relaxed enough to inject some humour into the proceedings.

The elected members actually knew things about Crichton that she did not know herself, because they had already had access to the results of a psychometric assessment which she had taken previously. The previous weekend, she had spent between two and three hours answering a series of questions provided by Donald Hudd, an independent consultant brought in by Smith, who is very keen on being able to provide psychometric assessments on each final candidate to help clients decide. Crichton, who had not been subjected to such tests before, was highly sceptical but, despite a conviction that this would be a waste of time, was prepared to do the tests properly, facing them with a mixture of trepidation and suspicion. They took the form of various multiple-choice questions looking at word associations and groups of like and unlike ideas and objects, to determine the candidate's powers of deductive reasoning and reaction to a range of options. She freely admits to being quite amazed subsequently at the accuracy and detail of the results, which she considered to be at least 90% on target.

Crichton never knew the relative importance which the councillors attached to the psychometric assessment, her presentation or her answers to their questions; but, after waiting less than an hour after the final candidate had been interviewed, she was recalled to the committee room. A member of the interviewing panel then informed her that the councillors had been unanimous in their decision to offer her the position. Smith took charge of the final negotiations about her contract, salary, conditions and, acting as an honest broker between Crichton and Notts, subsequently travelled back and forth to Nottingham twice.

Crichton signed the contract three weeks later in mid-April 1988, having already found herself a flat in which to live in Nottingham during the week.

This case study lends weight to the argument that headhunting can offer a creative and imaginative solution to a recruiting problem that might otherwise appear insoluble. For Smith's fee he not only presented a wide field of different but all able and qualified candidates, but also managed the entire process on behalf of his client in a highly effective and efficient manner. Notts County appreciated that they had received value for money, but not all of Smith's clients are so easily convinced. For instance, a few days after the Notts interviews, Smith travelled to Poole in Dorset to take part in a shoot-out for an assignment to find a Director of Works for Poole Borough Council. Smith's task was not only to compete against another search firm, but also to persuade the Poole councillors of the value of a combined search and advertising strategy run by an external consultant. Despite Smith's presentation, the Poole councillors felt that they could not justify the expenditure of £10 000 of public money, and decided to handle the recruiting themselves.

(A shortened version of this case study appeared in *Local Government Chronicle*, 30 September 1988.)

6

The Global Scene

Roddy Gow of Russell Reynolds was asked to comment on the global aspects of headhunting and suggested that search firms are perhaps most significantly differentiated by the extent of their international network. The largest of these have extensive coverage, and most international firms have offices in at least the three major financial centres of London, New York and Tokyo. Since the majority of high-level recruiting projects call – by definition – for the headhunter to find the best candidate possible, such searches are more international than domestic, more global than regional. It is the effective use of this international or global network which should be seen as a source of strength and added value by potential clients, and is frequently cited as a reason for choosing one firm in comparison with another. To be effective, however, such a network requires the existence of broadly accepted standards and procedures within a firm combined with the placing of a very high premium on the provision of assistance by one office or individual to another when requested; arguably, it also needs a method of measuring such contributions. In simple terms, the recruiter in Singapore must be prepared to work closely with, and support, colleagues in Sydney or San Francisco if asked to do so, and this global capability both in research and execution must subsequently be offered as a complete service to the client.

EVOLUTION

As with other service industries, so headhunting has expanded to meet the needs of its clients. Recruiting requirements have always been a principal stimulus to growth, although in many major firms, experienced recruiters with a desire to open a new office have been encouraged to do so on the basis that a person may create a market; but, however good a market, without the right person a business will not succeed. The early creation of a New York/London axis has been the feature of many major firms, Russell Reynolds having been formed in 1969 with the first overseas office in London opened three years later. While some offices were nurtured in their early stages by the existence of substantial international relationships with multinational and other corporations, an interesting counter-cultural phenomenon had developed. Frequently, a major company with few or slight links to a recruiting firm of the same nationality in its home country may make significantly greater use of its services in an overseas community: here difficulties in recruiting experienced professionals in a foreign centre such as London are caused as much by perception on the part of the potential employee of conditions within the firm that is recruiting as from an indifference or actual reluctance to work for a non-British company. It is under these circumstances that headhunters frequently find themselves providing the cultural bridge between overseas clients and the major companies who control recruiting effectively on a global basis. It is the decisions of geographic or sector heads which generally result in search firms being chosen for a specific project, and here the ability of the recruiter to bridge the gap first is often of paramount importance. Additionally, of course, however good the network and however fine the firm, a large part of a decision relating to which recruiter to use will also be based upon the chemistry established between client and headhunter, and the client's degree of comfort with the concept of a specific individual being his or her ambassador or agent in the market place, especially overseas.

As search firms have expanded and evolved to form networks of varying size and quality, their method of expansion can probably best be divided into two categories. Those that have gone for organic growth have, where possible, selected and recruited individuals who have been trained in an established office before subsequently moving to set up in a new location. From a fairly small initial core or critical mass of offices, satellites have been formed in this manner, linking newer offices and cementing the personal bonds between different recruiters. Another and also effective method has been through association where working agreements have been negotiated between firms with a presence in different market places, resulting in business referrals and formulae for calculating profit contributions.

GLOBAL SEARCH AT WORK

For research to be effective on an international or global basis, those involved must be familiar with working as a team. In the leading search firms, this teamwork is achieved in a number of ways. First, professional recruiters attend initial, and subsequently regular, training sessions to improve their skills and make them conscious of the need for what may be described as effective execution, first-class communication and up-dating of technological awareness. Second, annual planning confer-ences, either on a worldwide or regional basis, provide opportunities for the exchange of views and enable professionals to get to know each other, and this is particularly important in some of the larger, rapidly expanding search companies. Third, travel between offices is encouraged in the pursuit of business and to cement cross-border links. This is sometimes formalised with the appointment of liaison officers who, in addition to their normal recruiting work act as channels of information between one office and another. The result of these actions in a well-run recruiting business is to bind together the firm in a sense that makes individuals more aware of the cultural, economic and business differences of individual countries and regions. They then become used to providing help for, and requesting assistance from, other colleagues. From the clients' point of view, this emphasis on communication and networking should, if properly managed, speed the recruiting process, broaden the search coverage of an international project and reduce the need for recruiters to make long and sometimes fruitless journeys to other centres in order to interview potential candidates. Increasingly sophisticated computer-based data on clients, candidates and companies underpins such global work and enables relevant research information to be passed extremely rapidly to any part of the network. While not a substitute for highly inquisitive, well-planned original search, investment in sophisticated systems and on-line terminals equips the modern international recruiter with tools that increase effectiveness and improve the time of completion.

The global market place in which high-level search work is carried out is shrinking in terms of improved communications and better awareness of international developments and economic factors. There is, in theory, no reason why the use of high-level search should not extend in time to the Indian sub-continent, Africa, China and the Soviet bloc, as discussed in Chapter 7. Where demand outstrips supply and the need exists for first-class management to add value and enhance businesses, the demand and ingredients for search work then clearly exist.

Certainly a detailed knowledge of local culture and conditions is essential for an international firm to be effective. This will include an understanding of the law affecting the holding of information on individuals in West Germany, the implications of the Data Protection Act in the UK and other constantly changing rules and regulations. Other developments affecting particular industries and sectors are disseminated rapidly to those who need to know of them and, in a large firm such as Russell Reynolds, the grouping of sector specialists into practice areas improves such communication and provides a vehicle for the exchange of data in areas such as health care, hi-tech, retail and FMCG, investment management and investment banking.

As far as the initiation, execution and completion of international search work is concerned, a major project involving more than one office and recruiters in different countries essentially requires a high level of co-ordination and a great deal of co-operation. The general scope of a search having been assessed at the outset, individuals from different offices will expect to assemble for the client briefing, at which the project manager from within the recruiting firm will be introduced, and the members of the team formed to carry out the search identified. On a major project, the team may number three or more, differing from domestic search where, in Russell Reynolds, two recruiters are always allocated to each search to ensure continuity and facilitate an exchange of views. Typically, a Paris-based search might involve a briefing in France attended by a recruiter from Germany and the UK, with a telephone hook-up to an office in the USA or the Far East. Additionally, biographical details of recruiters not present but forming part of the project will be passed to clients so that they are aware of the full resources being made available to them.

Once a search is started, close co-ordination is ensured through the role of the project manager who will provide the principal interface with the client. Regular internal briefings keep the members of the team updated on progress and use of fax, telex and computer links ensure the rapid communication of reports to the clients. Video links are still fairly rare, although there is no doubt that they are likely to become an increasing feature in the future.

GLOBAL SEARCH OUTSIDE THE BIG FOUR

The majority of the search firms listed in the Select Directory offer an international search facility to their clients based not on offices overseas but on other search firms in other countries with whom they have an arrangement – either contractually or through a share swap – for undertaking global assignments. For example, Tyzack has a particularly long-established international network of this type.

The basic difference between the two possible ways of running an international search business lies in their manner of ownership. Many consultants in the Big Four and the other international firms have a stake in their local and/or the world business, but none has overall total ownership; within an association of international firms, such as the Tyzack-led network, the Ward Howell Group and Merton's Transearch, each firm is independent.

The amount of international business each partner undertakes varies considerably, usually according to business trends particular to their localities, and mostly outside the partners' control. For example, George Lim, who has run Tyzack's Hong Kong office since 1979, has found his business increasing with 1997 on the horizon; the anxious search of many Hong Kong Chinese businessmen and women for citizenship elsewhere – particularly Canada and, to a lesser extent, Australia – has left a void which is being filled by returning expatriates, at substantially higher salaries.

Nicholas Gardiner of Gardiner Stone International, Tyzack's New York-based representative – a breakaway from Haley International – claims that the transfer, over the last few years, of £46bn of investment from Britain to the USA has caused a substantial increase in his international search work. As a proportion of his total business, Gardiner has found that global assignments have risen overall from 30% in 1980 to 70% today. Friedbert Herbold and Armin Schmidt of Hofman, Herbold & Partners, Tyzack's associate in Frankfurt, have identified several new growth areas with the lead up to 1992, as has their colleague Jean Claude Lasante of Lasante et Associés in Paris.

International search, as with local headhunting, is inevitably dependent on changing patterns of demand and supply of certain functional specialisms. For example, MIS directors are in short supply in Switzerland and in Holland, and have to be looked for in other countries. Specialists in various sectors of financial services are being searched in London and New York for assignments elsewhere.

The appreciation and understanding of the concept of executive search varies substantially between countries, so the approaches of the different international partners varies accordingly. Global search began with multinationals and their demand for senior staff for their overseas offices; then search began to be used by non-multinational, indigenous companies. Lim suggests that this is beginning to happen among the younger generation of Hong Kong Chinese business leaders.

Gardiner, who works closely with many Japanese clients, emphasised the difficulties of explaining the search process to a business community which still regards it as alien and incomprehensible; for a headhunter on the international circuit, he half-jokingly claimed that a degree in anthropology was probably more useful than an MBA. Tyzack has a large number of Japanese clients in London, and still finds that some Japanese businessmen find headhunting difficult to understand, especially as they are not familiar with the wider concept of employing outside consultants. International search in the future will see the emergence of local headhunting firms; but there are few indigenous executive search companies in Japan. However, in late 1988 Merton Associates acquired a new Transearch partner, a Japanese businessman based in Tokyo who will undertake local searches on their behalf. Native Japanese headhunters, when they finally emerge in number, will find their services greatly in demand both by networks of associates looking for a greater Far Eastern presence, and multinational headhunters looking to expand by acquisition.

The most crucial problem in global search is the appreciation of the totally different business climates in different countries. In this matter the network-of-associates type of international search operation, where the offices are directed by nationals, has advantages over the branch-type global search business which tends to make greater or lesser use of expatriates from Head Office, at least when the business is first being set up. In this respect, Lasante – a graduate in business studies in Paris, and one of the pioneers of executive search in France – spoke of some medium-sized French family firms as dominated by Godfather characters and not dissimilar in closeness and nepotism to some of the Hong Kong Chinese businesses.

The truly international businessman or woman is not necessarily an ideal candidate in every global search assignment; they frequently have problems fitting in with the locals with whom they subsequently work, whose perspective may be more limited but nonetheless valid in the circumstances. Such candidates are very convincing in the 'courting' phase, but often disappointing when in position; knowledge of the world means little without understanding the subtleties of foreign cultures.

Responsibility for handling the assignment varies according to the nature of the client's need. The work can be shared by several offices, taken up by partners according to the markets which require being searched. Researchers play an especially crucial part in global searches, sometimes contributing more to an assignment than the consultants. Tyzack has been known to break down the fees for an assignment to separate the research element in various locations.

Some multinational clients maintain a considerable homogeneity between their branches in different countries; others vary enormously. Many try to establish a corporate uniformity, and fail to perceive the significance of different business cultures. Oil companies and banks can be quite similar wherever they are, but this is not the case with all conglomerates, even those with very powerful business cultures of their own. Unilever, for example, produces quite different executives in Holland when compared with those who staff its operations in London and New York. Serving such organisations can be a great challenge for the international headhunter.

A minority of international searches are best served by the consultant who was awarded the assignment, rather than being networked to partners on the spot. These include searches in countries where it may not be economic to support a partner – if one could be found – such as the Middle East, parts of Australasia and South America. Peter Bryant at the London office has led a number of pioneering assignments in such locations. To find local partners for a British bank in the Middle East, Bryant embarked on a one-man itinerant research programme; and an assignment for a Tropical Forestry Director with international expertise took him to Somaliland and New Zealand; this is an example of what a number of consultants call a 'Zanzibar job'.

Ways of paying each consultant involved in an international assignment vary and this can influence their attitude to the work. Saxton Bampfylde have an altruistic system of passing assignments to the most relevant partner overseas without payment, trusting that they will receive assignments in return; it is yet to be seen if this really works in practice. Russell Reynolds have a points system of rewarding every participating consultant according to the nature and extent of their contribution. Egon Zehnder partners share all international earnings equally.

Tyzack has instituted a general rule-of-thumb that the office through whom the search arose in the first place receives 20%, with the one executing the work taking the remainder, but this is always negotiable according to an assignment's individual merits. In all cases, the consultant who first won the assignment still maintains overall responsibility in satisfying the client, and acts as the liaison officer throughout. The partners all feel that the driving force behind a global search should be serving the client as widely and efficiently as possible, and that the firm's international research capability is seen to work, regardless of which office benefits most.

There is arguably a place for both types of international search firm, and frequently shoot-outs are held between them; Gardiner recently competed against Windle Priem of Korn/Ferry for a prestigious assignment with one of the major global commercial banks. International searches are certainly among the most sought-after of all assignments, in terms of their prestige. Most search firms quote a higher minimum fee for searches involving more than one office than for exclusively home-based work.

Yet global searches can be most prone to disaster and take much longer, both in execution and follow-up. One of the main reasons for failure in an international assignment is a breakdown in communications between the overseas branch of a multinational and the Head Office, or the insistence of a multinational in placing a candidate trained at home who appears to be an able ambassador of the corporate style but has not integrated into the foreign environment. It takes longer to investigate the viability of an overseas search, but spending this time is essential in order to maximise the chances of a successful outcome. The long-distance search process takes longer for simple technical and logistical reasons, and consultants, clients and candidates are naturally no less subject to jet-lag than anyone else, which can double the time-frame for an interview programme.

The possibility of firms offering longer guarantee periods for inter-office assignments has often been mooted. Gardiner maintains that the real duration of an international search assignment should be over three years, with the first part – from initiation to the candidate starting work – taking around a year, with at least two years 'to see if aspirations are met on both sides'.

The recruitment of foreigners by parent companies looking for a local to run an overseas operation is bound to be influenced by the fact that it is most unlikely that that person will reach the top of the organisation, which in almost every case is reserved for nationals of that company's head office. Global search at the very highest level is thus a continuing process.

HEADHUNTING IN EUROPE

In considering the wider international context of the executive search business, we have primarily been concerned with the importance of global contacts – through branch offices or affiliates – to the work of London-based search consultants. However, the creation of an internal European market planned for 1992 with all its implications justifies a closer examination of the headhunting business in Europe itself, and not only when it contributes to London-based pan-European assignments.

Here, the emphasis is mainly upon the firms now perceived as European market leaders: Egon Zehnder, with a European-wide fee income of over \$50m.; Spencer Stuart, with \$25m.; Russell Reynolds, with \$21m.; and Heidrick and Struggles with \$18m. But many others – listed in the Select Directory – have made, and continue to make, an important contribution to the expansion of the search business in Europe. These include Boyden, the Amrop group (represented by Canny Bowen in London), Carré Orban (who split off from Egon Zehnder), GKR, the Transearch network (Merton in London), Tasa and the Ward Howell Group (Whitehead Mann in London). Those expected to increase their interests in Europe in the future are Korn/Ferry and possibly Norman Broadbent and, through associates, Saxton Bampfylde and Tyzack.

It would be naive to suggest that the practice of executive search in Europe is radically different from elsewhere. At the very highest levels, especially on behalf of multinational clients, search is very much the same all over the world. It is still dominated by the leading international firms, for the main reason that many of these large, important clients will retain the same search firms in Paris, Frankfurt, The Hague, Milan, Madrid and Zurich as they employed in London, New York and Tokyo.

At this very top end of the market, Korn/Ferry have acquired a leading position in the USA, whilst Russell Reynolds have become number one (in fee earnings) in Britain; but, to an even greater extent, Egon Zehnder dominate the executive search scene throughout much of continental Europe. In the USA they are comparatively weak, ranking eleventh in US billings according to *Forbes Magazine*, July 1989; they make up for this to some extent in the Far East including Tokyo, yet in continental Europe, in their spread of offices, number of consultants and annual fee earnings, they are clearly market leaders, with an almost institutionalised image and strong brand name. This has been greatly helped by the fact that the firm began in mainland Europe, rather than in the USA, although as a rule the offices of all the major search firms operating in Europe are now staffed by nationals rather than expatriates.

To Egon Zehnder consultants, it is inaccurate to suggest that Europe is a decade behind Britain – and two decades behind the USA – in terms of the acceptability of executive search and the sophistication of users, precisely because a large proportion of their clients are international businesses seeking executives with an international perspective. Heidrick and Struggles, Spencer Stuart and Russell Reynolds – regarded by Egon Zehnder as their main competitors – also recognise this.

However, in headhunting on behalf of medium-sized national companies, it is apparent that national cultural differences have a more significant impact, and that some countries are more receptive to executive search than others. But this is changing: the trend overall is towards a convergence of practice, to the breaking down of regulations and customs which inhibit the acceptability of search, and this will accelerate with the approach of 1992. From the headhunting point of view, the cultural differences between European countries and the USA are considerably less than between the West and the East, particularly Japan.

A common feature of executive search throughout Europe is the consulting approach, away from more narrow transaction-style headhunting which is more popular in the USA. Fees are more frequently charged according to time and complexity, rather than as a proportion of the successful candidate's remuneration. Rarely – apart from in Britain – are the words 'executive search' used officially; in France, firms are *Conseillers de Direction*; in Germany, *Geschaeftsfuehrender Gesellschafter*; in Spain, *Consultores para el Reclutamiento de Directivos*. Far less is the word 'headhunter' – quite acceptable in the USA and increasingly so in Britain – palatable in Europe. *Chasseurs de têtes* and *cazadores de cerebros* are light-hearted terms seen occasionally in the popular press, although the former was daringly used in the title of a lively but informative book on headhunting in France by Jean Claude Lasante (associated with Tyzack in London) back in 1976.

As in Britain, European search consultants are conscious of their clients' insistence on total discretion and confidentiality; names of clients are closely-guarded secrets, not emblazoned on corporate brochures as in the USA. Coverage of the work of search firms in the media is unusual. Their promotional activities are very low-key; a good example is Heidrick and Struggles' Paris office's support and organisational input – jointly with Arthur Andersen – into 'Le Cercle 1992', a series of lunch meetings of leading politicians and businessmen discussing topical issues, held in Paris over the last 3 years. Another example of discreet PR is Egon Zehnder's publication of a range of well-documented economic surveys in conjunction with leading European business schools.

France

Executive search in France, unlike a number of other European countries, is almost entirely confined to the capital city. In Paris, senior-level headhunting in a modern and systematic manner dates back to the late 1960s, largely pioneered by Spencer Stuart and Egon Zehnder. Spencer Stuart, now with 20 years' experience here, has a significant presence in the French search market; with six consultants, it is, after London, one of the firm's more profitable offices in Europe. Egon Zehnder's Paris office opened in 1968. Dr Zehnder set up his own firm in Zurich in 1964 and opened branches in both Paris and Brussels four years later. In Paris, Egon Zehnder now have ten consultants and, according to competitors, a large share of the local search business; they dominate the most senior searches, and have recently taken on many mergers and acquisitions assignments which, with financial services, accounts for about one-third of their work. According to Eric Salmon, partner in charge of Western Europe, after London Paris is the principal centre for European M&A. The firm is about to open in Lyon.

Russell Reynolds, also with ten consultants, was established in Paris in 1977; and Heidrick and Struggles, now with fifteen consultants, was opened in 1978. The European offices of Heidrick and Struggles, including London, are co-ordinated from Paris; Gérard Cléry-Melin is President of the European division. As in London and Frankfurt, Heidrick and Struggles in Paris includes ESE, an executive-level (rather than director-level) search service recruiting within a slightly lower salary band. According to *Dynasteurs*, a French business magazine, in May 1989 Heidrick and Struggles was the clear leader of the French search scene, with a fee income of 38m. F. pa.

Although the use of search is increasingly commonplace among multinationals in France, there are special reasons why headhunting is less widely accepted by French compared with British and American companies. Allan Stewart, who spent nearly three years at Spencer Stuart's Paris office, suggested that by the broad measure of the number of search consultants per head of population, executive search is perhaps twice as widespread in Britain compared with France. He pointed to the innate suspicion of search in French business circles explained by two factors: the well-entrenched educational mafia based on the *grands écoles* network – with executives more loyal to their old school than their company – and the frequent movement of executives back and forth between companies and the government. There is a strong tradition of major French companies seeking staff from certain educational establishments, and in the substantial nationalised sector the government plays an important role certainly in the selection of corporate CEOs, and sometimes of other senior executives. Eric Salmon has noted an increase in the number of top civil servants moving into senior jobs in the private sector, and staying there.

Yet, over all, a survey in November 1988 by *Le Nouvel Observateur* of the super elite of France – top politicans and businessmen – questioned if it was for the benefit of the French economy that they were all from the same background, exhibiting a distinct standardisation of culture and outlook.

Brought originally by the multinationals, search in France began to take off (more recently than in Britain) not in the large, traditional French companies but in new businesses, such as hi-tech; in smaller firms outside the *grands écoles* network; and in those of the old traditional industries – like steel and chemicals – forced into rationalisation by changing demand. As many nationalised industries are denationalised, they too are calling upon headhunters; one example is Thomson SA, the part government-owned defence, consumer and electronics giant, who have retained Russell Reynolds for a number of searches, including a senior vice-presidency being searched in the USA, Europe and the Pacific. But the still-restricted use of search by France's top 100 companies explains why, for example, Spencer Stuart in Paris has a greater client mix here than in London, with more smaller and medium-sized companies. Egon Zehnder would appear to be capturing a large proportion of business from the larger French companies and the multi-nationals.

The growth of financial services in France has further helped the development of search. Seen as the fastest-growing sector by many search firms – accounting for an average of a third of their business, about half of which is for multinationals – Paris was chosen as the centre of Heidrick and Struggles' pan-European 'Fin$earch' sector. Similarly, as Eric Salmon pointed out, the highly-professional international luxury cosmetics/perfumery houses, such as Chanel, Yves St Laurent and Hermès, are also important users of search. However, despite this internationalism, there is still a great reluctance to hire non-French nationals.

The search business in France is highly fragmented, with very many headhunting firms, including those using both search and selection techniques. The tendency of consultants to leave the major firms and set up on their own is even more common in France than in Britain. Thus

Jean Michel Beigbeder and Messrs Carré and Orban left Spencer Stuart and Egon Zehnder respectively. Gérard Cléry-Melin, like Dr Zehnder, was originally with Spencer Stuart.

Many indigenous French search firms, without international networks, have remained small, with only a few clients and capitalising on their knowledge of the *grands écoles* network; they are subject to a high drop-out rate. As in the early days of search in Britain, many of the smaller firms are run by consultants without the qualifications and corporate experience of those in the larger firms. There has been some attempt to regulate the French search market with the foundation of APROCERD, a quasi-professional body; meanwhile market forces are less powerful, as fewer shoot-outs are held in France, and a greater proportion of French companies retain only one search firm.

Germany

Egon Zehnder's lead of the search business in Germany, with four offices – Dusseldorf (1975), Frankfurt (1982), Hamburg (1986) and Munich (1987) and a total of fourteen consultants – is striking. Spencer Stuart, also well established here, operates only from Frankfurt and Dusseldorf, with fewer consultants than it has in France. Russell Reynolds, established in Frankfurt in 1985, has six consultants here and is looking to expand the business. Heidrick and Struggles, with offices in Frankfurt, Munich and Dusseldorf, has a much stronger presence.

Headhunting in Germany is technically illegal, and even as management and industry consultants or advertising agencies, firms have occasionally faced prosecution. Thus they keep a low profile and there has been no attempt to form a professional body or group of consultants, as in the USA, Britain or France. All available positions must be advertised by law, and the search firms' problems are further exacerbated by the need to keep personnel records across the national borders. It is likely that, after 1992, Germany will face pressure to conform to the common European practice; despite the leverage of her officials at the EEC, it is less likely that the rest of Europe will have to conform to German practice. This may also affect the traditionally high levels of German salaries.

German clients, often highly suspicious of search firms, are more likely to regard executive search as a commodity, and are reluctant to accept a consulting approach. German executives, many of whom are academically qualified to doctoral level, are generally older than their contemporaries elsewhere in Europe, and are the least receptive of all Europeans to a headhunters' call. This was explained by Dr Albert Petersen, of Meyer-Mark in Dusseldorf (the German Transearch partner), who spent fifteen years recruiting in the German civil service before joining Tasa and then setting up on his own. Medium-sized family firms are vitally important in Germany, and many have survived to the fourth generation; they have been slow to use search and have relied on in-house executive succession, but now that they are turning to consultants they are calling on small, independent German firms, whilst the German multinationals more commonly employ the likes of Egon Zehnder. Now, according to Joel Markus (partner in charge of Egon Zehnder's mid-Europe offices) these large clients are welcoming a consulting rather than transactional approach to search, and appreciation of the role of executive search is expanding.

Benelux

Although headhunting was established earlier in Brussels, Holland is seen as a more mature market for search. With long experience of multinational presence such as Unilever, Philips and Shell, and many prestigious banks, such as Amrop, it is seen as being ahead of France and Germany in accepting headhunting. Spencer Stuart, operating from Amsterdam since the early 1970s, has a well-established business run by five consultants which it regards as more similar to London than all the other continental European offices. Egon Zehnder ran its Dutch executive search practice from Brussels before opening in The Hague in 1979.

   Amsterdam is seen as the most attractive city for a Dutch search office by Russell Reynolds, which plans to open there when the level of business justifies it; it strongly adheres to its policy of setting up only when it can establish a large office. This is in considerable contrast to the Egon Zehnder approach, which is to keep offices to a workable size, such that all the consultants – a maximum of twelve – can meet each week and discuss all their assignments together. If an office in one centre is expanding beyond such a point, this would influence the decision to set up a relatively nearby office. Thus The Hague office was established to serve Dutch clients yet prevent the Brussels, Copenhagen or Dusseldorf offices becoming too large.

Italy

Executive search in Italy is also perceived as dominated by Egon Zehnder. Some of its largest single clients worldwide – in terms of the number of assignments per company – are of Italian origin. It has been the last of the European countries to accept search, explained by the importance of family businesses and the prevalence of a form of 'organised anarchy', with vast variations in salaries and business practice. It is a major step for a traditional Italian family company to hire a search consultant, which favours the continued strength of Egon Zehnder; in

Milan since 1971, the firm enjoys such prestige that one of its leading Italian consultants accepted an invitation to become general manager of Gucci. A second office, in Rome, was opened in 1987. Spencer Stuart, in Milan since 1978, is perceived as Egon Zehnder's closest rival.

Russell Reynolds, keen to expand its European network, is opening an office in Milan in early 1989, and has already recruited a leading Italian businessman to run it. Italian clients are meanwhile being served from Paris: David Shellard, who runs Russell Reynolds' European-wide business, referred to six major searches for top Italian multinationals in progress in November 1988 being co-ordinated in Paris. Egon Zehnder, however, already handles over 100 assignments per year in Italy.

Spain

Conscious that they have much economic ground to make up, and eager to capitalise on their EEC membership, Spanish businessmen are taking to executive search, together with strategy and management consulting, which are presently expanding rapidly in Spain. Barcelona has now followed Madrid as a burgeoning business centre.

Egon Zehnder's Madrid office was established in 1973, and Spencer Stuart's in 1978; both have now opened in Barcelona. Heidrick and Struggles also operates from both centres. Russell Reynolds, a more recent arrival in Spain, are confined to Madrid but, now that this centre – according to Russell Reynolds – is as profitable as Paris and second only to London in billings, it is considering opening in Barcelona. Unlike London (where financial services brings in 55–60% of earnings), Russell Reynolds' income in Madrid is mixed with only 29% financial services. Originally mainly dependent on multinational clients, these now account for only 38% of Russell Reynolds' business, whilst 62% of its work is for Spanish companies.

Spain, with its booming gross national product, is viewed as the most fast-growing and exciting centre for search in Europe, as the Spanish are considered to be more open to outside ideas than the French or Germans. Headhunting is helping them to jump the development gap and, facing a scarcity of corporate talent, is encouraging more and more younger executives. All the leading search firms spoke of the quality of the consultants they were able to attract to join their firms in Spain; they also pointed to the readiness of Spanish clients to seek a general consulting approach to search, rather than offering only a narrow brief for a specific executive for a specific job. Egon Zehnder has eight consultants in Spain, and opened in Lisbon in early 1989. It faces strong competition in Madrid from Spencer Stuart, which has an especially effective team there.

Scandinavia

Egon Zehnder's Copenhagen office, opened in 1970, is also perceived by competitors as very strong. With eight consultants – two Danes, four Swedes and two Norwegians – it serves most of Scandinavia; Helsinki has its own office, formed in 1987 when the Copenhagen office threatened to become unwieldy in size. Spencer Stuart operates its Scandinavian search business out of Stockholm; neither Russell Reynolds nor Heidrick and Struggles maintain offices in this region, preferring to serve Scandinavian clients from Frankfurt and London. Other firms with Scandinavian offices are Boyden, the Amrop group, John Stork International (now merged with Korn/Ferry), Tasa, Transearch and the Ward Howell Group.

Switzerland

Outside the EEC and subject to restrictive employment legislation – affecting the hiring of non-nationals in particular – search on behalf of Swiss companies has enjoyed recent expansion with the increased pre-1992 M&A activity. Financial service sectors, because of their international nature and adaptability, have a long tradition as users of search, and this encouraged the early development of headhunting in Zurich by Spencer Stuart and Egon Zehnder. Swiss practice – i.e., the difficulty of obtaining work permits for foreigners, traditionally high salaries and Swiss men having to spend six weeks in every year on military service – is likely to remain unaltered.

As its place of origin, Egon Zehnder is strongly entrenched in the Swiss market. Much of the Egon Zehnder style emanates from its experience with Swiss clients, known for their demanding standards, and low toleration of lack of quality and attention to detail. The near-monopoly enjoyed by Egon Zehnder in Switzerland partly explains why Russell Reynolds was forced to close an office it opened in Geneva.

* * *

There is no doubt that Europe is seen as a key area for the expansion of executive search in the future. In-filling in Europe before striking out into completely new areas outside Europe is the priority of many market leaders as well as smaller firms.

7

Headhunting in the Future

There is no doubt that the executive search industry is constantly evolving and, as in the case of British and international business itself, will be significantly different by the twenty-first century. What are likely to be the comparative positions of the major executive search firms in the headhunting league table? Will there be changes in the corporate structure and manner of ownership of these firms? Will the nature of their work, in terms of level and function, be substantially altered? How and where will headhunting spread geographically? Will the large firms in Britain become even larger?

John Viney of Heidrick and Struggles was asked to analyse the possible ranking of British and multinational headhunting firms in the future. From the viewpoint of early 1988, he considered that potentially the strongest firm worldwide is Spencer Stuart. He saw them as having the best worldwide coverage, with strength in the USA, a formidable presence in Europe and one of the most successful firms in the third great economic area of the world, the Far East. Their international network of contacts is now so well developed that more than 50% of their business is derived from outside the USA. Spencer Stuart have apparently solved the problem of their future corporate structure and ownership. Now run with a partnership style but as a limited company, no partner holds more than 2% of the shares, thus encouraging teamwork and loyalty. A year later, he argued that this is still the case, borne out by *Business Week* figures of February 1989 showing Spencer Stuart clearly challenging the leadership worldwide of Korn/Ferry and Russell Reynolds.

Viney sees both Heidrick and Struggles and Egon Zehnder as potentially strong in the future, but both need to overcome specific problems first. Egon Zehnder are clearly very significant in Europe and have an important standing in the Far East, but they lack a credible US business, the most mature headhunting market of all. This problem could be solved through a strategic acquisition, but finding the right business in the States which would fit together with Egon Zehnder's predominantly European character would be difficult. Without a base in the USA, they clearly find themselves at a severe disadvantage and cannot truly be global players. They naturally disagree with this assessment, pointing out that the firm have had a New York office for twelve years, and with four branches in total they are the twelfth largest in the States.

Admittedly this is weaker, relatively, than the other leading firms, but further growth in America is planned and is being vigorously pursued.

Heidrick and Struggles, according to Viney, has experienced the opposite problem. It has a powerful and prestigious image in the USA – thanks especially to the efforts of Gerry Roche – but the firm has only belatedly started to make its international business work. Its Chicago roots have kept it predominantly in the USA and it has tried to start up its international businesses using American rather than local nationals, which has caused several difficulties. During the late 1980s it has built up an international business in Europe which will require further strengthening and development in the future; yet it still has no presence whatsoever in the Far East. In terms of economic activity, this is a major issue for the firm, especially as it has begun to win assignments on behalf of Far Eastern-based clients which it has to manage from London and elsewhere. The firm is actively seeking expansion in this region through acquisition. Based solely on geographical coverage, an obvious worldwide merger would be between Heidrick and Struggles and Egon Zehnder; but the two firms are culturally so different that this does not seem likely.

In looking at Korn/Ferry and Russell Reynolds, Viney sees their problems as emanating from their corporate structures: will the organisation and manner of ownership of the major headhunting firms change? Heidrick and Struggles and Spencer Stuart have already moved to a partnership structure, but Korn/Ferry, number one worldwide in fee billings and number of offices, is still 50% owned by the founders Lester Korn and Richard Ferry.

Stephen Rowlinson, the managing partner of Korn/Ferry's London office, pointed to the fact that Lester Korn, acting as US Ambassador to the United Nations, can play no part in his firm's activities during his tenure of office, and that the business worldwide is effectively run by a group of senior officers which meets every four months. Each of the senior officers has a substantial shareholding – Rowlinson has £100 000 in nominal value – and he is satisfied that there is little probability that Korn/Ferry will go public. Other leading headhunters question this assertion, asking what value will the shares have to the partners unless they make a market in them?

Viney, whose views are shared by a number of other British headhunters, questions the overall profitability of Korn/Ferry because of its possibly overstretched spread of offices. Until the future of Korn/Ferry is finally resolved, Viney wonders how the firm will progress. The best estimate at the moment, he maintains, is that it will be sold unless a group of the senior staff within the company can buy it out. Moving from strong ownership by two individuals to a different basis is going to be traumatic for them. Rowlinson points out that over the last year and a half, Korn/Ferry has been substantially reorganised as it has become larger, and its structure is more participative, with more emphasis on autonomy and consultation than ever before. He compares Korn/Ferry's present structure with that of the old-style McKinsey Management Consultancy.

Russell Reynolds also faces a succession problem. Like Spencer Stuart, it already operates effectively in the USA, the Far East and has a European presence which, although clearly very strong indeed in the UK, is relatively weak in mainland Europe. A change in the ownership and therefore the style of Russell Reynolds will inevitably occur once Reynolds himself effectively retires. Already, he is much less pro-prietorial, and the firm has adopted a collegiate-style organisation.

Viney is convinced, and most of the other major headhunters in Britain share his view, that no loose federation of local executive search businesses combining together under a global name – such as Ward Howell, Eurosearch and Transearch – will be able to make a sufficiently effective international presence to be able to compete with the big multinational firms. GKR appear to be trying this strategy, but they will need considerable financial resources to make it work. In the context of the rivalry between firms, time is clearly at a premium for GKR if it wishes to become a global player in executive search worldwide.

This study of headhunting has, from the outset, been predominantly concerned with executive search firms working at the top end of the market only. In the future, is it likely that these firms will move down-market in an attempt to sustain their level of growth at a high volume? Many find that they are increasingly offered lower-level searches by existing clients. Some, like GKR and Korn/Ferry, apparently refuse to take on this work. Heidrick and Struggles, on the other hand, whilst confining their core business to directors of Boards and Subsidiary Boards, has set up an associated business to take on executive and manager-level searches as a sideline, known as ESE. Many smaller, home-grown British search firms, including Norman Broadbent and Whitehead Mann, have adopted a similar strategy, offering lower level search and selection services.

Are the main functional areas of business in which headhunting has been most active likely to change? Financial services has long been the most controversial sector, in terms of the level of salaries and the intensity of the demand. The importance of this area has apparently fallen from around 50% in the case of Korn/Ferry and Russell Reynolds to about 40%; but despite this there has still been an overall increase, for the total volume has risen substantially and other sectors have become increasingly important. It was thought that recruiting in the financial services would suffer a temporary hiatus or at least a levelling-off after the Big Bang, but this did not prove to be the case. Similarly, Korn/Ferry and the other large firms were prepared for a drop in business with the stock market Crash of the late autumn of 1987; instead, they found that the number of assignments continued to increase, even from finance houses who had been shedding staff heavily.

As the trend to the further globalisation of big business continues, headhunting will eventually penetrate to even the most commercially remote places in the world. By the year 2000, the major multinational search firms expect to have opened several more branches. According to Stephen Rowlinson, Korn/Ferry are planning the continuing extension of their branches from the present 39 to more than 60 over the next decade.

It is likely that the further economic integration of the EEC in 1992 will encourage the opening of more European branches of the major firms. After 1992, local restrictions on movements of the labour market, such as in Germany, should be unified. Also after 1992, the labour law through-out Europe will gradually be harmonised, so that businessmen will eventually move freely between jobs across the Continent. Rowlinson suggests that if headhunting is 'part of the furniture' everywhere else, then countries like Germany will quickly be brought into line and become a significant market for search. Spain, too, is seen as a major growth area, and Korn/Ferry – already in Madrid – expect soon to follow Heidrick and Struggles by setting up a branch in Barcelona.

Expansion in Europe is less a case of pioneering than in-filling. Many major firms are considering increasing their number of branches in France, such as with Nice and Lyons; in Germany, in Munich and Hamburg, for instance; and also in major capitals in Scandinavia and across the Iberian peninsula.

More adventurously, search firms – possibly with Korn/Ferry taking the lead – will boldly go where no headhunter has been before. Six main areas are being targeted. First, the multinational search firms will renew their efforts to penetrate the Japanese market. They have already built up a considerable business on behalf of major American and European clients. Korn/Ferry became the first American-based search firm allowed to open in Japan in 1973–4, followed soon afterwards by Egon Zehnder. Yet it has proved difficult to gain assignments from Japanese clients, even though a great deal of work for them is carried out in Europe and the USA. But with increasing competition from Korea, for example, and with the inevitable breakdown of widespread lifetime employment as a result of the decline of some of Japan's major employers (such as shipbuilding) the labour market will become more mobile. Japanese culture will be forced to keep up with new, increasingly volatile trends in its business, and eventually a telephone call from a 'scoutman' will be welcomed, rather than regarded as an insult to an employee's principles of loyalty. Then search firms will strengthen their Japanese presence, with branches in Osaka, Yokohama and other commercial centres.

Second, a further penetration of the Far East is envisaged with the establishment of branches in Seoul, Bangkok, Indonesia and, ultimately, the People's Republic of China. Beijing, Shanghai and Canton are all being considered for branches when cultural barriers have been sufficiently broken down by the sheer weight of the expected competition which will come with the further opening up of China. Restrictions on labour recruitment and mobility will, like export licences and productivity quotas, have to be abandoned when they are seen as limits to growth. Maoist communism is still a powerful force, but China is changing more quickly than anyone could have envisaged.

Headhunting is also expected to make headway in Africa and in the Middle East. Presence in South Africa, as with any other business, depends on the nature of the political regime there; Korn/Ferry was offered the acquisition of a leading South African search firm, but refused to consider it. Nairobi and Harare offices are, however, projected.

Korn/Ferry has been seriously contemplating opening in India within the next few years, and Rowlinson explains exactly how this may be done. Expansion in such a high-risk business environment is only possible when an executive search firm has a critical mass of both clients and consultants. Before considering a move to untried headhunting terrain like India, there has to be a real demand. The level of business in the projected new country has to reach such a level that it is impossible to serve it adequately from nearby existing branches; this has already happened with Korn/Ferry's work in Scandinavia, hitherto served from Zurich and managed by a Norwegian consultant based there. Also, to maintain a consistent standard between Korn/Ferry offices throughout the world and promise the client the same brand of service in every location, Korn/Ferry cannot take the chance of simply taking over an existing executive search firm, as it did when it first came to London. Expansion by acquisition as a policy has been abandoned in favour of organic growth. In any case, Korn/Ferry would be unlikely to find suitable acquisition material in India. Consequently there must be enough consultants on hand, trained in the Korn/Ferry brand of search, to send them on this pioneering work.

The strategy for opening a branch in India would begin with recruiting new consultants with roots in the sub-continent who had been educated elsewhere, but nonetheless had experience of working with Indian companies in India and overseas. After two or three years in Korn/Ferry offices, chosen on the grounds that they would be expected to have frequent contact with a branch in India, two or three such strongly bi-cultural consultants would be sent to open up in Bombay. They would then need to recruit four or five locals of stature, influence and experience, who would be trained on the job.

Start-up costs, compared with beginning a large manufacturing enterprise, would be relatively modest but still significant. Office space
would have to be rented, expensive computer hardware purchased, and
salaries paid before substantial fee income could be expected. The
headhunting firm itself needs to have a critical mass of business to be
able to bear inevitable losses for a while.

The clients of a hypothetical Korn/Ferry (Bombay) on Day One would
come from three main sources. First, the firm could rely on business
from the Indian companies already served round the world in New
York, on the West Coast of the USA and in Europe, such as Tata and the
Taj Hotel group. It could also count on work from several international
clients who want to do business in India: demand from these clients for
an India-based Korn/Ferry office would have been instrumental in the
decision to open an Indian branch in the first place. Third, Korn/Ferry
would expect to serve multinational clients with existing or proposed
joint venture projects in India, comparable with Anglo-South American
joint-ventures.

Relying on these clients alone would not be enough to make such a
branch a real success. As elsewhere, the consultants on the spot – both
from other Korn/Ferry offices and recruited locally – would need to
create business and promote the concept of executive search in an
ignorant and even hostile environment. Successful early assignments
would lead to more work by word-of-mouth recommendations, but this
would all take time.

A much shorter time scale for start-up is envisaged for new branches
filling the gaps in Europe. A Barcelona office, for example, could be
opened with consultants, clients and even ready assignments from the
Madrid office. A recent opening of a new branch in Amsterdam, fuelled
with personnel and referrals from Brussels, made an overall profit
within its first quarter. In comparison, Rowlinson expects that the
Indian market would take as long to crack as Japan or China.

Perhaps one of the most exciting future headhunting markets of all
may be the Soviet Union. Glasnost and Gorbachev's new economic
strategy as a whole suggest that several new enterprises will emerge in
Russia to supply the demands of an expanding consumer society.
Rather than the usual pattern of state-supported and state-directed
corporations which frequently are allowed to become white elephants,
the new regime is looking towards creating new, truly commercial
individual enterprises. These businesses will be encouraged to be highly
profitable, to expand, and will be permitted to take over smaller firms.
The black market will control a reduced share of the economy with the
increasing deregulation of the white market. Rowlinson sees these as
ideal headhunting conditions. As we have seen in the origins of the
whole concept of executive search in post-war America, the Russians

will find themselves impatient with having to train up all their managers from scratch, and they will become frustrated with the bureaucratic machinery put into motion when they try to transfer people from other enterprises. This could happen even sooner in other Eastern bloc countries, such as Hungary. Russian headhunters trained in the West could play a significant part in cutting through Ministry red tape and will pave the way for radical changes in business strategy.

The creation of new business in new markets, in a constantly more competitive world, needs the services of new, especially entrepreneurial businessmen. If they are not necessarily apparent or thin in the ground, as in the Soviet Union, headhunting is the obvious solution. No major business venture can be truly successful in national isolation, and only international headhunting networks can effectively track down international talent. It may be some time before Korn/Ferry or anyone else takes a brief from the Kremlin; at least they will known in advance one item on the job specification: 'Has to be good Party Member'. Yet, it could well be that when the Soviets do begin to adopt the commercial trappings of the West, they will look to Britain to supply them. They are not likely to look to the USA, or to American companies; so home-grown British executive search firms may find a new source of demand for headhunting behind the Iron Curtain.

The headhunting business in Britain has, therefore, much room for expansion geographically. But it is also poised for further growth in other ways: into new business areas, such as more public sector work in universities and hospitals; into lower-level appointments, which can be searched more cost-effectively thanks to increased efficiency in the research department; and even, maybe, into Buckingham Palace itself. One prominent home-grown British search firm – obviously well-connected – has completed an assignment to find the new Land Steward for the Western District of the Duchy of Cornwall, effectively headhunting for the Prince of Wales.

Headhunting is also likely to continue to increase for another reason, beyond its expansion into new geographical areas and new functions/sectors. The declining birthrate and managerial shortage is making the search for talent more competitive. In the USA, the Association of Graduate Recruiters expect an annual graduate shortfall of 6000–9000 by the mid-1990s. Britain is facing a similar shortage of graduates which, with the demands of 1992, will result in greater usage of headhunters. The problem in Japan has become acute, with personnel managers – yet to use headhunters, on the whole – actually kidnapping graduates.

Conclusion:
The Headhunting Business

In the course of 3 years' investigation of the executive search business, from all four angles – consultant and researcher, client and candidate – the overall impression gained has been that, generally speaking, headhunting is a good thing. But this is not to say that this is always the case, and if this study appears to be unduly sympathetic to the headhunting fraternity it is because the firms discussed here have proved that they can make a substantial contribution to the effectiveness and performance of their clients. Yet, for every one of these firms, there are perhaps ten or more that are not necessarily to be recommended so highly, or are not trustworthy, discreet and reliable at all.

As intimated in the preface, this is a study of the top end of the headhuntering market. This does not mean that the literally hundreds of other firms not included here are to be avoided at all costs; but a client should be confident that he or she has a good reason for using them. As the headhunting process itself seeks to break down the old-boy network and establish a sounder and more systematic basis for choice of candidates, the manner by which clients choose search firms should be similarly precise, and based on first-hand recommendations and track record. As executive search becomes more widely accepted, clients are becoming more and more sophisticated users of search.

The early 1990s will be possibly even more exciting in the evolution of this industry. Headhunting in Britain was born in the late 1950s and 1960s, grew up – rather unsteadily at first – in the 1970s, and confidently celebrated its coming of age in the Big Bang era. Now more widely referred to by the more respectable term executive search, it has achieved a new maturity. The leading executive search firms who have, as we have seen, been jostling for position throughout the 1980s are settling down and a distinct pecking order has emerged. This development has occurred in parallel with the commercialisation and regrouping of the professional services, especially with the polarisation of the accountancy business between the eight major accounting firms. In the same context, the latest development in the headhunting industry has been the clear emergence of the Big Eight, each with its worldwide and more or less diversified empire, and its own own brand image and individual business culture.

Although there are many significant smaller firms – the most important of which are discussed in the Select Directory – the Big Eight together have captured the bulk of the top end of the market. They generate an aggregate annual fee income of well over £35m. through handling nearly 2000 of the most senior appointments searched. The hundred or so consultants within the leading search firms in Britain now earn salaries and bonuses on the same level as in the higher echelons of the professional services. The most senior 20 partners at Freshfields or Slaughter & May who take home over £½m. annually are now being joined as Britain's highest earners by top headhunters – the dozen or so individuals who lead each firm – whose incomes have doubled in the last three years. The most successful search consultants now earn as much as the people they recruit, and are clearly 'peers among peers'.

Finally, although *The Headhunting Business* has sought to be as wide-ranging as possible in its view of the industry, it omits one vitally significant element: professional ethics in executive search. This problem is inevitable in a proactive process whereby individuals in existing positions are directly approached and presented with the possibility of an opportunity elsewhere. This moral question, within the context of the wider issue of business ethics generally, is worthy of a separate study beyond the scope of this book. It includes such matters as poaching from clients, and whether or not the entire client company should be off-limits, and for how long; the deliberate limiting of the number of clients in a particular sector to keep hunting grounds open, and the behaviour of clients in engaging a number of search firms to reduce their vulnerability; the acceptance of assignments before the chance of success has been fully evaluated; maintaining client confidentiality; the charging of fees according to a proportion of the candidate's first year remuneration and bonuses, versus a fixed fee based on time and difficulty of the assignment regardless of salary level; fairness and truthfulness in the tracking down of candidates' names in headhunting research, and the use of elaborate cover stories to penetrate switchboards; and the independence of search firms from larger financial, industrial or service groups where there could be a conflict of interest with the parent company's clients. A further ethical issue is the use of headhunters by companies to side-step employment legislation, such as that relating to equal opportunities for men and women. A client can insist that the headhunter search only for a white Protestant English male, although it would be illegal to put this in an advertisement; but this only saves time and focuses the search. A client could as easily issue a general advertisement and discard the unwanted candidates. Really able minorities, the search firms argue, may even be helped by executive search, which can mean that a client is persuaded to consider a candidate previously seen as unacceptable.

These and many other questions are raised whenever the possibility of forming an official, professional body of executive search consultants is discussed. The most reputable firms – all those included here – have addressed these matters and have adopted a specific stance on each without the need for a professional association.

Select Directory: Leading Executive Search Firms in Britain

LEADING EXECUTIVE SEARCH FIRMS IN BRITAIN: CRITERIA

The following Select Directory summarises the basic details of 23 leading executive search firms operating in London. The criteria for inclusion were:

1. the firm is regularly undertaking assignments at the highest level, i.e. Main Board appointments;
2. the average salary level of successful candidates is over £50 000 (except in the public sector);
3. the firm uses search techniques rather than selection, except when advertising is mandatory (as in the public sector, when search is also used);
4. the firm's name was mentioned in the survey of clients and candidates in Chapter 3;
5. the firm has a proven track record, through several successful searches, with a fee income per year of a minimum of over £500 000 with a minimum of four consultants;
6. the firm has the facility to search for candidates overseas, either through its own offices or through affiliates.

Most firms meet all six conditions, with two exceptions: Baines Gwinner, who lack overseas offices, but recruit at very high levels in the City; and Succession Planning Associates, who work at the highest levels in the public sector, where salaries are lower and advertising is compulsory.

EVALUATING AN EXECUTIVE SEARCH FIRM

There is no scientific, objective way to evaluate a search firm as one could evaluate other service businesses. The search business in Britain has no professional body or association and thus firms are regulated by market forces only. The need for total confidentiality to their clients makes it very difficult indeed to gain an accurate picture of the performance of firms in specific assignments, unless the clients accept publicity. In this respect, the situation in Britain is completely different from that of the USA. Firms can be ranked by their numbers of consultants, experience in the search business, annual fee income and number of assignments, but these are not necessarily the most significant criteria by which to judge them from the point of view of a potential client or candidate.

SEARCH FIRMS AND CORPORATE CULTURE

Each consultant within each firm has different experience, ability, approach and style, which will suit some users and not others. Consultants with the greatest experience in a particular sector may not suit every client in that sector. The issue of corporate culture and style is crucial here: the attitude of a user determines the suitability of the search firm. There are two basic corporate styles, as far as the search firms are concerned, appreciating that there are many variants within each:

1. some companies are looking for a hunter of heads, to save time, to act as a middleman, to avoid the task of advertising and trawling around, but to cost as little as possible, and to be in and out of the assignment as soon as possible;
2. other companies are looking for a top-quality executive search consultancy, with a view to a long-term working relationship, to solve corporate problems before, when and after they happen, and to help in planning their executive succession in the future.

The search firms are trying to build up client lists of these latter companies; it is not in their interests to have too many clients, especially in one sector, because this limits their areas for searching.

THE SHOOT-OUT: A PRACTICAL TEST

For a new user, the best way to evaluate the quality of a search firm in the first instance is to invite a selection of firms – large and small, national and international – to a shoot-out (a competitive pitch for an assignment). As far as the particular assignment is concerned, the qualities and requirements the client should be looking for are summarised in Chapter 4, which considers four written proposals emanating from a shoot-out.

Professionalism

At the shoot-out, the client should be looking for industry knowledge, a speedy grasp of the problem in hand, enthusiasm, efficiency, confidence, confidentiality, a practical approach to planning the search and its timing, and an awareness of problems and pitfalls possible with this particular assignment.

Discretion and experience

It is not possible, through the need for discretion, for a search firm to be specific about its previous work and previous clients in a sector, except for the purposes of showing which firms are off-limits or not. For the same reasons, a search firm can summarise but not give specific information and evidence about its success rate (the proportion of completed searches to those which had to be abandoned).

Points to check

If the choice of search firm is mostly based on the personality and quality of the individual consultants – and there should always be two, not one on each assignment – the potential user should ensure that the consultants handling the presentation should be handling the search too. The user should also question the firm about their research resources; will a qualified researcher be assigned specifically to the task?

In the case of a search firm which a client has not used before, a cautious CEO or human resources director should contact other users and ask them to suggest a good firm, or request their opinion of one which has been tested in a shoot-out.

SELECTING SEARCH FIRMS FOR THE SHOOT-OUT

Which firms should be invited to the shoot-out and which should be discarded? It would be impossible to employ a rating system in the Select Directory, with points from one to three according to reputation, price and innovativeness as adopted in other business guides, such as those published by *The Economist*. The Select Directory is suggested as a guide to the style and approach of firms, so that this may be matched with that of the would-be client company. It would be inappropriate to use such ratings when discussing executive search firms.

Reputation and success rate

First, the reputation of a search firm cannot be judged as one would judge a school or college, for example: ex-students would have no reason not to give an opinion, and lists of past students are published; yet many clients of a search firm would not wish details of this relationship to be known, and no search firm in Britain publishes client lists. As noted above, discretion is an integral part of the executive search business, especially the confidentiality of clients.

As seen in the client survey, the majority of users of search did not disclose which search firms they have used. The Select Directory includes the comments made by one-third of the 30 users questioned who were prepared to make judgements on the reputation of search firms. Even if hundreds of users of search were questioned, their comments would only represent a minority of the market, and would depend on how much they wanted to reveal. Few users will admit to having employed poor quality, unsuccessful search firms, as this reflects on their judgement and lack of management of the consultants. Similarly, few users will admit to being overtly dependent on search firms or feeling indebted to them for good work because this may suggest that their own internal resources were inadequate. Companies will not reveal usage of a search firm in the way that they will readily publish the identity of their accountants, auditors and solicitors; indeed, they are not legally obliged to do so.

Creativity, performance and innovativeness

These qualities in a search firm cannot readily be measured for the same reasons which make it difficult to analyse reputation. Such qualities as these, in the executive search world, are more likely to be used to describe individuals rather than firms. Some consultants are clearly trail-blazers, others are willing to experiment and others follow the pack, and many search firms include examples of all three. It also depends on the sector and area of specialty of the assignment and, of course, the needs and style of the client. It would not be appropriate for a search consultancy to try to push a client towards a pioneering and novel solution if that client wanted to take a more conservative line. Also, such qualities are dependent on the perception of the client, and his or her own standpoint.

Cost

Although it would be a relatively simple matter to compare the level of fees charged, this would not be a valid exercise. In the wider perspective, when compared with the recruitment of a senior executive who will make a substantial contribution to the earnings of a company, the search consultant's fees appear minimal. Most search firms' fees are very broadly similar – based on one-third of the successful candidate's first year's remuneration, or approximately equivalent when based on time and difficulty – and this should not be a major factor in deciding between them.

If a potential user is faced with two firms equally appropriate for the task, then cost could be a deciding factor; but firms markedly less expensive than the norm – usually small, home-grown firms – may not be able to offer such a complete research service, may lack prestige and kudos with candidates in the market place and may have inadequate networks to mount an international search, if this is necessary. The large multinational search firms' fees are similar except for Egon Zehnder, whose fees are perhaps slightly higher.

The user should be wary of expenses, and request an estimate of these on commission. Some search firms use expenses to cover practically all their internal office costs; others, such as Baines Gwinner, a specialist City headhunter, refuse to charge expenses at all.

The most important criteria

The quality of the consultant assigned to the task required, his or her suitability for the needs of the particular assignment, and how he or she fits in with the culture of the client company are the most critical points a potential user should consider.

* * *

The information in the following directory has been presented in as standardised a form as possible, but this has inevitably varied according to the size and nature of each firm, and the amount of detail they were prepared to reveal. It is intended as a preliminary guide only, to give an idea of the approach and areas of speciality of each firm. This is intended primarily to assist users of search in making decisions about which firm to employ for a certain assignment. It may also help candidates to identify which firms to target when sending in CVs and, when they are interviewed by search firms, it may give them some idea of what to expect. In some cases, it would be helpful for both clients and candidates to request a copy of a firm's brochure, and to read any other publications either by or about them; these are referred to here and in the bibliography.

BAINES GWINNER

1 Founder's Court
Lothbury
EC2R 7HD
01–283 9801/992 7770
Fax 01–283 3790

Consultants in London Jonathan Baines, Martin Gwinner, Matthew Andrews and Martyn Pocock.
Founded in London 1986.
Owned by The directors and staff.
Worldwide No other branches as yet.
Annual fee income and number of assignments London, £1.2m.; approximately 40.
Basis of charges 30% of the first year's guaranteed compensation, with a minimum and maximum fee; first instalment to be paid when the assignment is commissioned; the second, when a firm offer is made and the balance when the candidate actually joins the client and begins work. Uniquely among search firms, Baines Gwinner does not usually charge expenses in addition to their fees.
Guarantees If the presentation of the short-list does not result in an offer, no fees other than the first instalment will be charged. The firm undertakes to continue searching until a suitable candidate is found. If the candidate placed leaves the client within six months, the search will be reinstated at no further charge.
Sector specialism Financial services including insurance.
Functional specialism Director and senior management level positions, in corporate finance, asset management, global equity and debt markets.
Salary range From £50 000, with an average of £100 000.
Associated and other activities None but executive search.
Publications Brochure, introducing the company and its approach.
Style, approach, future plans Through a period of explosive growth, the complex, village-like and almost incestuous nature of the fiercely competitive top job market in the City of London has spawned a shoal of small, specialist headhunting firms. Baines Gwinner is one of the few to have survived the post Big-Bang and post-Crash fall-out, and has now achieved sufficient maturity to ride out present and potential future upheavals. In its field, it can rival even the largest firms with the most costly resources; the golden rule for all at Baines Gwinner is to update their candidate/source data base constantly which, in finite markets such as equities and corporate finance, has total coverage. Such a 'big-brother' view of the business would be impossible outside financial services in the wider corporate sector.

The driving force of the firm is Jonathan Baines. Formerly with Brown Shipley merchant bank, he is refreshingly young, direct, honest and enthusiastic. He and his team work literally close to their market in offices overlooking the Bank of England, in contrast with their larger but more distant Piccadilly and Mayfair-based rivals. Baines Gwinner's four consultants and three assistant consultants work open-plan, like the dealing rooms and trading floors in which they search. The atmosphere is highly charged; information from screens and telephones flies constantly across the room.

Often the greatest edge a small firm can have on its large rivals is cost; Baines Gwinner goes a stage further than most in offering a maximum as well as a minimum fee, without charging expenses. If, the firm argues, the fee for a successful assignment is £45 000, why should the client be charged a further indeterminate amount on top? Generally, headhunting fees in the context of a successfully completed search – when the candidate is adding measurable value to the client – are deemed reasonable; but, in the shoot-out, these fees tend to excite considerably more comment, especially since the Crash. Baines Gwinner's fee income overall has not noticeably suffered as a result of adopting this unique basis of charging.

Sustained growth is dictated by a need to provide expertise in related business sectors, and to offer an international dimension. Baines Gwinner is already expanding its insurance search practice through Matthew Andrews, ex-Lloyds Reinsurance and Michael Page City, a selection agency. Baines Gwinner's investment banking sector has been further strengthened by the recent arrival of Martyn Pocock, who has bought a significant stake in the firm. He brings seventeen years' city experience, most recently with Bear Searns and Kleinwort Benson in London and New York. Prior to Pocock's arrival Jonathan Baines had numerous approaches from larger firms wishing to buy his business, which would have been one way of solving the problem of a lack of overseas contacts. The firm may now form a network with other independents abroad and even, ultimately, overseas branches. Currently assignments for clients in London requiring searches in New York and Tokyo, for example, have been undertaken from the City, fitting in with local hours.

Reputation Baines Gwinner was described as outstanding within its field in a survey of leading users of search within the financial services sector: the group personnel directors of one of Britain's principal clearing banks, and of one of the most prestigous of the Japanese banks in London, both spoke very highly of the effectiveness of Jonathan Baines and of his firm's data base and research services. Baines Gwinner's novel fee structure was regarded as a model which the rest of the industry ought to follow, in so far as it was weighted towards the successful completion of the assignment instead of expecting all, or most, of the fee up-front or on presentation of the short list. Users saw Baines Gwinner as much closer to the market – in terms of knowing all the players – than the multinational firms, and it is now competing for more senior, international Board level work.

BOYDEN INTERNATIONAL LIMITED

148 Buckingham Palace Road
SW1W 9TR
01–730 5292
Fax 01–730 8120

Consultants in London Michael Curlewis (Managing Director), Andrew Garner, Peter Skala, Nigel Godwin, Sarah Shiers and David Hutt.
Founded in London 1966, originally established in New York in 1946.
Owned by In London, the UK-based partners. The Boyden World Corporation in New York is owned equally by over a hundred partners worldwide.
Worldwide 250 staff worldwide, in Amsterdam, Atlanta, Bangkok, Bogota, Boston, Brussels, Chicago, Cleveland, Copenhagen, Dallas, Fort Lauderdale, Frankfurt, Geneva, Helsinki, Hong Kong, Houston, Johannesburg, Kuala Lumpur, Lisbon, London, Los Angeles, Madrid, Melbourne, Mexico City, Milan, Morristown, New York, Paris, Pittsburgh, Rome, San Francisco, São Paulo, Seoul, Singapore, Stamford, Stockholm, Sydney, Taipei, Tokyo, Toronto, Valencia, Vienna and Washington.
Annual fee income and number of assignments London, £1.5m., 75; worldwide, $35m., 1200+. According to a survey in *Fortune*, Boyden's recruiting fees worldwide were only $26.8m. for 1987. *Business Week* reported them as $34.6m. for 1988.
Basis of charges A fee based on one-third of the first year's annual salary plus any cash bonus is charged in three equal instalments over the first three months: on taking the assignment, after 30 days and after 60 days. The client may cancel the work at any time, although the first instalment is not refundable. The fee is increased for international searches involving two or more offices. Boyden is now committing itself to producing shortlists in only four weeks.
Guarantees In certain circumstances, if the candidate placed leaves the client within twelve months, Boyden will carry out a further search at no additional fee.
Sector specialism Consumer goods, 19%; electronics and hi-tech, 18%; banking, 12%; industrial manufacture, 11%; construction and mining, 9%; retail and distribution, 6%; energy, 6%; printing and publishing, 4%; healthcare and biotechnology 9%; and other 6%.
Functional specialism Over 50% of searches by Boyden in 1987 were for new positions rather than replacements. General management, 34%; sales and marketing, 29%; finance, 12%; technical, 7%; manufacturing, 6%; human resources, 6%; planning, 2% and other, 4%. One-third of the assignments were for UK public companies, with another third for US multinationals.
Salary range £45 000 +.
Associated and other activities Boyden's activities worldwide are confined to executive search.
Publications Brochure of Boyden in London, reviewing the general business climate and Boyden's search activities, with potted biographies of the consultants; a general brochure about Boyden's approach to executive search; and a large format international brochure, mainly concerned with the firm's interest in the USA.
Style, approach, future plans Chapter 1 described how Boyden was one of the first of the international search firms to come to Britain. It enjoyed early success led by the highly-regarded Reece Hatchitt, but then experienced problems from the mid-1970s to the early 1980s. The departure of the then President of Boyden

International in March 1984 marked the beginning of recovery and a period of rapid growth worldwide. Michael Curlewis and his colleagues have helped to turn the business around, although they decided not to become as deeply involved in the Big Bang as they might have done, especially in comparison with Russell Reynolds. Instead, they have established a lucrative market working for international commercial banks, helped by their worldwide network. They have achieved a high level of growth over the last few years, with a remarkable number of searches per consultant, helped by the prominent role played by researchers. The present consultants have strong international backgrounds, with Michael Curlewis having been a senior partner with Coopers & Lybrand in Tehran and acting as the principal financial adviser to the Iranian Government on international oil consortium operations there; Andrew Garner has a background in international marketing with Mars Electronics; Nigel Godwin has experience of banking in the USA, and for a Canadian and a Mexican bank in London; Peter Skala was based in Chicago and Brussels, principally in food-related industries; and David Hutt managed two businesses across Europe and before then an Australian company. Internationally, Boyden is moving in exciting new directions. For example, in New York, the firm has established a special Japan Division, headed by a Japanese national, to help Japanese clients in the USA to add American managers to their teams, and to identify Japanese managers in the USA who might return to their homeland in executive positions with Japan-based multinational subsidiaries; a Japanese specialist with a similar role in Europe now operates from Germany. Even more significant, Boyden seems to be breaking completely new ground by having formed a relationship with the leading recruiting firm in India. It has become the first of the large firms to rejoin the Association of Executive Search Consultants in the USA, which appears to be gaining a new respect.

Reputation Boyden has an apparently high success rate of about 80%, but is not generally known for the really high-level searches where the market would appear to be more or less cornered by Russell Reynolds and Norman Broadbent. The firm regards as its best asset long experience in the headhunting business, and takes pride in its openness and honesty with both clients and candidates which, from their comments, would appear to be justified. Michael Curlewis particularly exemplifies this aspect of Boyden's reputation, with a refreshing directness in attitude and in his belief that he can help candidates as much as they can help him. He spoke particularly of one executive placed in a new hi-tech venture, who enjoyed a rise in earnings from £30 000 to £70 000 when the company's business increased tenfold. This particular executive had initially been most reluctant to move; Curlewis declared, 'I spent months dragging him up from the beach.' More recent – and higher-level – assignments include the search for an MD Europe for Murjani/Coca-Cola clothes, and on behalf of the organisation currently involved in the building of the Channel Tunnel. The firm also found the MD of the leading British sailboat manufacturer, Sadler, just as it went into receivership, suggesting the wide variety of Boyden's work.

CANNY BOWEN & ASSOCIATES LIMITED

Dorland House
14–16 Regent Street
SW1Y 4PH
01–839 2561
Fax 01–925 2690

Consultants in London J. Robin Russell, J. Michael Brown, Robert Usher, Basil Evans, James Curtis and Mrs C. Bond.
Founded in London 1967, originally established in New York in 1954.
Owned by The directors operating in the business, without outside shareholdings.
Worldwide 63 principals with 42 research staff working within Amrop International, of which Canny Bowen is a member: this organisation has offices in Amsterdam, Argentina, Austria, Berlin, Boston, Brussels, Buenos Aires, Copenhagen, Dusseldorf, Frankfurt, Hamburg, Hong Kong, Ireland, Johannesburg, Kuala Lumpur, London, Melbourne, Milan, Montreal, Munich, New York, Paris, São Paulo, Singapore, Spain, Sydney, Toronto and Zurich.
Annual fee income and number of assignments $30–40m. worldwide, 820; including 70 in London; *Executive Recruiter News* quotes total billings for year ending May 1988 as $26m., ranking ninth worldwide.
Basis of charges The firm charges a fee based on a percentage of the successful candidate's first year's remuneration, but in certain cases a fixed fee will be quoted which relates to the importance of the search to the client and the degree of difficulty involved. International searches may be subject to a special quotation, but in all cases a minimum fee of £15000 operates, charged in three equal instalments at intervals of 30, 60 and 90 days following authorisation of the search.
Guarantees If the position has not been filled by the end of the invoicing period, the search will continue on expenses only; if an executive recruited by Canny Bowen leaves within a year for reasons of his or her own deficiency which Canny Bowen should have uncovered but did not, or leaves through his or her own volition for reasons which are not of the client's making, the firm will repeat the assignment for no further professional fee.
Sector specialism Canny Bowen see themselves as a broad-based firm, operating in all the market sectors; the principals have special skills and experience in consumer goods, hi-tech, oil, chemicals and engineering.
Functional specialism The firm works mainly at the main board level, and within division boards of plcs.
Salary range £45000+.
Associated and other activities The firm specialises exclusively in executive search, but does also provide advice on the management resource implications of acquisition, divestment, diversification, expansion into new geographical areas and products, leveraged buy-outs and in start-up situations.
Publications Small brochure describing Canny Bowen and Amrop International, briefly introducing their style, background, approach and international capability, with inserts describing the consultants; *The British Chief Executive; Time Allocation Review; Company Performance; The Future*, based on completed questionnaires received from over a hundred CEOs from the 500 largest companies in the UK; *US Presidential Study* produced by Canny Bowen in the USA, analysing the opinions of nearly 200 American CEOs; and a large brochure with photographs and résumés of all the Amrop International principals worldwide.

Style, approach, future plans The firm is strongly research-based, and the partners pride themselves on their ethical and thorough approach. They also justifiably point to their wide spectrum of interests: Robin Russell, a graduate of St Andrews University, worked in industry and engineering with the De La Rue Group and founded an oil distribution company for one of the oil giants; Michael Brown graduated from Cambridge before his 20 years in Shell all over the world. Basil Evans graduated from Imperial College London, and spent eleven years as MD of an engineering company before becoming a director in a merchant bank's corporate finance division. Robert Usher, the youngest Canny Bowen consultant, was educated at Sandhurst before serving as a regular officer in the Scots Guards in Europe and the Far East, from which he entered banking.

Overall, the firm is seen as low profile, very discreet, seeking to offer a high quality service without necessarily concentrating on pushing to increase its volume of business. With the approach of 1992, the Amrop connection, bringing together 14 offices in Europe, will assume even greater importance. Plans are well advanced for a United Amrop in Europe, specialising in identifying Euro-managers. Relatively rare among search firms, Canny Bowen features a management consistency in which there has been only one change – due to retirement – since its foundation in 1967. Although one partner is assigned to each search, to ensure continuity and quality a second partner will be consulted at all key stages as 'devil's advocate'.

Reputation Canny Bowen is well known for its high level of repeat business; for example, it has worked for one medium-sized engineering plc for sixteen years, having undertaken 23 assignments for them. It has enjoyed a similarly close relationship with a financial services group over a ten-year period.

CARRÉ, ORBAN & PARTNERS INTERNATIONAL

7 Curzon Street
W1Y 7FL
01–491 1266
Fax 01–491 4609

Consultants in London Charles Betz (Managing Director), Peter Giblin (Chairman) and Giles Brady (Director).
Founded in London 1982, originally established in Brussels by Georges Orban and Michael Carré in 1978, with offices in Geneva and Paris that same year.
Owned by A privately-held group.
Worldwide Offices – all wholly-owned subsidiaries – in Amsterdam, Barcelona, Brussels, Dusseldorf, Geneva, Madrid, Milan, New York, Paris, Rome and Zurich.
Annual fee income and number of assignments Billings of $13m. from about 600 corporate clients were achieved in 1986; the estimated fee income for 1987–9 is confidential.
Basis of charges This information is regarded as confidential and is discussed with clients only; but all fees are agreed with the client before an assignment is commenced.
Guarantees The firm undertakes to complete all assignments to the client's and the candidate's satisfaction.
Sector specialism The firm's London office has a balanced concentration on financial markets, in marketing and management. In 1986 assignments worldwide were industrial products and services, 36%; consumer products and services 27%; holdings, banks and insurance companies, 26%; other services (medical, software, trading, shipping) and Government and international institutions, 4%. This has not changed dramatically since.
Functional specialism 22% of Carré Orban searches in 1986 were for presidents, CEOs, general managers or Board members; 20% for marketing, sales and diversification executives; 18% for finance and accounting executives; 21% for banks and insurance executives; 11% for senior specialists (Information Technology, Legal, Personnel, R&D traders) and 8% for manufacturing and engineering executives.
Salary range About 40% of searches are for positions paying £100 000 a year or more; 21% are for below £50 000.
Association and other activities The firm offers, separate from its search activities, a management appraisal service, providing clients with objective, confidential assessments of the strengths and weaknesses of their key executives, in relation to corporate strategies, especially prior to significant corporate changes such as reorganisations or acquisitions. These assessments may evaluate a functional segment of the management or provide a comprehensive audit of the client's human resources. The firm's management consultancy service includes searches for suitable businesses as merger or acquisition candidates. Services have ranged from assistance in defining strategic objectives to the integration of acquired companies, for clients in Europe, the USA and Japan. Carré Orban's management consultancy work may include the comprehension and definition of client strategy; confidential industry screening and evaluation; approaches to acquisition targets; selection of acquisition targets; negotiations and integration of the acquired company.
Publications *Carré Orban Annual Report*, produced in English, French and German, which includes overseas addresses, a statistical review, the firm's

approach to search and management consultancy and notes on the professional staff worldwide; the firm also contributed substantially to an article in *Business Week* of 18 August 1986.

Style, approach, future plans The firm has grown steadily by an annual rate of between 30% and 50% from 1981, recording 32% growth in 1987, which has been sustained. It attributes much of that success to its emphasis on personal networking between offices. The inception and growth of Carré Orban has been based on what the organisation calls a one-firm concept, in which all offices are interdependent and multi-resourced, i.e. one particular office might be handling a specific assignment, but they may call upon the resources within other offices. The firm sees itself as a group of professional practitioners as opposed to academicians or accountants, strongly consultancy-based, concentrating on the needs of their clients and establishing a firm basis for effective client relationship management. It aims to become a temporary extension of the client, bringing its accumulated skills, techniques and contacts to bear on the client's behalf; this is seen as more important than growth as an end in itself. The London office reflects the firm's strongly international flavour, run by American Charles Betz, a graduate of the American Graduate School, Stanford and the London Business School, who had previously worked as Regional Vice-President for the Nordic Region of the Bank of America in London and had been Vice-President of Administration for the Bank of America in New York. Fellow American Peter Giblin, who graduated from Columbia and Yale, previously Managing Director of Samuel Montagu, is also based in London. Hilary Sears, one of the most outstanding women consultants in executive search, referred to in Chapter 4, used to work for Carré Orban.

Reputation The firm is seen as a highly professional international and multi-national consultancy-based practice, with a name for quality and attention to detail. It may arguably be seen rather like a smaller and more recently-formed version of Egon Zehnder, but they dispute this, claiming they are more important in some particular markets. The level of repeat business is 74%, with a substantial proportion of new clients from referrals. A particularly successful search, quoted in *Business Week*, was the appointment of Anthony Lund, previously head of Shearson Lehman Brothers in Britain, to become CEO of European Banking Corp., the British subsidiary of Amsterdam-Rotterdam Bank; this was a nine-month effort, spanning five countries and seriously considering over 60 candidates, for which Carré Orban's resources were ideally suited.

CLIVE & STOKES INTERNATIONAL

14 Bolton Street
W1Y 8JL
01–408 0370
Fax 01–493 1322

Consultants in London Hamish Kidd, Malcolm Campbell, Bryan McCleery, Alan Tipper and Michael Springman, with two more consultants in Leeds.
Founded in London 1959.
Owned by A. H. Kidd, 80% and D. M. Morgan, 20%, as a limited company.
Worldwide Part of ISA, a partnership of independent firms with offices in Amsterdam, Athens, Atlanta, Boston, Brussels, Chicago, Cleveland, Dallas, Frankfurt, Guadalajara, Leeds, Los Angeles, Melbourne, Mexico City, Miami, New York, Newport Beach, Paris, San Francisco, San José, São Paulo, Stockholm, Tampa and Toronto.
Annual fee income and number of assignments London, £1m., 63.
Basis of charges The average fee per assignment is approximately £16 000, based on one-third of the first year's remuneration, invoiced in three equal parts at the end of the first, second and third months. Expenses incurred during the assignment are invoiced monthly.
Guarantees If it is felt that an inappropriate appointment has been made, and the firm bears some responsibility, the assignment is repeated at no further fee.
Sector specialism Manufacturing (with an emphasis on electronics and hi-tech), commerce, retailing, financial services and the City, the service industries and the professions. The 63 assignments conducted in 1987–8 were distributed accordingly: financial services, 14%; professions, 11%; not for profit/ Government, 3%; consumer products, 13%; hi-tech, 10%; energy, 5%; manufacturing industry, 20%; building, construction, property, 8%; distributive trades, 14%; service industry, the remainder.
Functional specialism Many chief executive assignments, and mostly Board-level work assignments in 1987–8 were for general management, 32%; sales/ marketing, 13%; finance, 19%; production, 9%; R&D/technical, 8%; personnel, 8%; professional 8% and systems, 3%.
Salary range From £35 000 to over £100 000.
Association and other activities An organisational consultancy, offering advice to clients.
Publications A brochure is being prepared for publication; the firm has not felt the need for one until now. An ISA brochure is available.
Style, approach, future plans As one of the oldest firms in the business, Clive & Stokes – bought out from the original founding partners by Hamish Kidd in 1980 – is still very traditional but professional. The firm's offices are unglamorous and unpretentious but equipped with modern on-line computerised control systems, research back-up and an in-house data bank containing 20 000 entries. The reception area is gloomy and reminiscent of one of the older gentlemen's clubs. The consultants are jovial and friendly but ethical, cautious and critical of younger and newer rivals. Hamish Kidd, whose background has been in general management consulting, is proprietorial about his firm, feeling that executive search itself is even more rewarding when running one's own company and he also undertakes various organisational consulting assignments. He has been asked why, in view of the fact that Clive & Stokes has been in existence for nearly 30 years, this firm has not grown more than it has; he insists that the aim has always been to provide the highest-quality service, not the largest volume

growth. Although the firm has to be a minimum critical size – probably five consultants – to afford the systems and research overheads but not necessarily glamorous office, the optimum size may not be much larger if the firm wants to avoid off-limits problems and also remain closely knit. Clive & Stokes' consultants have been able to convince the most cautious and reluctant clients of the value of executive search as a business tool through their unaggressive and matter-of-fact manner; but because they are so reluctant to appear pushy and sales-orientated, and because they have deliberately not paid attention to marketing and promoting their business, they have inevitably lost out to more dynamic rivals.

Reputation Clive & Stokes would not reveal the names of any of their clients, pointing out that much of their work was confidential in the extreme, including searches to replace existing directors who were unknowingly about to be fired; but they were mentioned by two of the client companies approached in the client survey within Chapter 3, as having provided satsifactory service. The fact that the firm has remained in existence for so long mainly due to repeat business and referrals to other companies by previous clients to some extent speaks for itself.

GODDARD KAY ROGERS & ASSOCIATES LIMITED

Old London House
32 St James's Square
SW1Y 4JR
01–930 5100
Fax 01–930 7470

Consultants in London David Kay (Chairman), Paul Buchanan-Barrow (Managing Director), Ron Begley, Dickie Birch Reynardson, Brian Burwash, Gill Carrick, Andrew Clowes, Graham Potter, Simon Pratt, Sir John Trelawny and Paul Turner.
Founded in London 1970.
Owned by The partners, as a private UK company.
Worldwide 28 consultants worldwide, with a total staff of 42 in London; offices in Bath, Dusseldorf, Frankfurt, Leeds, Madrid, Manchester, Tokyo, Atlanta and Dallas in the US and a research office in Hong Kong.
Annual fee income and number of assignments UK an estimated £6.5m.; worldwide approximately £10m.; the firm would not reveal their number of assignments per year, but did indicate that those completed in 1988 reflected an increase of 30% over 1987, and growth has continued.
Basis of charges Fees are based on an estimate of the complexity of the assignment and the amount of time that a comprehensive search is likely to take. A proposal is given to the client for agreement prior to the search and the fee is due and payable at each of the following stages: a third on commencement of the assignment as a retainer, a third on submission of the short list and a third on the acceptance by the candidate of an offer, and when he or she has signed up with the client.
Guarantees Since the firm is not paid the second instalment of its fee until suitable candidates are produced, it is obviously in GKR's interest, as well their clients', to find the successful candidate for an assignment as soon as possible. In eighteen years of search, only two successful candidates have left their employment within six months of their appointment. The firm does not apparently offer a specific guarantee.
Sector specialism Financial services, 35%; professional services, 21%; manufacturing, 22%; construction, 5%; distribution, 7%; petroleum, 4%; food and drink, 6%.
Functional specialism Senior management, 30%; finance, 20%; operations, 18%; marketing, 11%; personnel, 10%; legal, 11%.
Salary range £50 000+ in London; £35 000+ in other UK offices. 1988 assignments according to salary range were 37% up to £75 000; 41% between £75 000 and £100 000; 22% over £100 000.
Associated and other activities GKR is engaged in top-level executive search only.
Publications *Annual Report* 1988–9, which analyses the past year's business, both regionally and in terms of assignments, and includes a useful flow diagram of the search process as GKR sees it.
Style, approach, future plans GKR are among the most low profile of all search firms, to the extent that it has been very difficult to make contact with consultants to gauge an impression of the firm's style. They clearly place a great deal of importance on the quality of their research, as they employ more than 20 researchers in the UK. They see their work as so discreet and professional that they scorn all publicity, but this has not apparently been bad for business; as we

saw in Chapter 1, this firm has become an immensely profitable concern, and other headhunters complain that, without trying, GKR turn away more business than many smaller firms can hope to attract. Yet they are not particularly interested in volume growth, being more interested in reputation than size. The firm's aim in the future is to expand further into the USA, Europe and the Pacific basin.

GKR's offices, based like many others in St James' and Piccadilly, have not suffered the intrusion of modern trappings, they have preserved the dignified and historical interiors of the Bishop's residence for which purpose their building previously served. The consultants have impressive commercial and industrial backgrounds, and quickly win respect in even the most cautious Boardrooms. David Kay, an Oxford graduate, worked for ICI, Rank Xerox and the Bechtel Corporation before joining another search firm – Alexander Hughes – and then helping set up GKR. Paul Buchanan-Barrow, educated at the University of St Andrews, joined Cadbury's export department before working at IBM UK, selling computers to the Government; then he ran County Bank's advertising and PR, finally planning the strategic development of the National Westminster Group in international capital markets before coming to GKR in 1986. The increases in UK business for the firm during 1988 continued in two of its sectors in particular: management consulting partners in the major accountancy firms and commercial partners in the ambitious and expanding law firms. This demand is likely to be sustained. GKR have also been active recruiting in corporate financial and investor relations management, and in non-executive directors.

Reputation The firm enjoys at least 70% repeat business, higher than many of their competitors, without having had to put great resources into business development. Companies in the client survey in Chapter 3 praised GKR particularly highly, and other headhunters consistently speak well of them. In keeping with their image, they were not prepared themselves to mention the names of any clients. GKR was both best-known and favourably regarded by respondents of a MORI survey conducted among human resource directors of *The Times 500* companies.

HEIDRICK AND STRUGGLES INTERNATIONAL, INC.

100 Piccadilly
W1V 9FN
01–491 3124
Fax 01–734 9581

Consultants in London Dr John Viney (Managing Partner), Dr Peter Basset, Mina Gouran, Peter Breen, Robert Meadows, Nick Fitzgerald, Geoff Brown, Penny Powell, Les Hart, Richard Wall and Mark Weedon.
Founded in London 1968, first established in Chicago in 1953.
Owned by The international partners in Europe and the USA.
Worldwide 130 consultants and over 200 support staff in Atlanta, Barcelona, Boston, Brussels, Chicago, Cleveland, Dallas, Dusseldorf, Frankfurt, Greenwich, Houston, Los Angeles, Madrid, Menlo Park, Minneapolis, Munich, New York, Paris, San Francisco, Toronto, Washington and Zurich.
Annual fee income and number of assignments London, £4.6m., over 170; worldwide, $48m., nearly 1500 in 1988; according to a survey in *Fortune*, global recruiting fees were $38.9m. in 1987. *Business Week* published 1988 revenues of $55m.
Basis of charges Fees are agreed with the client in advance, based on one-third of the first year's compensation, payable in three equal stages: authorisation, one month later and two months later, plus VAT and expenses. The minimum fee chargeable in the UK is £18000 per assignment.
Guarantees If the search is not completed after three months, the firm will continue to work on an expenses-only basis for up to a further six months. If the candidate is dismissed or leaves the client for reasons outside the control of the client, the firm will reinstate the search for expenses only. The firm operates Europe-wide practice matrices in financial services (Fin$earch), IT (TekSearch) and for multinational clients (TNS).
Sector specialism Financial services, information technology, health care, professional practices, consumer products and retail.
Functional specialism Mostly general management at Board level, but also finance, sales and marketing, manufacturing, research and development, personnel and information technology.
Salary range £50000+
Associated and other activites ESE Consultants was acquired to handle searches for younger executives for positions with salaries from £30000 to £45000, with a minimum fee of £13000, turnover £700000 in 1988–9.
Publications Besides the international brochure, Heidrick & Struggles publishes research reports on particular functional skills and management trends, including *Le Talent de Diriger*, 1985; *The University and College President*, 1987; *The Role of the Chairman*, 1987; *The Managing Partner and Partnership Firms* 1989, and *The Information Technology Director*, forthcoming, 1989.
Style, approach, future plans The growth of Heidrick and Struggles in London has been discussed in Chapter 1: the firm's strong leadership since the arrival of John Viney has enabled it to become one of the major players, through attracting a range of new clients and developing a comprehensive research base. The next phase of growth is being geared towards the Far East, where Heidrick and Struggles is seeking representation initially through acquisition. Overall, the firm sees itself as outgoing, open and very much of today, the most clearly contemporary of the major firms. Certainly the consultants are significantly younger than many of their competitors, both in terms of actual age and, more

significantly, in terms of outlook and approach. Yet this is not at the cost of industry experience, consulting background or professional qualifications. They are enthusiastic rather than pushy, confident rather than arrogant, energetic rather than laid-back. The partners are flexible in approach, internationally-focused, but at the same time with a distinct boutique style, concentrating on clients matching their own outlook. They argue that their attitude to executive search and their close attention to detail in their work enable them to attract both important clients with challenging problems and high-quality candidates to help solve them. There is an exceptionally strong emphasis on research, with as many researchers as consultants; and research is seen as a training ground, as discussed in Chapter 4. The firm seems to be the least susceptible to PR hype and clients are clearly treated as equals; the consultants are neither overbearing nor obsequious. The glamorous new offices at 100 Piccadilly are practical and workmanlike, the Boardroom's specially-commissioned modern art freize depicting an abstract view of headhunting in both its interpretations – although not to everyone's taste – is a welcome change for the usual hunting prints and scenes of old London.

Reputation The firm's reputation has grown substantially since the arrival of Dr John Viney in 1985, as attested by three clients in the client survey within Chapter 3, including Kingfisher. Others speaking highly of the firm include Quaker, Reebok, Moss Bros, Midland Bank, Nomura, Salomon Brothers and the Hongkong and Shanghai Banking Corporation. The firm is often scorned by competitors for its apparent youth culture, but admired by several firms for its attitude to the importance of research. One occupational psychologist who had come into contact with Heidrick and Struggles through applying psychometric testing to their candidates saw them as one of the premier firms in this regard.

ALEXANDER HUGHES & ASSOCIATES UK LIMITED

4/5 De Walden Court
85 New Cavendish Street
W1M 7RA
01–636 9184

Consultants in London Bert Young (Chairman), Ian Telfer (Managing Director), James Hollins, Jim Mackay, Jeremy Melhuish and Elaine Sunderland.
Founded in London 1964.
Owned by Director-shareholders, the consultants themselves.
Worldwide Part of ES International Group, a partnership of independent firms; a total of 63 staff in Barcelona, Brussels, Chicago, Dallas, Honolulu, Madrid, Milan, New York, Paris, São Paulo, The Hague, and Tokyo.
Annual fee income and number of assignments London, £1m., 65; worldwide, £17m., 700.
Basis of charges All assignments are on a quoted fee basis. Average fees are £15 000. Fees are invoiced over a 60 day period.
Guarantees Assignments will be continued beyond the 60-day period as long as is necessary to provide clients with a short list of quality candidates. Otherwise specific guarantees are not provided.
Sector specialism Industrial and manufacturing, 41% (engineering – process, electrical, electronic and mechanical; building and construction; paper, printing and packaging; chemical; energy and mining); retail and consumer goods, 18% (FMCGs; consumer durables; distributive and retail trades; leisure industries); information technology and communications, 12% (media – press and publishing, radio and television; advertising – PR and market research agencies; information technology and data processing); financial services, 21% (banking, insurance, building societies, investment services, chartered accountancy and business consultancy); public sector, 8% and other professional services.
Functional specialism Chief executives and general management, 33%; sales and marketing, 20%; personnel, 12%; production and technical, 12%; finance, 23%.
Salary range £40 000+, with 30% over £50 000.
Associated and other activities No other associated companies in other activities, but advertised recruitment is offered when appropriate to the particular assignment, and a counselling service is available for chief executives and Board members on organisation and management matters. Psychometric testing and assessment is carried out by Jim Mackay.
Publications Brochure, with diagram of search methodology, and inserts listing names and addresses of members of ES International Group, analysis of previous assignments of Alexander Hughes by sector and function, and personal information and photographs of consultants, research associates and the research manager; various articles in the national and business press, including *The Times*, 22 January 1987, p. 25 (Bert Young on the importance of decision-making chief executives in British business) and *The Times*, 12 November 1987, p. 35 (Elaine Sunderland on emancipation in the Boardroom: challenging for prizes in the former male club).
Style, approach, future plans Alexander Hughes and the other companies in the ES International Group are strongly research-orientated and are deliberately small and specialised, seeking quality rather than quantity and not geared towards dramatic growth or maximising turnover of business. The firm aims to subject every assignment to a particularly thorough analytical review before

commencing an intensive, systematic search programme, developed over its 25 years of operation. All candidates are referenced and checked before they are considered for the short list and before they are presented to the client. The consultants are businesslike without stuffiness, quietly professional but not slick or showy, with a good mix of academic and commercial credentials. Bert Young is down-to-earth, knowledgeable and precise if slightly bossy, and clearly proud of his long association with headhunting; Elaine Sunderland is one of the outstanding women in this business. The offices are reminiscent of an upper-middle class town house, chintzy and comfortable rather than glamorous and ritzy or brash and hi-tech. Very British in style and approach, Alexander Hughes would especially suit the smaller, more old-established client – generally British rather than multinational in ownership – seeking sympathetic and not necessarily revolutionary attention to its recruiting and general management problems.

Reputation The firm enjoys a high level of repeat business – of at least 75% – through its emphasis on maintaining client goodwill, and its long tradition in executive search. Successful assignments, attested by clients, include placing the member for finance and central services of the Civil Aviation Authority; the Director-General of the Irish Management Institute; the Chief Executive of the British Technology Group; the Personnel Director for British Rail; the Group Finance Director for Meyer International; the Group Marketing Director for Wedgwood; and the Head of the Legal Department for British American Tobacco. The firm has also advised the Boards of Renault in France and Hickson International, but 80% of its clients are UK-based.

KORN/FERRY INTERNATIONAL LIMITED (*see also under* **John Stork**)

Norfolk House
31 St James's Square
SW1Y 4JL
01–930 4334
Fax 01–930 8085

Consultants in London Stephen Rowlinson (Chief Executive), Simon Clay, Michael Brandon, Edward Kelley, Earl LeGrand, Madeleine Stanford, Fiona Barltrop, Lucinda Skeggs, Yvonne Sarch, Jane Pollard and Colin Grand-Wilson.
Founded in London In 1973, through the acquisition of G. K. Dickinson, established in 1967; Korn/Ferry was originally established in the USA in 1969.
Owned by Majority shares by Lester Korn and Dick Ferry – just over 25% each – in the USA, with other international partners holding the remainder.
Worldwide 550 staff, with offices in Amsterdam, Atlanta, Boston, Brussels, Caracas, Chicago, Cleveland, Dallas, Denver, Frankfurt, Geneva, Guadalajara, Hong Kong, Houston, Kuala Lumpur, Los Angeles, Madrid, Melbourne, Mexico City, Milan, Minneapolis, Monterrey, Newport Beach, New York, Palo Alto, Paris, Rio de Janeiro, San Francisco, São Paulo, Seattle, Singapore, Stamford, Sydney, Tokyo, Toronto, Washington DC and Zurich. Korn/Ferry also has offices in Scandinavia through the merger with John Stork.
Annual fee income and number of assignments London, an estimated £2.8m., approximately 110, with figures for 1989 estimated as £3.5m. and 150; worldwide, $95m.; around 2000. 1989 final results could be much higher as a result of the merger with John Stork.
Basis of charges On one-third of the first year's annual earnings. There is a fixed minimum fee of £15 000, invoiced in three equal stages on day one, day 30 and day 60 from confirmation, with expenses charged additionally.
Guarantees All clients retain the right to cancel an assignment within the first 90 days, should the unforeseen occur and an appointment be no longer necessary. In this case charges are made only for those professional hours actually expended. Korn/Ferry will reactivate a search, at no additional fee charge, in the event that a candidate leaves within a six-month period, for reasons other than the failure of the client to adhere to the agreed conditions of employment.
Sector specialism There are specialist divisions relating to financial services, hi-tech, the Middle East and Africa, general consultancy, hotel and leisure, multinationals and the public sector. Key sectors are banking, energy, public sector, electronics, professional services, consumer marketing and retailing.
Functional specialism Chairman/chief executive, 38%; banking, 20%; finance/administration/MIS, 17%; marketing/sales, 10%; personnel, 5%; manufacturing, 4%; other 6%.
Salary range £40 000, 15%; £50 000, 20%; £60 000, 15%; £70 000, 15%; £80 000, 10%; £80 000+, 25%.
Associated and other activities None outside high-level executive search.
Publications Brochure, with addresses of offices worldwide, general notes on executive search, including a statement of Code of Business Conduct; and a series of studies including *The Independent Director in the British Company* (with the Oxford Centre for Management Studies), *The Outside Director of the Public Corporation* (with the University of Pennsylvania Law School), *The Nominating Committee: Trends in Selecting Directors of Major US Corporations* (with the Yale School of Organisation and Management), *Korn/Ferry International's Executive Profile: A Survey of Corporate Leaders* (with the Graduate School of Managment,

UCLA), *National Index of Executive Vacancies* (published quarterly in the USA), *Boards of Directors Study* (annually in the USA), *Boards of Directors Study* (annually in the UK), *Boards of Directors Study* (annually in Australia), *British Corporate Leaders – A profile* (with the London Business School), *Profile of a Successful Personnel Executive* (with the Graduate School of Management, UCLA), *Repatriating the Multinational Executive* and *Profile of Women Senior Executives* (with the Graduate School of Management, UCLA).

Style, approach, future plans As discussed in Chapter 1, Korn/Ferry entered the London market through taking over an indigenous firm. It has been recently developed by Stephen Rowlinson, who took over in May 1985 and replaced a number of consultants with fellow-McKinsey people. In contrast with a boutique firm like Heidrick and Struggles, Korn/Ferry has more of a general approach, offering a senior recruiting service for a large number of clients across a range of functions and sectors. The consultants are a mixture of personalities: from the easy-going, approachable American style of Ed Kelley, to the mature Simon Clay and the determined, uncompromising Stephen Rowlinson. Korn/Ferry is the most ambitious and expansionist of the leading firms, seeking to open more and more branches in new areas worldwide, as discussed in Chapter 7; Rowlinson maintains that in the next decade, Korn/Ferry will become twice as large as any other search firm in London. A recent move in this direction has been the merger with John Stork's London and Scandinavian offices in December 1988. With revenues of $91.5m. worldwide, Korn/Ferry was described by *Business Week* as aggressively expanding.

Reputation Many of the companies in the client survey in Chapter 3 referred to extensive use of Korn/Ferry's services and were generally satisfied; however, a minority expressed some reservations. Korn/Ferry seems to have acquired a reputation for relatively speedy solutions, and it could be domineering in manner and tended to dictate its views strongly. Korn/Ferry was criticised by one survey respondent as having a formula approach and concentrating on developing its volume business. Yet Korn/Ferry is, on the whole, generally more highly spoken of by clients than by fellow-headhunters, who have made attacking Korn/Ferry a corporate sport. Inevitably, the largest headhunting firm in the world attracts the dislike of its rivals, and there must be an element of sour grapes in this.

Stephen Rowlinson quotes the latest findings of a MORI survey conducted among Human Resource Directors of *The Times 500*, which shows that Korn/Ferry was regarded 'favourably' by 33% of respondents. The survey identified the three most 'favoured' search firms in the UK as GKR (34%), Korn/Ferry (33%), and Spencer Stuart (32%); the remaining ratings were Whitehead Mann (29%), Heidrick and Struggles (25%), Egon Zehnder (24%), Russell Reynolds (19%) and Norman Broadbent (9%). The lower-rated firms probably have fewer dealings with human resource directors, and have greater contact with CEOs and MDs.

MERTON ASSOCIATES (CONSULTANTS) LIMITED

Merton House
70 Grafton Way
W1P 5LE
01–388 2051
Fax 01–387 5324

Consultants in London Michael Silverman (Managing Director), Air Vice-Marshal William L. Gill (Chairman), Christopher Ashton, John Gelling, Ian Hamilton, Bryan Thomas and Clive Baker.
Founded in London 1976.
Owned by The partners, as an independent private company.
Worldwide Merton has another office in Leeds, with five consultants, and is part of Transearch, an international network of independent search firms. With 225 staff including 73 consultants; the organisation has offices in Adelaide, Barcelona, Brussels, Chicago, Dusseldorf, Essen, Hilversum, Milan, Oslo, Paris, São Paulo, Singapore, Stockholm, Tokyo and Toronto.
Annual fee income and number of assignments In the UK, £2.3m., 103; worldwide, excluding London, $2.3m., 58.
Basis of charges 35% of the agreed notional gross remuneration, payable in three stages: on commissioning of the assignment, on the submission of a short list, and on completion. Work may be charged on a daily rate and modest expenses, charged separately, are quoted in advance. For management consultancy work, fees are based upon an all-inclusive charge per consultant per day. Work within the area of acquisitions, divestments and mergers is undertaken only to meet specific objectives. Fees are chargeable based on time spent within a pre-agreed budget.
Guarantees Should employment of the candidate be terminated within a year of appointment, in circumstances which would reasonably indicate that the candidate did not meet the agreed criteria for the appointment, the firm will repeat the assignment free of charge.
Sector specialism consumer products, retail and distribution, 16%; financial and professional services, 14%; food and drink, 13%; hi-tech, aerospace and defence, 14%; property and construction, 20%; hotels, catering and leisure, 11%; manufacturing and engineering, 9%; healthcare, 2% and public sector, 1%.
Functional specialism Chairmen, Board members, chief executives, 26%; marketing and sales, 18%; production, manufacturing, engineering, 15%; finance and administration, 13%; general management, subsidiary Board directors, 12%; property and construction specialists, 9%; personnel, 6%; and non-executive directors, 1%.
Salary range Over £100 000, 11%; £75 000–£100 000, 18%; £50 000–£75 000, 48%; below £50 000, 23%.
Associated and other activities Management consultancy advice, including the compilation of industry surveys, especially related to salaries; services in connection with acquisitions, divestments and mergers.
Publications Brochure, outlining the Merton approach to executive search and management consultancy and describing the Transearch network; surveys on 'Board Directors' Executive Remuneration', 'Rewards for Management: Ghost Share Option Schemes', 'The Reorganisation of the National Health Sevice', 'Remuneration in Conglomerate PLCs' and 'Living and Working in Hong Kong'; Managing Director Michael Silverman has featured extensively in the press on

executive search and problems of industry as a whole, from an early article on the impact of rising house prices in restricting the movement of executives ('The High Price of Mobility', *Management Today*, June 1980) to a recent exposé of unsatisfactory service from British Telecom in a number of national newspapers. **Style, approach, future plans** The origins of Merton and its market research-based approach are discussed in Chapter 1; the firm sees a client company as a market place, and an executive as a product, with the overall need to establish maximum brand share. As part of this strategy, Merton views investment in information technology as of high priority: the resources it has established are examined in Chapter 4, featuring an insight into the work of Robert Birkett, the firm's research manager. Future plans include seeking to expand their inter-European operations with the advent of 1992, and further developing their management consultancy business to offer a wide range of services to key clients. The atmosphere at Merton's Fitzrovia-based office is professional and industrious, but also convivial and relatively relaxing, especially compared with the somewhat daunting formality of headhunters' reception rooms in St James'. The partners' backgrounds are largely more industry- than consulting-based, and thus they deal with businessmen on a level; helped by well-researched industry analysis, they take a real interest in their work, looking at it in the context of the sector as a whole, rather than just in terms of each assignment. **Reputation** Over the last ten years, repeat business has grown from 60% to over 80%, aided by the fact that Merton is able to offer management consultancy services as well as executive search to its clients. As discussed in Chapter 1, Merton has undertaken several prestigious assignments, including searches in connection with Rosehaugh Stanhope's Broadgate development; finding aerospace engineers for Canadair; and tracking down new sector directors for Tesco during its expansion and reorganisation period. The firm has tendered for and won important assignments in the public sector, such as for Deputy Chief Executive of the Crown Estate Commissioners, completed in December 1987. Merton has also worked on a search for Westminster City Council and, at the end of 1988 completed an assignment leading to the appointment of a new Land Steward for the Western District of The Duchy of Cornwall.

CHRISTOPHER MILL AND PARTNERS

Russell Chambers
Covent Garden
WC2E 8AA
01–379 5996
Fax 01–836 4587

Consultants in London Christopher Mill (Managing Partner), Paul Paroissien, Allan Cummings and two others.
Founded in London 1977.
Owned by Christopher Mill.
Worldwide Total staff of 30, in London and associates in San Francisco, Washington DC, (Leon A. Farley Associates), Melbourne (Fish and Nankwell Pty), and Hong Kong (Wilfred Chan Management Consultants Ltd).
Annual fee income and number of assignments Worldwide, including associate firms approximately £2.4m.; 120.
Basis of charges A fixed fee is agreed with the client, normally one-third of the first year's cash remuneration forecast for the position, which is charged in three equal parts over the duration of the assignment.
Guarantees The firm undertakes to continue the search until there is agreement that all sensible avenues have been satisfactorily explored. If a placement leaves within one year the firm undertakes to conduct a further search, charging only out-of-pocket expenses. The firm will not approach any employee of the client organisation for two years after a search.
Sector specialism Manufacturing, with particular emphasis on hi-tech industries such as computing, communications and automation; professional services, especially management consultancy; financial services, including venture capital; and international operations including multi-country searches.
Functional specialism Senior positions across a variety of functions.
Salary range Average fee in London £20 000, reflecting a range of £40 000–£100 000.
Associated and other activities None but high-level executive search.
Publications Brochures with relevant industry emphasis are produced when they receive an enquiry.
Style, approach, future plans This relatively small firm has succeeded over the last decade through its emphasis on a highly personal consulting approach. The firm's style is quiet, low-key and fairly relaxed with an atmosphere unlike other search firms: its offices in the heart of Covent Garden have lent themselves to arty yet simple and effective interior design, with low ceilings and semi-circular windows. Christopher Mill – a London University Sociology graduate with a Master's degree from the London Business School – claims a strong international dimension to his work, having carried out assignments in Western Europe, the Middle East and North America. The emphasis on a consulting approach comes from his previous career in international personnel management with Honey-well Europe and the Memorex Corporation. Mill has no pretensions about his calling and is prepared to look at the human side of search with a sense of humour; but he is closely involved – he has been a member of the Board of Directors – with the Association of Executive Search Consultants in the USA, where until very recently he was Chairman of the International Committee, and he takes a keen interest in the headhunting business as a whole. The early meetings of the Executive Research Association, whose current work is dis-cussed in Chapter 4, were held in these offices.

Reputation Among smaller firms, Christopher Mill was highly spoken of by three respondents in the client survey in Chapter 3, and is generally respected by its competitors. In March 1988, the firm received an award from the American Association of Executive Search Consultants for its 'outstanding contribution to the profession', the sixth such reward made and the first outside the USA. The aim is to become very closely involved in the strategic development of client businesses, offering industry knowledge in several key areas; judging by the relatively high level of repeat business which they apparently enjoy, this is being achieved.

MSL GROUP INTERNATIONAL LIMITED

32 Aybrook Street
W1M 3JL
01–487 5000
Fax 01–487 4374

Consultants in London (Major Contacts) Barry Curnow (Chairman & Chief Executive), John H. Woodger (Director) and John Hodgson (Director).
Founded in London In 1955.
Owned by Saatchi & Saatchi plc as a wholly-owned subsidiary.
Worldwide 200 consultants, in Britain (Belfast, Birmingham, Bristol, Glasgow, Leeds, London, Manchester, Nottingham, and Windsor) and Brussels, Dublin, Dusseldorf, Hong Kong, Lisbon, Milan, Paris, Sydney, Utrecht and Washington DC.
Annual fee income and number of assignments Not disclosed.
Basis of charges Fees and the basis of associated expenses are quoted and agreed in writing when the assignment survey report is presented to the client after the initial briefing discussion. Fees are normally based on the first year's salary to be paid to the successful candidate; some adjustment is made where there is a guaranteed bonus or where a performance-related bonus represents a large proportion of the first year's earnings. Fees are invoiced in stages: when the assignment is authorised, signalling that MSL has been retained, and thereafter fees are invoiced as is appropriate to the progress of the assignment. In terms of expenses, advertising – when used – is charged at normal media rates, and telephone, courier, travel and accommodation charges are passed on when they have been seen as necessary to the assignment.
Guarantees An assignment will be restarted if necessary at no extra cost, but subject to a review of the reasons why the candidate left.
Sector specialism Across a range of sectors, but specialist units operate in marketing, finance, retailing, engineering, information technology, distribution, retail financial services, the public sector and for Middle East clients. Now all MSL consultants have specialist niches, such as in stockbroking, merchant banking, marketing and engineering.
Functional specialism A variety of middle and senior management posts, including specialist positions not always searched, such as for chartered secretaries, for whom four MSL consultants are constantly looking.
Salary range £30 000–£200 000.
Associated and other activities Advertised Selection and Recruitment Advertising.
Publications Two major brochures are available; the UK version states MSL's approach to search and the addresses of UK branches. MSL has also begun to produce a regular *Boardroom Briefing*, which describes the activities of the company and includes various statistical surveys, such as an analysis of motivational factors involved in why a candidate was attracted to a certain position. The MSL Index, which measures advertised demand for managers, executives and senior technical/design/production staff, is well known as a tool for gauging underlying trends in the economy and the general level of business confidence, and press releases of results are issued.
Style, approach, future plans MSL has a wide appeal and extensive coverage of the recruitment field, very much a supermarket-style operation rather than a boutique, but is developing a specialist niche approach in response to market demand over the last four years. MSL has been a very useful training-ground for

a number of researchers and consultants now in the other leading firms, including Dr John Viney of Heidrick and Struggles. It has pioneered much of the technological progress made in the search process in the development of computer-based candidate files. MSL as a brand name in the search business is being further developed in the long term by John Woodger, a food industry man, John Hodgson, a down-to-earth and friendly Cumbrian who handles day-to-day promotion and by Barry Curnow, who used to run the Hay Group. MSL have managed to achieve a workable mix between consultancy work and search; this has been more effective, perhaps, than many of their rivals, including PA. MSL's worldwide coverage is being extended; for example, they previously handled their Far Eastern work through a referral arrangement with an associate company, but now MSL Pacific is being launched as a directly managed operation, run by an experienced Hong Kong search manager, Robert Friend. MSL is also expanding its consulting services, and has set up The Boardroom Appointments Consulting Team to provide a general management perspective in advising clients. After 35 years in the recruiting business, MSL is undergoing evolution rather than revolution, but is adapting to changing demands, especially relating to Europe post-1992.

Reputation The inclusion of MSL here is perhaps surprising because it extensively uses advertising and much of its business is within the marzipan layer of recruitment. However, the firm did play an important part in the early days of search in Britain, and in systematising the recruiting methods of the day, and now handles an increasing number of more senior appointments. Under J. P. P. (John) Smith – who has now left to set up his own firm, Succession Planning Associates – MSL made a strong name for itself in the public sector; this is discussed in case study III in Chapter 5. This part of MSL's work is, because of its nature, more open to analysis, and it would appear that MSL has made greater inroads into this sector than even firms within Britain's Big Eight, such as Korn/Ferry.

NORMAN BROADBENT INTERNATIONAL LIMITED

65 Curzon Street
W1Y 7PE
01–629 9626
Fax 01–629 9900

Consultants in London Miles Broadbent (Chief Executive), Julian Sainty, Nicolas Crosthwaite, Robert Hutton, Ian Jones, Gary Luddington and Christopher Beatson-Hird.
Founded in London 1 July 1983.
Owned by Charles Barker plc.
Worldwide Seven professional staff in London, six in New York and five in Hong Kong; through the International Search Partnership, Norman Broadbent is also represented in Dusseldorf, Milan, Paris, Sydney, Tokyo, Turin and Zurich.
Annual fee income and number of assignments London, around £5m., 180; Hong Kong, around £2m., 110; New York, around £1m., 60.
Basis of charges Details not provided.
Guarantees Details not provided.
Sector specialism 50% in financial services, 50% in industry and commerce.
Functional specialism Chairmen, chief executives and managing directors, 40%; foreign exchange, bond and equity traders and salesmen, over 10%; analysts and fund managers, over 10%; in other finance positions, over 10%; the remainder includes marketing, personnel, technical and legal. International business accounts for nearly a quarter of the company's work.
Salary range £60 000–£400 000 within financial services, of which 35% of assignments were for positions paying more than £100 000; within industry, 20% of placements earned more than £100 000. Only about 20% of Norman Broadbent's work is with positions paying less than £40 000, and these are mainly non-executive directors.
Associated and other activities NB Selection Ltd, opened in London in September 1987, which handles assignments within the salary range £30 000–£60 000. Regionally-based offices are planned for 1989 to a total of eight in number.
Publications Brochure, most recent edition published in March 1989, with a detailed management report and statistical review of searches, followed by photographs and summaries of the consultants' biographies.
Style, approach, future plans In Chapter 1, the origins and development of Norman Broadbent were discussed in the context of the MacGregor and Colin Marshall searches, and the defection of the original partners from Russell Reynolds, emphasising the superb sense of timing involved. The firm specialises exclusively in executive search, rather than offering a range of consulting services, as in the manner of Egon Zehnder. However, it has developed a strong business in middle-management recruitment, with the first of a network of regional offices opened in Slough in January 1989. The London office of NB Selection, with five consultants, handled 116 assignments in 1988. Although a relatively new business, the partners are well used to working with each other from their Russell Reynolds days: David Norman, Miles Broadbent, Julian Sainty, Robert Hutton and Nicolas Crosthwaite have worked together on search assignments over the last eight years, so there is a strong sense of continuity. The consultants have impressive qualifications and strong commercial backgrounds: Miles Broadbent – well known for his recruitment of several industry leaders – graduated from Cambridge, gained an MBA from Harvard, and worked in IBM and Grand Metropolitan; Julian Sainty trained with Pinchin

Denny of the London Stock Exchange, worked for the Anglo-American Corporation, and served as a Business Development Officer with Standard Bank National Industrial Credit Corporation. Nicolas Crosthwaite graduated from the Wharton Business School of the University of Pennsylvania, and spent ten years with Citicorp both in London and New York. Robert Hutton is a chartered engineer, having worked with Tube Investments, Shield Packaging and Sea Containers. Ian Jones is a qualified chartered accountant, ex-Peat Marwick Mitchell, for whom he opened and ran an office in Lyons before becoming UK managing director of Fabergé. They are dedicated and discreet but much more approachable than their close rivals GKR; Miles Broadbent in particular is avuncular and down-to-earth. The firm's new offices in Curzon St. suggest their growing prosperity.

Reputation In 1986, 66% of Norman Broadbent's business was for existing clients, and this level has been maintained. The firm has become increasingly in demand for very high level work, ever since David Norman's recruitment of Ian MacGregor in 1980, as in the recruitment of John Craven for Morgan Grenfell, discussed in Chapter 1. In 1988 the number of assignments to recruit chairmen, CEOs and MDs increased to 30% compared with 28% in 1987 and 26% in 1986. Its reputation for financial services headhunting is arguably equal to that of Russell Reynolds, and accounts for half its work. Some of Miles Broadbent's searches are described by him in Chapter 4. About 1200 searches have been undertaken in the past six years. 82% of the UK assignments granted in 1988 were completed successfully; 19% of them had an international dimension.

RUSSELL REYNOLDS ASSOCIATES INC

24 St James's Square SW1Y 4HZ
01–839 7788
Fax 01–839 9395

Consultants in London David Shellard (Managing Director, Europe), Roderick Gow (Managing Director, London), Bruce Beringer, Olivia Bloomfield, Michael Cottrell, Giles Crewdson, Barry Dow, Patrick Fearon, Caroline Foster, Barry Gould, Mathewson Green, David Henderson, Jane Kingsley, David Moorhouse, John Morris, Robin Rogers, Jeffrey von der Schulenburg, Rae Sedel, Victoria Sharp, Valerie Stogdale, Francis Wilkin and Alan Winton.
Founded in London 1972, originally established in New York in 1969.
Owned by A substantial number of key employees, registered as a private US company. Originally, 60% of shares were held by Russell Reynolds, but this has recently been considerably diluted, especially as a result of the departure of David Norman and his colleagues in 1982–3; although Russell Reynolds is still the holder of the largest single individual block of shares, over 60 senior consultants – about one-third of the firm's total – own a significant amount of equity. Even the US staff pension plan is now invested in shares in the company.
Worldwide 170 professional staff with an overall total, including support staff, of 450 in Boston, Chicago, Cleveland, Dallas, Frankfurt, Hong Kong, Houston, Los Angeles, Madrid, Melbourne, Minneapolis/St Paul, New York, Paris, San Francisco, Singapore, Stamford, Sydney, Tokyo and Washington.
Annual fee income and number of assignments Annual fee income in London in 1988 was £7m. with £10m. estimated for 1989. More than 75 Chief Executive and MD appointments were searched by the firm in 1988. *Fortune* (in 1988) ranked Russell Reynolds as second behind Korn/Ferry with recruiting fees worldwide and in the USA, of $67.7m. and $44m. respectively. *Business Week* in February 1989 quoted the firm's latest annual revenues as $91m. and described them as cultivating 'high-level work and an elite image'.
Basis of charges Fees are based on one-third of the first year's total remuneration including the successful candidate's salary, bonus, profit-sharing arrangements and any cash compensation, invoiced in equal interim fees over three months. Minimum fees are fixed from time to time, according to rates ruling in the market. In 1988, half of the assignments were for positions paying £70 000+.
Guarantees None, but if for some unforeseeable reason an assignment is not completed within the stipulated three-month period, the search will be continued at no extra fee except out-of-pocket expenses.
Sector specialism Among the firm's assignments, financial services occupies a prominent – but not dominant – position of 55%; unlike many other search firms, who have suffered a decline in business in this sector in late 1987, 1988 and early 1989, Russell Reynolds' work in this area continues to grow. Personnel, MIS and management consultancy assignments are still expanding. The distribution of assignments between sectors is commercial banking, 24%; merchant and investment banking, 38%; industrial products and services, 16%; professional and business services, 13%; and consumer products and services, 9%.
Functional specialism Assignments are mostly for top-level appointments – chairmen, chief executives, general managers – but include many financial executives, such as capital markets and securities managers, investment managers and personnel directors and MIS directors for commercial, merchant and investment banks. Other assignments include Board-level directors for consumer

and industrial products and services companies and in the field of professional and business services. Assignments by function in 1988 were chairmen, chief executives and general managers, 28%; capital markets and securities management, 23%; personnel, MIS and other, 16%; investment management, 12%; financial executives, 10%; consultancy, 6% and engineering and manufacturing, 1%; others, 4%.

Salary range Three years ago, 51% of assignments were for positions paying upwards of £60 000 in total, and the average is now much higher. This is partly due to the globalisation of salary levels, and to a proliferation of executive share option schemes and the payment by companies of 'up-front' compensation for loss of options on executive moves, indicating that neither stock option schemes nor pension schemes are necessarily a strong obstacle to executive mobility.

Associated and other activities None besides top-level executive search.

Publications Annual brochure produced by the London office, with review of assignments, outlook for the future, philosophy and approach to executive search, and with photographs and short biographies of consultants and senior support staff; overall corporate brochure produced in New York, regularly updated, with current review of search activities worldwide, featuring not only the consultants in each office but also satisfied clients in a variety of industries; a series of short leaflets, produced from Head Office, serving specialised areas, geographical and by sector, such as *The City, The Fashion Industry, The Real Estate Industry, The Investment Management Industry* and *Organisations with Business Interests in the Middle East.*

Style, approach, future plans Russell Reynolds see their success as the result of their great attention to teamwork within the London office and networking with the other nineteen offices around the world, as described by Roddy Gow in Chapter 6. Future international and domestic expansion is planned but the firm is not willing to reveal how or when. As we saw in Chapter 1, Russell Reynolds himself inspired a strong elitist image in the business and, unlike other search firms, planned a system of career progression within the firm to nurture and develop new recruits. Russell Reynolds has perhaps the strongest business culture of the major headhunting companies; but, although this is American-inspired, it has adapted extremely well to the British business scene. This, combined with their international reputation for financial services work, helps to explain their continued predominance in the British search market. Although Russell Reynolds' offices are shoulder-to-shoulder among their competitors in St James's Square, they are clearly distancing themselves from the opposition by the strength of their ranks of consultants and their ability to work closely together in harness. The consultants do not appear isolated, trying to work as one-man-bands under the umbrella of a large firm, as in the case of many other firms. Together, the consultants combine a distinct Britishness with international, especially American, business experience. Roddy Gow was described by a colleague – quoted by John Byrne – as running 'the business like Salomon Brothers' trading room' and, with 'a phone at each ear, he knows more about what's going on in the City than anyone in the marketplace'.

Reputation As declared in the firm's brochure, it is rare that Russell Reynolds mentions specific examples of their work:

> but it is public knowledge that we were retained in 1986 by Beecham Group plc to recruit their new Chairman, resulting in the appointment of Mr Robert Bauman. This is a fine example of our international capability, where the assignment was handled jointly by our London and New York offices and involved a trans-national search throughout every major industrialised country in the world.

Although sounding like PR-talk, it is arguable that only the Big Four and Egon Zehnder could handle an assignment of such prestige and international ramifications. The firm's reputation – both with clients and competitors – is riding high, but there is a danger of continued volume growth producing a standardised, formula, depersonalised approach. Maintaining turnover without losing quality could be one of its greatest future problems.

SAXTON BAMPFYLDE INTERNATIONAL LIMITED

35 Old Queen Street
London
SW1 9TB
01–799 1433
Fax 01–222 0489

Consultants in London Anthony Saxton, Stephen Bampfylde, Lilias Graham, Marion Capriles and Douglas Board.
Founded in London September 1986.
Owned by Anthony Saxton and Stephen Bampfylde (35% each), with 30% held by three outside shareholders, private friends of the founding partners.
Worldwide 26 staff in London, and partner offices in Dusseldorf, Frankfurt, Hamburg, Malmo, Munich, New York, Paris, Stockholm and Zurich.
Annual fee income and number of assignments £1.6m. in London, from approximately 75 assignments and consulting projects.
Basis of charges On one-third of the first year's remuneration of the successful candidate, paid in four equal monthly retainers, plus expenses.
Guarantees No specific guarantees are offered, except the firm's reputation.
Sector specialism The firm operates in most industry sectors, but especially in banking (particularly investment banking), retailing, communications, property, the media, hi-tech, venture capital and for consulting firms.
Functional specialism Board-level appointments in most functions.
Salary range The average fee charged is approximately £20 000, so average salaries of jobs searched are principally between £40 000 and £80 000.
Associated and other activities Besides high-level search work, the firm offers the services of a wholly-owned division named Cannon Rosen, where Ben Cannon runs management coaching to increase the effectiveness of already effective senior executives further as well as providing advice to clients to help newcomers fit into existing management teams. Ben Cannon's work was discussed by John Spicer in *The Times*, 19 February 1988. The firm also offers sophisticated psychological assessment services managed by John Burnard.
Publications A 'Manifesto', entitled *Twenty Points to Consider Before You Headhunt Another Director* which lists 20 critical issues between a search consultant and a client, illustrated with apt quotations and rather puzzling but arty inkblots, much praised in *Marketing Week*.
Style, approach, future plans As discussed in Chapter 1, Saxton Bampfylde was formed as a result of the departure of the founding partners from John Stork. They had strongly held feelings on the way that international search business should develop, and see themselves as having a passionate (their word) attachment towards the use of research in headhunting, and employ a large number of researchers compared with the number of consultants, claiming that the calibre of their research team is such that in other firms many of them could expect to be employed as consultants. They see their aim as to achieve a close working relationship with a relatively small number of clients.

Internationally their strategy is to work closely with excellent partner firms in key countries, to provide a chain of search and consulting services without weak links; they differentiate this from search firms who have loose international affiliation arrangements, maintaining that their overseas partners have exclusive working relationships with Saxton Bampfylde and share their philosophy and standards. In an international assignment, the overseas partners will take the brief personally, flying in from Europe or the USA if necessary. The firm is looking to develop a similar relationship with a Far East-based consultancy. No money changes hands when Saxton Bampfylde introduces a London-based client to one of its overseas partners; the firm handling the work receives the fee. This apparently excessively altruistic method of business does actually work in practice, as Saxton Bampfylde have received as much work in return as they have handed over. In the run up to 1992, the firm has experienced significant growth in pan-European assignments: over ten in the last twelve months.

Reputation The partners brought with them an already prestigious name from their days at John Stork, enough to enable the firm to set up on their own with two assignments already in hand. They envisaged much knocking on doors to develop further opportunities, but did not realise that they already had such a strong client following, and their first new assignment came from a telephone call at 9 a.m. on Day One. The partners have been able to fund the business with profits as they came in. A number of clients and other search consultants see them as among the most promising of the new firms.

SPENCER STUART & ASSOCIATES LIMITED

Brook House
113 Park Lane
W1Y 4HJ
01–493 1238
Fax 01–491 8068

Consultants in London Christopher Power (Chairman), David Kimbell (Managing Director), Nigel Dyckhoff, Carolyn Eadie, John Lawton, Stephen Patrick, Allan Stewart, Peter Williamson and Tim Pethybridge; Michael Holford, John Murray and John Sellers in Manchester.

Founded in London 1961, with Manchester office opened 1976; originally established in the USA in 1956.

Owned by The consultants, spread throughout the 30 offices with no single consultant owning more than 2% of the equity; 42% is held in Europe and 42% in the Americas, with the remaining 16% in the Pacific Basin.

Worldwide Total staff worldwide is 400, including nine consultants in London and three in Manchester; other offices are in Amsterdam, Atlanta, Barcelona, Brussels, Chicago, Dallas, Dusseldorf, Frankfurt, Geneva, Hong Kong, Houston, Los Angeles, Madrid, Melbourne, Milan, Montreal, New York, Paris, Philadelphia, San Francisco, São Paulo, Singapore, Stamford, Stockholm, Sydney, Tokyo, Toronto and Zurich.

Annual fee income and number of assignments Revenue income in the UK an estimated £5m. 170; worldwide an estimated £49m., 2000. According to *Fortune* (counting only recruiting fees, excluding expenses), Spencer Stuart worldwide earned $56m., ranking third, and $26.2m. in the USA, ranking fourth. The latest issue of the American *Executive Recruiter News* lists Spencer Stuart's total world billings as $59.3m.

Basis of charges Like Egon Zehnder but unlike the other major international firms, Spencer Stuart charges on a fixed fee basis rather than on a third of the successful candidate's salary. The minimum fee in the UK is £20 000, charged on the basis of work completed monthly.

Guarantees Standard replacement search on an expenses-only basis.

Sector specialism Spencer Stuart covers the full spectrum of senior-level search work; on average around 35% of the business is derived from financial services, especially relating to capital markets and fund management.

Functional specialism Main Board level, and specialised financial services functions.

Salary range As the firm charges fixed fees, salary levels are of less concern than other firms; minimum salaries of £50 000–£60 000 are currently the norm.

Associated and other activities Board reviews, organisation and remuneration studies, and senior level short- and long-term performance-related reward schemes.

Publications Brochure, describing the firm, its approach and search method; *Point of View*, a series of regularly-produced discussion papers for leaders of management, generally well-written and of considerable general interest. The following are available: *Chairman & Chief Executive – One and the Same or Not?; The Deployment of Talent; What Future for Work? – Changes in the Pattern of Employment; What Future for the Personnel Manager?; Science and Industry – Towards an Entente; Organisation and Enterprise – The Cycle of Management Style; Financial Incentives,* with Appendix; *The Japanese Economic Drive – Threat or Promise?; Leadership – Managing the Team; The Independent Director,* with Appendix. David Kimbell recently contributed an article on search in Europe with 1992 in *First* magazine April 1989.

Style, approach, future plans As we saw in Chapter 1, Spencer Stuart was the first of the Big Four to arrive in London, and the firm successfully took root in a quite different business climate through recruiting consultants with sound British commercial and industrial backgrounds who would be acceptable with British clients, at a time when executive search in Britain was still at an embryonic stage. Their competitors in the late 1960s and early 1970s, Heidrick and Struggles, were less successful, apparently – according to Spencer Stuart – because they employed a number of American consultants who failed to understand British business and thus did not work so well with British clients. Spencer Stuart's business has continued to prosper by instilling a strong sense of firm loyalty among consultants, and the attraction and retention of several prestigious clients. Plans for the future include the continuing but slower expansion of its network of overseas offices to grow to 35 or 40. As another area of growth, consideration is being given to the possibility of providing other services besides the core executive search business, such as temporary management resourcing at a senior level; Egon Zehnder has recently launched such a service in London. Consulting staff in London and Manchester are to be increased to fifteen, with a parallel growth in the number of researchers. The firm appears to be coping with the problem of an increasing age profile among consultants – inevitable in a long-established firm without frequent consultant defection – by recruiting younger consultants; the average age is now 46. The image and style of Spencer Stuart is clearly evident in its Park Lane offices, well apart from the other search firms crowding St James' and Piccadilly; the furnishings are traditional and comfortable, slightly clubby with framed cartoons of famous Spencer Stuart characters and lots of polished wood. The consultants are relatively quiet-natured, unaggressive, and appear reasonable and sympathetic.

Reputation Spencer Stuart, like GKR, are known for their low profile and very strong emphasis on discretion; as such, they were most reluctant to mention any clients for whom they have worked, although they received enthusiastic praise from companies in the client survey in Chapter 3 and are very highly spoken of in the executive search world. The firm has always seen itself as strong in assignments where the definition of the job and the best solution are not obvious. Examples of such work are their appointment of the first Chief Executive of the Stock Exchange and the last three CBI Director-Generals.

JOHN STORK INTERNATIONAL LIMITED

(*see under* **KORN/FERRY**)

Consultants in London John Stork, Mike Eggers, Jeff Elder, Donald Macleod and Charles Oswin.

Founded in London 1973.

Owned by John Stork majority shareholder, with other partners, formed into a private limited company. The London and Scandinavian offices were merged with Korn/Ferry in December 1988.

Worldwide 65 staff worldwide, in John Stork International Offices in London, Amsterdam, Brussels, Frankfurt, Geneva, Gothenburg, Paris, Stavanger and Stockholm. The company is also represented in North America through Paul Stafford Associates, in Atlanta, Chicago, New York, Princeton and Washington.

Annual fee income and number of assignments in London before the merger, £2m., 150; Europe £4.5m., 350; worldwide, $11.5m., around 500.

Basis of charges One-third of expected first-year remuneration, subject to a minimum retainer generally charged over four months, with fees fixed in advance if required.

Guarantees The retainer fee paid by the client is valid for six months. If the candidate leaves within the subsequent six months, there will probably be no further charge except for expenses.

Sector specialism Consumer, technology, financial services, property, professional firms, marketing services.

Functional specialism Especially general management, but across all industries and job functions.

Salary range Over 80% £50 000+

Associated and other activities Haymarket Consultants, specialising in sales and marketing appointments, up to Sales Director and Marketing Director level in consumer goods and services businesses, retailing and related areas; Pintab Associates, concerned with psychological assessment of internal and external candidates, team building and other management motivational issues, which employs several psychologists in the UK and Europe.

Publications Brochure, entitled *Introduction to John Stork & Partners*, which discusses the search process carried out by the firm without details, and short papers entitled *Briefings*; these are guides to clients in dealing with recruiting senior personnel, especially at Board level. The firm does not issue details of the backgrounds of consultants with its literature, but will do so with specific assignment proposals.

Style, approach, future plans In Chapter 1, the origins and background of this firm were discussed in detail: how John Stork himself came into the business, how his style of headhunting evolved from direct experience and trial and error, and how the firm survived the defection of Anthony Saxton, Stephen Bampfylde and a senior researcher. John Stork himself, who used to dominate the business just as he used to dominate the share-out of equity, is friendly, unpretentious and relaxed. He is justly proud of his business, and glad to demonstrate the thoroughness and effectiveness of the research facilities, which plat a vital role in the firm's method and approach. The offices in Haymarket were slightly rambling, chaotic and confusing, rather at odds with the professional image which the firm seeks to convey. The remaining John Stork consultants now share offices with Korn/Ferry.

Reputation According to three of the companies responding to the client survey in Chapter 3, John Stork offers a very professional and thorough approach, and is especially appropriate for international searches covering Europe. Marketing companies especially speak particularly highly of the firm.

SUCCESSION PLANNING ASSOCIATES

34 Old Queen Street
SW1H 9HP
01–233 0311
Fax 01–233 0456

Consultants in London John Smith and four others.
Founded in London 1988.
Owned by The consultants.
Worldwide No other branches yet.
Annual fee income and number of assignments London, £0.5m., over 30.
Basis of Charges Fixed fee based on estimate of time and difficulty of the assignment, payable in three equal instalments: on confirmation of the assignment; on presentation of the short list; and on the appointment of the successful candidate. Expenses are charged in addition.
Guarantees Visits are made to check on the progress of the appointee in three months and in six months. If it is clear, after six months, that the appointment has not been successful, the firm undertakes to bear the cost of outplacement, and to find new candidates. Similarly, if the incumbent leaves within six months, a replacement will be found free of charge.
Sector specialism Public sector only, but within this central and local government, the health service, education, nationalised industry, the environment and many more. Eventually, the firm may move into other sectors, but it has no specific plans in this direction at the moment.
Functional specialism All functions in the public sector, from CEOs to directors of planning, economic development, engineering, education, etc.
Salary range From £30 000 upwards (public sector positions are rarely as well paid as in the private sector).
Associated and other activities Beside executive search, selection work (all positions in the public sector have, by custom and practice, to be advertised) and management consultancy advice on organisational structures in the context of the top management team of a local authority (although not throughout an authority). Those advised in the past include both water and health authorities.
Publications No brochure, by design, as all assignments are seen as individual and one brochure would not be relevent to them all.
Style, approach, future plans Succession Planning Associates (SPA) was founded by John Smith as a breakaway from MSL and, in a wider context, the entire Hay/MSL group, for whom Smith worked first as head of Hay's nationalised industry consulting group, and then as director of MSL's public sector executive search practice.

In justifying the establishment of the firm, Smith argued that the larger, general search firms in the public sector were too large, corporate and heavy in style for this specialised sector. They tended to concentrate purely on searching for candidates to fill vacancies, rather than offering the sort of specialist management consultancy advice which many local authorities needed. They also tended to be over-commercialised and to send their best sales-driven consultants to shoot-outs and then other less experienced consultants would do the work.

Public sector clients, on the whole, are less knowledgeable than corporations in the hiring of consultants and, in Smith's experience, they prefer a specialist firm which can handle a range of consultancy requirements and which does not insist on treating them like just another production-orientated company. With large Boards and committees of councillors, many of whom have little experience of consultants or, indeed, of the business world, the public sector is very different from the corporate world.

However, large Civil Service departments have much in common with large companies with powerful cultures; the Ministry of Defence, the Treasury, the Diplomatic Service and the Home Office are arguably similar to ICI, Unilever, Procter & Gamble and IBM in their hiring of graduates straight from university and their well-known training schemes. But whereas fifteen to twenty years ago, the Civil Service was seen as the most popular destination for high-powered graduates, this is no longer the case; it is now difficult to recruit people to the public sector.

This adds to Smith's problems: at least a quarter of his successful candidates have come from the private sector, and they have to cope with the reputation of the Civil Service as hidebound and rulebound, with a poor public image and low morale, as well as generally lower salaries. Smith feels that the identification of candidates suitable to work in this sector is a skill altogether different from general headhunting, and thus his firm is deliberately kept small and specialised. Partly because of the different interpersonal skills needed in this area of work, the greater part of public sector appointments involve the moving of people from one sector to another.

The style of SPA is indicated by its name: it aims to help authorities plan their succession for the future, often a slower process than in the corporate world because of the need to consult large bodies of councillors and because of the publicity surrounding the plans of an authority and its appointments. It also indicates the firm's wider interest in management consulting and not just in hunting heads.

SPA has frequently brought candidates over from the EEC government in Brussels and elsewhere for opportunities with British local and central authorities; they have been able to do this without the aid of overseas offices, but the opening of branches in European cities may be a development for the future.

Reputation Smith brought his own reputation from MSL to SPA, and has enjoyed a large volume of business from the beginning, partly due to the perception that his main competitors – Korn/Ferry, PA and MSL – are too commercial and impersonal for many smaller authorities. The large accountancy firms with management consultancy/executive search divisions have tried to penetrate this market, through the clients they have acquired in this sector in their auditing work; yet many authorities are concerned that these firms are not independent and there may be a conflict of interest.

In the public domain, appointments are well known and talked about; personnel directors and chief executives in this sector meet frequently and discuss their mutual problems, quite unlike the corporate sector. Thus news of good and poor quality headhunting and consultancy work travels quickly. So far, Smith's publicly acknowledged assignments have included work for the Local Government International Bureau, Ipswich Borough Council, the London Boroughs of Barnet, Enfield and Bexley, the City of Bath, Three Rivers District, Dartford Borough Council, the Isle of Man, Nottinghamshire County Council, and the second generation Urban Development Corporation and the Enterprise Council, who underpin the Department of Trade and Industry's Enterprise Initiative.

TASA INTERNATIONAL AG

c/o Stephenson Cobbold Limited
84 Palace Court
W2 4JE
01–727 5335
Fax 01–221 2628

Consultants in London Nicholas Cobbold, Tim Stephenson, Andrew Mackenzie and David Bateson.

Founded in London 1971; the firm was created in 1972 as a result of the merger of two search firms that were founded in the early 1960s: Tasa (which had extended widely into South American markets) and Consulting Partners (which had grown up in the major European business centres). Worldwide headquarters are in Zurich.

Owned by A Swiss corporation; the London office of Tasa is managed by Stephenson Cobbold, an independent company.

Worldwide Tasa has offices in Barcelona, Bogota, Brussels, Buenos Aires, Calgary, Caracas, Edmonton, Frankfurt, Hong Kong, Johannesburg, Madrid, Melbourne, Mexico City, Miami, Milan, Montreal, Munich, New York, Palo Alto, Paris, São Paulo, Scandinavia, Sydney, Tokyo, Toronto, Vancouver, Vienna and Zurich.

Annual fee income and number of assignments 1988 estimated worldwide fee income is US $20m., on about 400.

Basis of charges Tasa charges a fixed fee, as agreed upon with the client, or one-third of the first year's compensation. The total fee consists of the initial retainer followed by three equal monthly instalments. Different arrangements may be made for particularly complex international searches, with a minimum fee of £15 000. Stephenson Cobbold charge 35% of the first year's compensation payable in three equal monthly instalments.

Guarantees The firm guarantees to replace an executive who leaves within six months unless the client company's circumstances radically alter the entire placement situation, such as in the case of a merger or problem with a particular product.

Sector specialism Tasa specialises in seeking to fill positions where an international business profile is necessary, and overseas recruitments generally. These include recruiting UK nationals for overseas positions, especially for difficult locations in Asia, the Middle East and Africa. Much of Tasa's work is in canvassing continental European talent to come to work for international operations run from the UK. Industry sectors covered include banking, chemicals, construction, consulting, consumer, cosmetics, electronics, engineering, information technology, pharmaceuticals and telecommunications. Location of assignments may be categorised into UK, 25%; Europe, 50%, Middle East, 20% and Africa, 5%.

Functional specialism Chairman/managing director, 20%; marketing director, 15%; finance director, 20%; personnel, 10%; technical/engineering/manufacturing, 20%; other, 15%.

Salary range £40 000–£50 000, 25%; over £50 000, 75%.

Associated and other activities None but executive search.

Publications Brochure, introducing the search process as Tasa sees it; *US Company Headquarters in Europe – Some Interesting Trends*, looking at European bases of US multinationals, based on nearly 200 examples based in London, Brussels, Amsterdam, Paris and Geneva; *The Manager of the Year 200*, an investigation into the executive of tomorrow, based on round-table discussions with over a hundred directors from a variety of sectors.

Style, approach, future plans Tasa consultants are bright and enthusiastic, with a contemporary, informal style, and a mixture of European and American cultures. Andrea Wine, who used to run Tasa's office in London and is now in Brussels, is outgoing and determined, but flexible and sympathetic to complex international recruiting problems. The London office is strongly linked to the overseas branches run by Stephenson Cobbold which runs all Tasa's UK searches as well as conducting their own business, mostly in financial and service industry sectors.

Reputation Sound within its specialty of overseas searches, but the firm has yet to establish a strong niche in the UK market comparable with the top dozen firms; perhaps it appears so strongly internationally-biased that it does not yet appeal sufficiently to British clients. The link-up with Stephenson Cobbold may change this.

TYZACK & PARTNERS LIMITED

10 Hallam Street
W1N 6DJ
01–580 2924
Fax 01–631 5317

Consultants in London Nigel Humphreys (Managing Director), Richard Addis, Peter Ohlson, Neal Wyman, Alex Gibson, Anthony Gilbert and Antony Longland; Peter Bryant works mainly in Bristol, and Tim Bowdler and Brian Gordon in Leeds.
Founded in London 1959.
Owned by Employee trust, 75%; partners, 25%.
Worldwide 75 total staff in Bristol, Frankfurt, Hong Kong, Leeds, London, New York and Paris.
Annual fee income and number of assignments UK £2.75m., 130; worldwide $12m., 376.
Basis of charges Fees are agreed in advance and, although they bear some relationship to one-third of the first year's rumuneration, they also take into account the complexity and amount of work required. Invoices are sent in three equal monthly instalments. Current minimum fees are London £17 500, Leeds and Bristol, £13 500.
Guarantees The firm's work continues until an appointment is made or the client agrees that there are no suitable solutions available. If a candidate leaves within six months and the nature of the position has not changed, the assignment will be continued on an expenses-only basis. All offices work to a common code of conduct established seven years ago.
Sector specialism Tyzack consultants have handled assignments for all functions in industry and commerce but with particular reference to banking, technology, State enterprises, the professions and what the firm calls 'top level management of change'. Recent appointments have been made in the following areas: brewing, construction, consultancy, financial services, hi-tech, insurance, leisure, manufacturing, the media, property, the public sector, retail and in international trading.
Functional specialism The firm has undertaken assignments within nearly every senior function; besides chairmen, chief executives and MDs, they have also searched for vice-presidents of MIS, directors of international planning, commercial directors, finance directors, technical directors, international operations directors, acquisitions directors, sales directors, marketing directors, information systems directors, personnel directors, chief actuaries, vice-presidents of legal affairs, heads of PR, sales directors in regional broadcasting, heads of radio and television production, editors-in-chief, and heads of corporate banking, treasury, securities, foreign exchange and money markets.
Salary range Between £40 000 and £250 000.
Associated and other activities A number of Tyzack consultants have been trained in the techniques of psychometric testing; this can be called upon by clients as an activity quite separate from search. Remuneration planning is assuming an increasing importance as a further Tyzack service.
Publications Brochure, outlining the approach of the firm, with photographs and brief résumés of the consultants, both in London and internationally; the *Tyzack Review*, a regular publication discussing current business trends with which the firm has become familiar through its search work.
Style, approach, future plans As we saw in Chapter 1, Tyzack began in 1959 in

high-level recruitment advertising, and the firm's name became almost a household word from the plethora of Tyzack advertisements in the *Financial Times* and *The Sunday Times*; in 1981, however, it was recognised that future growth in top-level recruitment was in search rather than in advertising. The firm then underwent a dramatic metamorphosis, dropping advertising completely and building up a sophisticated research department. Tyzack's high profile disappeared, and the new emphasis was firmly placed on high-level executive search with a strongly research-driven consultancy approach.

Tyzack is known for its relatively low turnover of consultants, with average length of service of at least seven years. One of the possible drawbacks of a long established firm with continuity and stability is the problem of the increasing age of consultants: but Tyzack has overcome this by an early retirement age and bringing in relatively young blood, such as Neal Wyman, London School of Economics industrial economics graduate and chartered accountant with experience in the City and the Far East, and Oxbridge-educated Alex Gibson, who has also been closely involved in financial services work internationally. Anthony Gilbert, who recently joined the team in Bristol, had gained an MSc in Computer Science after his MBA, and worked in the management consultancy side of Ernst & Whinney, before becoming head of information technology at Britain's largest R&D organisation. The more senior consultants, mainly with Oxbridge backgrounds, provide a strong basis of industrial expertise supplementing the financial skills of the younger recruits. Nigel Humphreys, the urbane yet thrusting managing director who has been involved with the firm since its great policy change of 1981, which he helped promote and develop, has a background in manufacturing, construction and international consultancy. Richard Addis was in international textiles, manufacturing and financial services; and Peter Ohlson was previously a chief executive in Grand Metropolitan. From consulting backgrounds in PE and McKinsey respectively, Antony Longland and Peter Bryant have wide international experience in executive search. Brian Gordon followed his MBA with a general management career in industry before obtaining seven years experience in executive search in the North of England.

Tyzack offers its clients the benefits of a well-developed international network – as discussed in Chapter 6 – based on a combination of its own firms and associates, all run by nationals: George Lim's Hong Kong research office plays an important part in Tyzack's Far Eastern and Pacific Rim work, whilst Nicholas Gardiner handles US referrals, Friedbert Herbold takes care of German contacts and Jean Claude Lasante represents Tyzack in Paris.

Reputation Tyzack has always enjoyed a significant proportion of repeat business, 66% in the last year; representing a continuing high level of work from existing clients now augmented by a higher proportion of new business. The firm's remuneration surveys – which provide detailed and specific guidelines on corporate salaries across the board for one of Britain's largest construction companies, one of the Big Eight accountancy firms and a leading merchant bank – help account for this growth. Tyzack was often favourably mentioned by companies in the client survey in Chapter 3, and is held in high esteem in the headhunting fraternity generally.

WHITEHEAD MANN GROUP PLC

44 Welbeck Street
W1M 7HF
01–935 8978
Fax 01–935 8356

Consultants in London Dr Anna Mann, Clive Mann, Nigel Smith, Chris Leslie, Peter Williamson (Directors) and eight other senior consultants.
Founded in London 1976.
Owned by The directors, and the chairman, Sir Peter Parker.
Worldwide Whitehead Mann is part of the Ward Howell International Group, an extensive international network of independent, well-established executive search firms who have strong local businesses in their own right but who nevertheless benefit greatly from global contacts. Ward Howell used to have over a hundred consultants, now only 45, in offices in Amsterdam, Auckland, Barcelona, Brussels, Chicago, Copenhagen, Dallas, Dusseldorf, Hong Kong, Houston, Los Angeles, Madrid, Melbourne, Mexico City, Milan, Munich, New York, Oslo, Paris, San Francisco, Singapore, Stamford, Stockholm, Sydney, Tokyo, Toronto, Vienna and Zurich. Ward Howell itself began in the USA in 1951; this group has been established and developed over the last eight years.
Annual fee income and number of assignments London, the second-largest office in the Ward Howell International Group, last year earned £4m. from search, from 150–70 assignments overall, of which 20% were international; worldwide the group earned $40m., ranking fourth of all US-based search firms, with the largest proportion of non-US work – nearly two-thirds – of all the multinational headhunters, on approximately 1200 assignments. In the USA, $13.9m. was earned by Ward Howell in 1988, with 45 consultants heading 610 searches.
Basis of charges For search work, usually one-third of the first year's remuneration, taking into account other factors such as the geographical scope of the assignment, with a minimum fee of £18 000. The fee is payable in three equal parts: a retainer becomes due immediately the assignment is authorised, and is non-returnable. The second and third payments become due at subsequent monthly intervals. The payments are not contingent upon any particular phase of the search. Where an appointment is made at a significantly higher salary than that upon which the fee was quoted, a fourth payment may become due based on one-third of the salary difference. Expenses are billed to the client company to a maximum of 15% of the fee. In the event of expenses exceeding this sum, prior authorisation will be sought.
Management assessment is subject to a minimum fee of £800 for each assessment, including a full report; consultancy assignments are charged at per diem rate of between £800 and £2000.
Guarantees Whitehead Mann undertakes to continue a search until it is brought to a successful conclusion; in cases where the search is not completed due to circumstances beyond its control – where the client changes his or her mind about the specification, or where a job disappears as a result of an internal reorganisation, for example – the full fee will still be payable, but the firm will be prepared to consider a reduction, proportionate to the extent to which the search remains uncompleted, if the consultant in charge is notified of the change before the date on which the third payment falls due.
Sector specialism Financial services, 20%; manufacturing, 20%; retail, 15%; FMCGs, 12%; professional services, 8%; others, 25% – including some public

sector work, such as for Water Boards, the Post Office, the Ministry of Defence and the Department of Trade and Industry. The firm seeks to cover a wide spectrum of sectors, and has clients in such diverse areas as leisure, insurance, PR, the legal profession and property; this avoids off-limits problems.

Functional specialism Dr Mann is well known for specialising in very senior appointments of chairmen and CEOs, and of non-executive directors; further work covers general management and the full spectrum of professional disciplines.

Salary range The firm employs a rigid cut-off point in terms of the salary level at which they will work; most assignments of below £55 000 are referred to Whitehead Rice Ltd (see below) or are not undertaken.

Associated and other activities An Audit & Assessment Centre is operated by Whitehead Mann within the Welbeck Street offices and is run by Dr Rob Irving with a professional staff of three others; this provides organisations with an analysis of their personnel structure and an enquiry into the capability of its human resources to meet existing and projected needs. This service is particularly effective for companies involved in acquisitions or mergers; in corporate reorganisation; in developing new ventures; in evaluating inherited management teams on behalf of newly-appointed chief executives; and in strategic planning. Comprehensive individual psychological assessments can also be arranged, for senior selection and management counselling, covering all aspects of psychometric testing; the Centre maintains contact with the major test producing agencies in the UK, with academic occupational psychology departments and with recognised bodies such as the Independent Assessment and Research Centre in London.

A management selection company, Whitehead Rice Ltd, is run entirely separately and independently and carries out advertising and selection recruiting work for positions attracting salaries of between £25 000 and £55 000; a further three professional staff are employed here. These two associated activities have a turnover of nearly £1m. per annum.

Publications Brochure, describing the firm's approach to executive search but without any biographical details of directors or consultants.

Style, approach, future plans As discussed in Chapter 1, the style of Whitehead Mann reflects the influence of its founder; any firm run by an entrepreneurial businesswoman attracts unfavourable attention from the popular press and the firm has tended to avoid publicity. The firm, however, has a highly research-orientated approach, with as many researchers as consultants. The researchers act like deputies to the consultants, meeting the clients and undertaking much of the telephone contact work, and receiving training in interviewing. Dr John Viney of Heidrick and Struggles worked here, and shares the same belief in recruiting researchers with the understanding that they can become potential consultant material. Other successful graduates of the Whitehead Mann school include Stephen Bampfylde. Whitehead Mann aims to build strong client relationships, believing that loyalty is a two-way process in search; thus, they would not favour clients who employed several other search firms at the same time. The firm's offices are quietly traditional and understated, apparently anonymous in a row of similar Edwardian town houses north of Oxford Street; not for them the glitter of Piccadilly. Looking to the future, the firm is especially interested in the growing opportunities for search on behalf of Japanese clients; in this respect they are helped by Chairman Sir Peter Parker, who speaks Japanese and is involved in Government liaison work with Japanese politicians and businessmen. International work is seen as increasingly important, and Clive Mann, who acts as the firm's liaison officer in global searches, is keen to ensure that quality remains high and that close co-ordination is maintained throughout Ward Howell offices.

Reputation The firm is known for working across a spread of sector interests much wider than most and includes two unusual areas of speciality; start-up and smaller companies and non-executive directors. The former is discussed in Simon Bartholomew's article in *The Times* (see bibliography). Although Whitehead Mann's clients include 24 of *The Times 1000* top 100 companies and two of the largest insurance companies – which they see as their bread and butter work – they also welcome unusual and creative searches, such as finding a second layer of management for a leisure company that had become too large to be managed exclusively by its founders and finding a management team to run a regional franchise of convenience stores. Second, Dr Mann has established a reputation for non-executive director searches, and argues strongly that the role of these businessmen is becoming increasingly important. No longer are non-executive directors just names to grace the notepaper; many boards of important plcs include up to one-third non-executive directors to two-thirds executive directors. Despite – or perhaps partly because of – its air of mystery, even more strongly maintained than GKR, Whitehead Mann's reputation is envied by many other British firms and respected by the multinationals. Not surprisingly, the firm does not publish a client list which could furnish user comment.

WRIGHTSON WOOD LIMITED

11 Grosvenor Place
SW1X 7HH
01–245 9871
Fax 01–235 0659

Consultants in London Christopher Wysock Wright (Chairman and founder), Jeffrey Bonas, Guy Hitchings, Barry Dinan, James Edmiston, Ted Edwards and Alan Bradley.
Founded in London 1979.
Owned by The partners.
Worldwide Wrightson Wood has an office in Bristol and is associated with independent firms in New York and Sydney; a total of 35 consultants and support staff. They are in the process of establishing links with firms in Paris, Frankfurt, Madrid and elsewhere.
Annual fee income and number of assignments London and Bristol, £2m.; 105; worldwide, £4m.
Basis of charges Fees, based on first year's salary, are normally 35% payable in three stages, over three months, beginning at the end of the first month of an assignment. If an assignment is cancelled in the first month, the first month's fee is always payable, and thereafter on a pro-rata basis. Expenses, charged additionally, are normally between 10% and 15% of the fee.
Guarantees The firm undertakes to continue searching beyond three months at no extra charge. If, within one year, an appointment is not a success, a replacement will be found with no further financial commitment.
Sector specialism None.
Functional specialism Mainly general management.
Salary range £40 000+.
Associated and other activities No other activities besides high-level executive search; but Jeffrey Bonas, who is responsible for the operational side of Wrightson Wood, assists clients in the wider aspects of their business such as company restructuring, fund raising, acquisitions and flotations.
Publications Brochure, *Wrightson Wood Executive Search: A Pocket Guide*, containing addresses of Bristol, New York and Sydney offices; a general introduction to their services; and résumés of the consultants. A quarterly bulletin, *Wrightson Wood Search* with articles by staff and by distinguished outside contributors – such as John Plender of the *Financial Times* and Channel Four's Business Programme – has recently been launched.
Style, approach, future plans Most of the consultants share public-school, Oxbridge and service backgrounds. Christopher Wysock Wright is ex-St Albans School, Sandhurst and the Royal Northumberland Fusiliers; Jeffrey Bonas was at Harrow and Oriel College, Oxford; Guy Hitchings was educated at Wellington, Clare College, Cambridge and served in the Fleet Air Arm; Barry Dinan went to Downside and became a regular officer in the Irish Guards; James Edmiston was at Rugby and Brasenose College, Oxford; Ted Edwards graduated from Jesus College, Cambridge; and Alan Bradley, another Cambridge man, followed a short-service commission in the Royal Air Force. Together they also boast a wide range of commercial experience, in computers, FMCG, and quality consumer goods retailing, publishing, textiles, precision engineering, insurance broking, and the marine, aviation and motor industries. Some of the consultants hold non- executive directorships in other businesses, including mail order, financial services, retail, venture capital and aviation. Wrightson Wood's style is traditional

and discreet. They see themselves as problem-solvers, whose professional approach and methods of search enable them to be totally flexible in terms of sector and function. Their business is expanding at a faster rate than many of their competitors among the more long-established British search firms, apparently through continuing work based on their wide range of previous assignments.

Reputation The firm measures its success by the amount of repeat business it enjoys from core clients; they quote a number of leading blue-chip industrials and finance houses for whom they have worked on more than one occasion. Wrightson Wood are known for their very effective handling of a comparatively large number of searches for loyal clients; the fact that they have worked with them in the past enables the firm to complete assignments relatively quickly and increases the chances of success.

EGON ZEHNDER INTERNATIONAL

Devonshire House
Mayfair Place
W1X 5FH
01–493 3882
Fac 01–629 9552

Consultants in London John Grumbar (Managing Partner), Robin Gowlland, Hugh Murray, David Rogers, Philip Vivian, Anthony Couchman, Julia Budd, Ian Maurice, Damien O'Brien, Andrew Lowenthal and Stephen Sampson.
Founded in London 1970, first established in Zurich in 1964.
Owned by Equal ownership by – currently – 60 partners worldwide, each of whom owns 1.66% of the equity.
Worldwide 150 professional staff, with an overall total of 320, in Atlanta, Barcelona, Brussels, Buenos Aires, Chicago, Copenhagen, Dusseldorf, Frankfurt, Geneva, The Hague, Hamburg, Helsinki, Hong Kong, Lisbon, London, Los Angeles, Madrid, Melbourne, Mexico City, Milan, Munich, New York, Paris, Rome, São Paulo, Singapore, Sydney, Tokyo, Vienna, Zurich, with Lyon opening in 1990.
Annual fee income and number of assignments Worldwide, £45m., 2500; no specific office figures are released, but London office income has been independently estimated at £3m.
Basis of charges Fixed fees: 1989 minimum £22 000, rather than one-third of the successful candidate's salary, paid over 3–4 months, plus expenses of between 5% and 15% of total fee.
Guarantees The firm will undertake to keep working for no further fee until the search is successfully concluded; if a placed candidate leaves within six months, the firm will reactivate the search for expenses only.
Sector specialism In London, financial services, 30%; manufacturing, 20%; computers/electronics, 15–20%; FMCG/retail, 15–20%; professional services, 5%; with the remainder in a wide range of other sectors.
Functional specialism In London, top management, 60–70%; first line directors and specialists, 30–40%; international clients, 50–60% and local clients, 40–50%.
Salary range Between £40 000 and £100 000+: the average fee received is £26 000 in London. The average fee in international searches – including two or more countries – is £32 000, with a 1989 minimum of £28 000.
Associated and other activities Also attached to Egon Zehnder in London is Executive Interim Management (tel. 01–629 2832), run by Robert Mark, MD. This is a new venture between Egon Zehnder, Boer & Croon and Euroventures, which provides senior managers to undertake specific assignments on a temporary basis for organisations within both the private and public sectors. The need for such temporary managers frequently arises during sudden vacancies, before a replacement can be searched: for example, in preparation for a management buy-out or any other sudden change in policy. Egon Zehnder in London and worldwide also offers practices in acquisitions and divestments, and in management appraisals, alongside executive search.
Publications Jointly with the London Business School, *Acquisitions: The Human Factor* and *Management Resources: Present Problems and Future Trends*; and brochure describing the entire firm and its worldwide operations, with statistics of growth, an outline of the firm's philosophy and how it handles search assignments, its professional ethics and fees, with photographs and potted résumés of its consultants worldwide. Egon Zehnder consultants also contribute directly

to the press, such as John Grumbar's article in *Acquisitions Monthly* on 'Professional Assessment of the Human Factor in Acquisitions and Divestments'. Worldwide, many other publications are produced annually, such as *Banking and Finance Industry Survey of Australian Chief Executives; Annual Banking Survey of Chief Executive Officers (USA); Survey of Bank Chief Executives in Asia;* and *Corporate Issues Monitor: A Quarterly Survey of Executive Opinion on Topical Issues (USA)*, published from 1986 onwards.

Style, approach, future plans The discussion of the arrival of the international firms in London in Chapter 1 has considered how Egon Zehnder became established, and looked at its similarities with Spencer Stuart in terms of the way it operates and how it is able to retain its consultants for long periods. The firm has a strong European, rather than American or British, style, deliberately playing down the headhunter image. It is the only major international search firm to offer management consultancy advice on as high a level as its executive search practice. Egon Zehnder's consultants are clearly professional and high-powered. Their new offices, spacious and functional rather than overly grand, are more in tune with their image than their previous long-standing accommodation in slightly crumbling, genteel Jermyn Street. Egon Zehnder consultants see themselves as very much one firm, enjoying equal ownership, in which clients are always put first. With a consulting rather than transaction-orientated approach, the firm is relatively rare in offering secure long-term career prospects for its staff. There is none of the uneasiness associated with the constant movement of consultants and dramatic ups and downs of the business experienced by many other search firms. Egon Zehnder is keen on a modest patronage of the arts and has also sponsored awards for enterprise and achievement by graduate MBAs or MBA students in industry from 1986 outwards.

Reputation Egon Zehnder is arguably the Rolls Royce of headhunting in London and even perhaps the world, outside the USA; Russell Reynolds, equally elite and sought-after but with greater business volume, may be seen as the Jaguar of the business. The firm's work is known for its high quality, and is seen as rather expensive, but worth it. Especially successful searches include the chief executive for BAA, as described in case study I in Chapter 5; subsequently Egon Zehnder also found BAA's finance director. An extensive worldwide search has just been completed for the chief executive of Galileo, a major new venture in airline reservations. At the time of the Big Bang, Egon Zehnder successfully moved several teams. For example, a team was found for UDT, a finance house owned by TSB and then run by Don McCrickard, now Chief Executive, Banking, for TSB; and other teams were recruited for a prominent merchant bank.

Appendix: Hints on How to be Headhunted

Although *The Headhunting Business* is primarily aimed at users of search, and the general business reader wishing to understand the growth of a new industry, it also seeks to provide an insight into the workings of top-level recruitment which can help would-be candidates to maximise their potential, and to use the mechanisms of executive search to climb the corporate ladder. The discussion of the headhunting process in Chapter 4 and the problems consultants face in pin-pointing candidates, interviewing them and presenting them to clients, gives incidental information on how candidates are identified in the first place and how they are most likely to progress to the short-list stage; this section will concentrate on the whole question of how ambitious executives can reap the benefits of the more widespread acceptance of headhunting. It falls into three main parts: first, how a would-be candidate can attract a headhunter's attention; second, how to react most effectively to a headhunter's call; and third, how to handle an interview with a search consultant and then with a client. Many of the suggestions offered here are inevitably common sense and not necessarily new but, emanating from consultants and clients, they can be viewed very much as 'horse's-mouth' advice.

The obvious first step to being headhunted is to send in a CV, but this is always a long shot as leading search firms receive hundreds of 'write-ins' per week. Some firms consign most to the nearest waste-paper bin, but all will retain those that look impressive and interesting. It is vital that this CV is especially tailored for headhunting consumption; this often means a completely different document from that required by an employer or by an academic institution. A CV will have a greater chance of being retained and stored on a search firm's computer files if it is brief and factual, basically chronological rather than thematic, with the type of information that can be easily entered on to a computer and, of course, as up to date as possible. It should be specific about the candidate's principal industry sector, so that this can be keyed in according to standard industry codes. Candidates should investigate which search firms specialise in certain industry sectors, and be sure to target their CVs accordingly. A longer, more detailed CV can always be provided later, and in any case the search consultant will prepare the candidate's CV for presentation to the client.

CVs for search firms should always include salary details and age, and include any unusual qualifications that might catch a consultant's eye. Although it is always wise to seek advice on the ideal layout of a CV, those that are too polished may give the impression that they have been specially prepared by a professional CV company; individuality, to a certain extent, is an advantage. And, in this context, each CV should be an original, not a photocopy, and should be accompanied by an individually typed covering letter summarising the key information included in the CV, finishing off with a bold and confident signature. It is not necessarily a good idea to write that one is actively seeking a new position, but the impression of being open to opportunity should be clearly given, although this is naturally apparent from the sending in of a CV in the first place. It is generally a good idea to send one's CV to the search firm's research director, who is usually closely involved in all the searches being undertaken by the particular search firm at any one time, and would know who to forward it to; in any case, research directors receive fewer CVs than consultants, and may well give them more attention. Most headhunting firms include details of their research staff in their brochures.

Although no instant results should be expected, it is a good move to send in CVs to a variety of search firms, both international and British-based, to obtain a good coverage and maximise chances of being approached, if only as a source. A much more positive step, and one which is much more likely to result in contact with a headhunter, is to ask an influential friend, especially an existing user of search, to make a direct recommendation on one's behalf. Most headhunters will willingly give time to a would-be candidate who is introduced by a client or a particularly useful source. Again, this is unlikely to lead quickly to an executive position, but it makes a stronger impression on a consultant than a CV alone. Some search firms will give time to 'walk-ins' or hopefuls literally walking in to their offices from the street; but this is not to be recommended for the most ambitious and high-flying candidates.

Many executives feel that the headhunter should make the first move, and that they should play hard to get. But in this strategy, the potential candidate must become visible and attractive whilst he or she is in secure employment, not when the business climate has changed and they desperately need a new job. John Wareham, writing in 1981 in his *Secrets of a Corporate Headhunter*, gives advice on these lines for American executives; the globalisation of business since then has been such as to render his suggestions also appropriate to British businessmen and women too. He suggests ten ways of attracting a headhunter's attention, starting with the need for a degree or an MBA, or both; this is not just for the educational experience, but because without being a graduate one cannot easily become a member of the business elite.

A university degree is a passport to useful mailing lists in the USA; this is not necessarily the case in Britain, but it is always a good idea to feature in such lists because they are frequently used by researchers looking in specific industries. By joining relevant trade associations and subscribing to appropriate journals, a potential candidate's name is likely to appear in the initial trawling rather than fishing phase of a search.

Subscribing to a professional or trade association is not necessarily enough; a further plan is to become appointed to its committee. This enables an ambitious executive to become well known among the leading lights of his or her industry sector, which could well lead to an indirect approach from a headhunter via a source. In addition, it is always a good idea to write articles and contribute short pieces for such publications, which are read by both competitors and search firms. Such work will give an impression of commitment, industry and enthusiasm beyond the call of duty, and it is not as difficult as it might sound. Many prestigious journals and top newspapers are willing to accept freelance material, as long as it is pithy, original, makes a clear point and is no more than 700–800 words. Longer articles are more difficult to place and may wait several months in production. If this sounds daunting, short but effective letters to the press can receive equal attention and are almost as impressive. At least the ambitious executive should be sure that his or her promotions are recorded, and that they feature within in-house corporate productions (preferably with a photograph), in the company brochure and in the annual report, both oft-used sources for the headhunting researcher.

A final strategy by which to make a headhunter call, which should not be taken too seriously but may be worth a try, is to return an imaginary call from one, saying that the particular consultant – whose name one failed to catch – asked to set up an interview. This may be dangerous in view of the fact that most headhunters keep detailed records of all their calls, and can immediately summon up such information on their desk-top screens. But it does give one the chance to mention one's qualifications and industrial sector. It is perhaps an even better strategy to ask a friend to return an imaginary call to him or her as a source, who can then make enthusiastic recommendations on one's behalf.

In the headhunting business, it is not necessarily a disadvantage to belong to a minority. In the USA, by law minority candidates must receive special attention and some are able to assume senior management positions on these grounds alone and, since it is illegal to ask a person about their age or background, it is possible to change one's name to give the impression of being in a minority. Such laws are not current in Britain, but many companies see it as a plus to have an international Board and one with women directors, for instance. Certainly headhunters discriminate between candidates; clients, after all, use them to find an executive who is ideal for them, and this inevitably involves a preference for people with a certain background, experience, age and sex. On the other hand, a consultant can persuade a client to consider a candidate outside his or her specification because of their strong qualifications for a job. Many successful candidates are not at all what the client first envisaged, especially in terms of age, sex or industry sector background.

Once an executive is clearly visible in his or her industry for their qualifications, achievements and ambitions, and features in common reference sources, as well as having ensured that their CVs are selectively and strategically placed, a call from a search firm is likely although not, of course, certain. The next step is being able to handle that call to maximise the chances of reaching the short-list stage, or at least gaining the consultant's respect and interest.

REACTING TO THE HEADHUNTER'S CALL

Writing in *The Sunday Times*, Geoffrey Golzen compared being telephoned for the first time by a headhunter as 'the career equivalent of one's first serious kiss'. But this is no time to be carried away, and the would-be candidate should be as businesslike and professional as possible for the minute or so that this will take.

At the outset, it is wise to close the door and make sure that no one else is listening; if in doubt, and if, as in many financial institutions, calls are taped or on a conference line, it is a good idea to suggest a call later or at home. The conversation will necessarily be highly confidential, and it is important for the executive to concentrate on what he or she is being told; after all, this could really be a once-in-a-lifetime opportunity.

It is important to know exactly which consultant or researcher from which company is telephoning, and in this context it is useful to know the names of the leading firms. An executive should ensure that he or she is talking to a trustworthy, bona fide search consultant or researcher. If necessary, the headhunter can be asked to call back to allow time to make checks; if they are listed in *The Headhunting Business*, the would-be candidate can proceed with a greater degree of confidence and background information. This can also help a candidate to assess the significance of the opportunity on offer, in view of the fact that certain search firms deal with opportunities at a higher level and in different sectors than others. Some search firms employ researchers to do the cold-calling only; at others they do all telephone work.

It is crucial to establish then if the call is to a potential candidate for the job, or to a source for further names to contact. Many would-be candidates are convinced that when they are asked if they know anyone suitable for a certain job, the headhunter is obliquely making an approach to them; this is rarely the case, and professional search consultants and researchers would make this clear from the beginning of the call.

Why should a potential candidate help a consultant as a source? Many executives are loath to help in this regard but they may be among the first to hope that someone might recommend them. Even if the job on offer is not attractive, then it is always a good idea to recommend an industry colleague who will certainly appreciate the favour and may return it in the future.

Even if one's first contact with a headhunter is as a source, it is an opportunity to make a good impression and make sure one is remembered. Thus the most effective reaction is a crisp, efficient, highly professional telephone manner, which in itself can be very revealing to an experienced consultant. One of the worst – yet very common – mistakes that an executive unused to headhunting can make is to ask how the headhunter came across his or her name. Such a question suggests an awe and certainly inexperience of search. It is much better to imply that approaches by search consultants are frequently received and that one is accustomed to such calls. As it is a testimony to one's standing in the industry, the call should never be queried. If a candidate has been suggested by a specific source, the source's name would only be revealed with their permission.

Even if the search firm is clearly reputable, and the candidate is eager to be as forthcoming as possible, he or she should never give away confidential information. A good executive should show shrewd judgement and an ability to handle confidences. A headhunter will have immediate doubts about a candidate who openly discusses what they know of their employer's plans, and/or criticises their policies. An executive would expect a headhunter to be totally discreet with personal information about themselves, and also assumes that same rules in the relationship between the search firm and their clients.

Other common mistakes made by candidates include trying to play games with the caller, thinking that their value will be enhanced if they appear aloof and hard to get. Many candidates simply do not listen to the nuances and significance of what the consultant is saying, and ask – and answer – the wrong questions. A number of executives have lost their chance by talking too much and appearing too brash and over-confident.

A call from a headhunter is a time for taking in information; he or she will already know something of the candidate, and wants to explore their initial interest and reaction. Rather than going into great detail about achievements and qualifications at this stage, a candidate can offer to send a CV. The candidate should be ready to find out as much about the opportunity as possible, by asking relevant and pertinent questions.

The search consultant will not necessarily be able to state the client's name – often the greater the confidentiality, the more senior and important the job – but will provide information on what the job entails and what qualifications and experience are required; on the level of the job expressed in terms of reporting relationships within the company; on why the appointment is being made and why an external search is being conducted, and on the position of the client company in the market. Is it a well-established or a new business, and is it expanding, stabilising or restructuring? What is the company's size, by market capitalisation and number of employees, and what is its current turnover, profit and recent performance? At this stage, it is comparatively rare for a salary to be mentioned, although the headhunter may mention a base figure, indicative that the client has a specific remuneration policy and a maximum figure in mind. If the search consultant has carried out his or her research properly, some idea of each candidate's salary will have been already ascertained, and that will have been taken into account in seeking to fill the job on offer.

The first telephone call to a potential candidate is the first stage of a sifting process. It should, if successful, lead to short listing for the appointment and the next hurdle: an interview, first with the consultant and then, ideally, with the client.

THE FIRST INTERVIEW WITH A HEADHUNTER

Experienced search consultants can quickly appraise a candidate at an interview, but because the executive search industry is growing so quickly, and because a more junior executive may be interviewed by a researcher rather than a consultant, it is very important to ensure that one is careful to give as good an impression as possible.

From the beginning, the interviewer should be impressed by the appearance of the candidate, who should look the epitome of a rising executive. Too many interviewees wear pinstripes, so it may be a good idea to wear plain, dark colours, to appear generally conservative but with a hint of individuality in a tie or tasteful piece of jewellery. Shoes should look clean and smart without outrageous socks or stockings.

Candidates do not help themselves by lying about their salary, especially to experienced consultants who will have a shrewd idea of what they may be earning according to their age and recent responsibility. If a candidate exaggerates his or her salary, the consultant will immediately suspect a lie, or think that the candidate is being overpaid because the employer has not been able to attract others of a higher calibre. The candidate should always be scrupulously frank and honest, yet at the same time emphasise the strong, positive reason for the main changes in their careers. It does not sound impressive to say one left a job because of a personality clash, but if one was dismissed, this should not be concealed; if the headhunter is really interested in the candidate, this will be discovered in any case.

The interview should be taken seriously, but it is not advisable for candidates to try and sell themselves too strongly at this point. After all, one is not applying for a position, but has been approached oneself, and the impression should be given that all is well at work and a new job is not actively being sought unless, of course, one is unemployed, when it should be clear that the candidate has many irons in the fire and is not desperate. If this is in any way a selling exercise, it is one by the consultant of the opportunity on offer, not of the candidate to the client. At this point the name of the client will generally be revealed – unless the assignment is especially confidential – and more detail about the firm. If a candidate has very strong reservations about that particular company, such as moral qualms about their products or geographical field of operations, these should be voiced at this stage. As discussed in Chapter 4, at the beginning of the contact between the consultant and the candidate the latter is in a stronger position, especially until it has been ascertained if the job is of real interest or not. The best line for a candidate to take at this stage is to be circumspect but not off-hand, and to ask many relevant questions.

Yet oblique reference may be made to one's achievements – beyond the more obvious ones which the consultant will already know about – especially those showing commitment and effort, such as gaining degrees part-time by evening classes. Copies of any articles and corporate material to which one has contributed – as long as it is not confidential – should be brought along. A candidate should appear hard-working, capable, secure, well adjusted and basically happy. The consultant is looking for industry knowledge and experience, but also at the way the personal chemistry between the client and the candidate would work.

Although most of the interview will be concerned with direct work experience, a further sense of commitment can be imparted from one's activities outside the office, especially one's reading: *The Economist, Business Week* and the monthlies *Business, Management Today* and *The Director* give a good impression, as do books such as Sir John Harvey-Jones's *Making it Happen; Reflections on Leadership* on his time at ICI, John Byrne's *John Sculley: Odyssey* on his move from Pepsi-Cola to Apple, Goldsmith and Clutterbuck's *The Winning Streak* and Nick Kochan's *The Guinness Affair*. There is also certainly now a very strong accent on personal fitness, and many companies offer work-out facilities for employees.

At the end of the interview – after about 1½–2 hours – when candidates feel that all their questions have been answered and that they have given the best impression possible, they should then politely break off, explaining that work is pressing, but that the opportunity has been much appreciated. If one is interested in the position, one should say so, but always being aware that there will be many other candidates and this does not mean that a meeting with the client and offer of the job is next on the horizon. It will still be very competitive, and the candidate should be prepared for the possibility of undergoing a 5–6 hour psychometric test, the results of which will be considered by the client. Before an offer is made, certain reference checks will be carried out (and many afterwards) and the veracity of qualifications will be ascertained.

The meeting with the client will be less of a case of giving and receiving of information, because the candidate will have been briefed about the client and vice versa. The format will vary enormously according to the personality of the chief executive or Board director entrusted with the task, but if the consultant has done his or her job properly, both should more or less happily interact together. But it is by no means unusual for a search to come unstuck at the last moment, because the candidate's present firm has made a better offer, or family circumstances have intervened, or the candidate has just decided not to move after all. As Geoffrey Golzen suggests, 'headhunters accept the realities of the marketplace but they resent being let down at the last minute for no good reason or without warning; and they like to be told if a candidate has other irons in the fire which can, of course, make that candidate seem even more desirable'.

However, if all goes well, it is at this point that the doubtful candidate can begin to appreciate the role of a headhunter, who will be on hand to discuss progress at every stage and may well, in the final stages of a successful assignment, negotiate terms which are an improvement on the original offer. Once a candidate has finally been headhunted – which may occur as the result of the first contact, or the fifth contact, or the tenth contact – he or she will have their own advice for the would-be candidate.

Glossary

These are the words in most common parlance in the executive search world, but it must be emphasised that not all firms and consultants use them, and definitions are inevitably subjective and may vary slightly in application and usage between different headhunters. These words do not all appear in this book, but all have been used more or less frequently by headhunters in conversation with the author. This listing is intended as a guide to users of search, candidates and sources. Consultants should – ideally – always define their terms to new contacts who may be unfamiliar with the search process. Some headhunters appear to be trying to blind with science, others cannot see the wood for the trees and simply forget to explain themselves, and many are afraid of insulting the intelligence of those whose support and interest they are anxious to gain. As a result, many people in the headhunting business may seem to be speaking a foreign language.

ASSIGNMENT A commission from a client to a headhunter to carry out a search to fill a specific position; the assignment officially begins when the client decides on a particular search firm, and agrees to their initial brief.

ASSOCIATE A ranking within a search firm, sometimes below consultant and certainly below partner.

BATTERY OF INSTRUMENTS A group of psychometric tests specially selected by a psychometric tester to test for specific skills and reactions for a particular job in a particular company.

BEAUTY PARADE Like a shoot-out, but when the individual firms merely display their credentials and argue their case generally, rather than pitching for a specific assignment.

BIG BANG, THE The deregulation of the London stock market which took place in October 1986 and brought an unprecedented demand for headhunting in Britain, especially in the financial services sector.

BIG EIGHT, THE The leading search firms in Britain, seen as having the strongest brand images, who dominate high-level search in London. They are Russell Reynolds, Norman Broadbent, Spencer Stuart, GKR, Whitehead Mann, Heidrick and Struggles, Egon Zehnder and Korn/Ferry.

BIG FOUR, THE The first major American search firms which have subsequently spread their operations worldwide, discussed in Chapter 1: Heidrick and Struggles, Spencer Stuart, Russell Reynolds and Korn/Ferry.

BIG-NAME BUSINESSMAN A well-known figure in the business world needed to lead a company through important changes, especially where public support is needed, as in a privatisation flotation. An example is the search for a chief executive of BAA, case study I in Chapter 5.

BILLINGS An American term used to denote the fee income, including expenses of search firms and individual consultants.

BIODATA Within psychometric testing of candidates, biographical data which is scored and analysed as a preselection device; in other words, a way of looking at a CV for career patterns and indications of future behaviour.

BLOCKAGE A problem faced by a search firm with too many clients within a limited sector, leaving no poaching grounds in which to search for candidates, because too many companies are off-limits or no-touch. This can cause severe limits to growth of volume business for a specialist company and for a specialist headhunter.

BOUTIQUE-STYLE A method of approach of a headhunting firm in terms of the clients it hopes to attract and the service it seeks to offer, in the same way that one would go to a boutique for a limited range of quality products of a consistent style and quality, as opposed to visiting a supermarket or general store. An example of a boutique-style firm is Heidrick and Struggles, which promotes an individual style not necessarily appealing to all possible clients, but which will be attractive to those who welcome this approach. The opposite is Korn/Ferry, which is more interested in building volume business overall, seeking to be all things to all people.

BRIEF, THE In contrast with the initial brief, this is a detailed document which acts as a control on the search programme and outlines the expected time-span and the headhunter's fee. It follows the formal commission of the assignment.

BUSINESS CLIMATE The overall state of play of the economy; headhunting thrives on changes in either upward or downward directions, and finds least work in a stable and static business climate.

BUSINESS CULTURE The nature of a company in terms of what it is like to work there, the sort of people favoured, and its attitude to change. Companies with strong business cultures are keen on developing the skills of their own people and use headhunters little. They are seen as ideal poaching grounds, but are very difficult to penetrate, because they promote and gain strong company loyalty. Many of the key operators in these companies are clearly identifiable as a type, such as Xeroids, or for their Unileverness. They are subjected to corporate guidelines for behaviour and attitudes, such as *The IBM Way*. Seven different business cultures have been identified and analysed in Chapter 4. Understanding the nature of the business culture of a client is crucial to the researcher and consultant, as frequently the success of a candidate will depend not just on his or her technical ability and qualifications, but on an ability to fit into the business culture of the new firm without undue culture shock.

BUSINESS DEVELOPMENT Work promoting the activities of a search firm trying to gain more clients, by strategic mail-shot of brochures, cold-calling, business presentations such as beauty parades and making opportunities to join shoot-outs. This is crucial for new search firms, those that do not have a high level of repeat business and those that are eager to expand their volume of assignments, such as transaction-orientated search firms.

CANDIDATE Definitions vary from all persons contacted in a wide trawl to fill an assignment, (sometimes, referred to as 'prospects') to only those who have expressed a real interest in the job and in whom the client is interested (sometimes called 'warm bodies'). Technically, candidates are just the front-runners, or those who appear on the final short list.

CANDIDATE REPORTS Produced by the search firm for the client, providing background information on each candidate on the short list before the client enters the interview programme/process. They add to the basic CV, suggesting why the headhunter thinks the candidate is especially suitable, perhaps emphasising their pluses and minimising their weaknesses, or at least preparing the client for them. Some include photographs; some are accompanied by videoed interviews, especially for global searches where considerable expense is involved in the candidate meeting the client. Candidate reports are known as confidential reports at Korn/Ferry and Spencer Stuart.

CLIENT The company, firm or organisation employing the search firm.

CLOAK-AND-DAGGER HEADHUNTING An assignment where the search must be a particularly confidential one, because the person currently occupying the position must not know that his or her replacement is being sought, or because the chairman does not want the rest of the Board to know that a search is in progress, for example. Such cloak-and-dagger headhunting was current in the early days of headhunting, when clients felt they could use advertising or the old-boy network for more open, conventional recruiting problems. These assignments were sometimes seen as having to do a company's dirty work for them, and are not now necessarily regarded as popular or attractive to consultants.

CODE OF BUSINESS CONDUCT All headhunting firms have to operate by a formal or informal code of conduct in order to establish a reputation and gain repeat business. One of the most obvious rules is not poaching from one's clients for up to two years and maintaining strict confidentiality. Korn/Ferry publish a specific 'Code of Business Conduct', which includes performing assignments in a timely and cost-effective manner; preparing candidate reports without distortion or omission; using discretion over expenses; never recruiting people they have placed; withdrawing from an assignment if conditions change and impair their ability to complete it; offering a guarantee that they will reactivate a search at no additional fee charge if the candidate leaves the client within six months; never presenting a candidate to different clients for different assignments at the same time; and keeping close contact with the client at all stages of the search and in the follow-up. Attitudes to these points are fundamental to the ethics of headhunting.

CODING OF CANDIDATE FILES A task of many researchers creating and maintaining an in-house data bank as a source of information on candidates and sources. Information has to be coded in such a way that it can be utilised to the maximum advantage by researchers and consultants, many of whom will have their own screens and instant access to these files.

COLD-CALLING When a consultant or – more usually – a researcher has to make an initial call to a candidate or source not contacted before. The most effective cold-calls follow extensive homework on the person. Often elaborate cover stories are needed to ascertain the name of the person to be cold-called. This is seen as one of the worst chores of headhunting, and is minimised by developing a specialism in a particular sector and, of course, by more experience in executive search generally.

CONFIDENTIAL SEARCH An assignment in which the consultant is not able to reveal the name of their client to candidates until the final stages, making the search process very difficult; it may be that the client needs cloak-and-dagger headhunting, but it may have perfectly sound and honourable intentions in wanting to keep the search very secret. Of course, all assignments are confidential to a greater or lesser degree, and many first cold-calls do not reveal the client's name.

CONSULTANCY-ORIENTATED SEARCH FIRM Those firms who make a particular point of cultivating existing clients and offering a more total, rounded service than transaction-orientated search firms who seek to maximise their number of assignments and business volume. Consultancy-orientated search firms are likely to enjoy a high level of repeat business, especially those who have been in the business a long time.

CONSULTANT A general term loosely applied to all headhunters, as opposed to researchers. It can technically refer to a senior member of a headhunting firm before he or she becomes a partner.

CONTINGENCY-BASED FEES/CONTINGENCY WORK Where the consultant's payment is dependent on the success of an assignment, rather like the 'no cure, no pay' practice of marine salvage firms in marine insurance. Contingency work was common in the early days of headhunting, especially in the USA, but it is obviously very unpopular among search firms, who now nearly all work on a retainer basis except for very exceptional circumstances.

COVER STORIES/UNDERCOVER RESEARCH Ploys by researchers to discover the names of persons occupying specific positions in companies, to cold-call them subsequently as possible candidates or sources; a typical cover story is pretending that a conference is being organised for which names of invitees are sought. This, and other aspects of undercover research – any kind of enquiry in which the purpose is not made entirely clear – is frowned upon by many concerned about the ethics of headhunting, but it would be very difficult to obtain all necessary information without a minor form of semi-deception.

CROSS-VECTORING A term used by some researchers to describe discovering details and pinning down suitable candidates by means of various research methods, both direct and indirect, to minimise the amount of cold-calling involved, and to reduce the time taken in homework on potential candidates and sources.

CULTURE SHOCK Can be suffered by a successful candidate entering a new company with a different business culture (qv), especially someone leaving a company with a strong business culture in which they have worked for some time. Culture shock may also be suffered within the headhunting world itself, when consultants defect from one search firm to another, and perhaps accounts for the lack of success of certain defections.

CV Curriculum Vitae, known as 'résumé' in the USA; an outline of one's personal details, qualifications, and experience. CVs prepared for headhunters are not necessarily the same as those favoured by potential employers; search consultants look for very brief outlines in a clear chronological order, not thematic appraisals which smack of careers advisers and CV-producing companies. CVs for headhunters should always include salary details.

DEFECT/DEFECTION When a headhunter moves from one search firm to another, often due to an uneasiness with the business culture, and a lack of opportunity to gain a share of the equity; it can simply mean a move to a rival firm, or a desire to set up on one's own.

DESIRE TO HIRE Intention on the part of a client engaging a search consultant to appoint a candidate to a specific position, as opposed to a client who is not necessarily interested in making a placing, but wants to appraise the quality of the market generally. Whether or not there is a desire to hire should always be made clear at the outset, otherwise candidates will become interested in a position and will inevitably be disappointed. Client ethics should be seen as just as important as the ethics of headhunting.

DESK-RESEARCH See librarianship phase.

DINOSAURS A pejorative term given by smaller, home-grown British head-hunters to the Big Four and other international headhunters, insinuating that they have become so large, unwieldy and unable to adapt to a changing environment that they must inevitably become extinct. The large firms, on the other hand, argue that they have the resources to expand and take advantage of new business opportunites, unlike the smaller companies, who are merely voicing a form of sour grapes.

EQUITY The capital of a company, what a business is worth; one of the main problems suffered by headhunting firms is dealing with consultants who demand a share of the equity, and a proportion of the profits earned, rather than just a salary and bonuses.

ETHICS OF HEADHUNTING Most search firms appear concerned about this problem when discussing their code of business conduct, and many claim to be consistently honest and open in their approach, denying the use of cover stories and undercover research. Companies most reluctant to use search frequently quote their suspicions about the ethics of headhunting as a reason for their caution. Some aspects of search, including poaching and the movement of teams, are seen as most questionable in terms of ethics.

EXECUTIVE SEARCH Used in *The Headhunting Business* synonymously with headhunting, but many firms much prefer this more formal and professional label, and never refer to themselves in any other way.

EXPENSES Charged by a headhunting firm to a client, counted within revenue but not fee income. An estimate of the expenses, at least as a percentage of the total bill for an assignment, should be sought by the client commissioning the headhunter. This normally works out at between 15% and 25% of the total cost; but some headhunters have been known almost to double their bills through expenses.

EXTERNAL CANDIDATES Candidates for a position to be filled who are working for an outside company, as opposed to internal candidates.

FACTORY A pejorative term used about dinosaurs, The Big Four and other international headhunters who tend to adopt a standardised, formula approach to assignments, by transaction-orientated search firms seeking to maximise their business volume. It is a criticism often levelled at some of the larger firms by clients, as discussed in the client survey in Chapter 3.

FEE INCOME The income a search firm receives from fees charged to the client, excluding expenses.

FIRST, SECOND AND THIRD GENERATION RESEARCH The historical development of attitudes to research by search firms since the early days of headhunting in Britain. First generation research depended largely on personal contacts within the old-boy network; second generation research was supplemented by published secondary sources and circulation lists of particular business magazines and alumni which, being rather imprecise, may be seen as fishing rather than trawling; third generation research is that practised in the most modern and successful firms today, involving systematic and creative cross-vectoring of a variety of sources, through desk-research or the librarianship phase, on-line information, cold-calling and telephoning existing contacts. Most search firms combine all three generations of research, but in varying proportions.

FOLLOW-UP The period after the successful completion of an assignment, after the candidate starts work, in which a good search consultant will keep in contact with both client and candidate to monitor the progress of both, seen as good for business development, and as a part of the search firm's code of business conduct.

FRONT-RUNNER A candidate in the final short list who is presented to the client and has an equal chance with the others of winning the position. Sometimes this term is used by the headhunter to refer to his or her favourite candidate, who will be recommended most strongly to the client.

GAMEKEEPER The term given by a headhunter to a personnel director, especially one in a company which is a frequent user of search and often used as a poaching ground, particularly in the context of the phenomenon of poacher-turned-gamekeeper, whereby a search consultant defects to join a company. Gamekeepers, of course, can and do become poachers, and many search firms are actively seeking new recruits from this source.

GENERALIST HEADHUNTERS Consultants within search firms who do not specialise in any particular industry or functional sector and will take on assignments in a range of areas. Generalist headhunters are becoming rarer in relation to specialist headhunters because of the increasing sophistication of business; but specialists are more tied to fluctuations in the market, and some search firms have suffered heavy losses in business when a particular specialty becomes less profitable, such as the impact of the stock market Crash of the autumn of 1987 on headhunting in financial services. Some firms have also taken knocks when certain specialist headhunters have defected to other search firms.

GLOBAL SEARCH International networking within the headhunting business, acting for multinational clients across a range of different branches, carried out by the Big Four and other international headhunters, as discussed in Chapter 6.

GOLDEN HANDCUFF An incentive, usually financial, applied by a company to key executives as an inducement for them to stay and not be tempted by headhunters to move to a rival. Headhunting firms also use golden handcuffs themselves to keep their top earners, such as offering guaranteed bonuses. Like golden hello, this term entered common parlance in the era of the Big Bang.

GOLDEN HELLO A bonus, usually financial, paid on the arrival of a new recruit headhunted into a company; the headhunter, if the firm normally charges one-third of the first year's salary of the candidate, will also receive a third of the golden hello, especially if he or she has played a part in negotiating this. The golden hello can tempt a candidate to join a company but will not necessarily keep him or her there for long; golden handcuffs are needed for this.

GRAPHOLOGY/GRAPHOANALYSIS The interpretation of hand-writing style and form as a method of selecting and analysing candidates. It is more common on the Continent than in Britain, where many psychometric testers consider that it is of dubious predictive value.

GUARANTEE Offered by many search firms to clients in the case of an assignment which is not completed in a specific period of time, where none of the short-listed candidates is acceptable to the client, and if the successful candidate leaves within a period of six months or a year. Such guarantees usually take the form of an offer to continue or reactivate the assignment on an expenses-only basis until a suitable candidate has been found.

HATCHET MAN An executive required to scale down and reorganise a company in great need of a turnaround. Qualities sought would include aggression, ruthlessness and a lack of sentimentality combined with a shrewd assessment of business situations. Many of the most famous hatchet men have been headhunted, because by definition someone from outside an organisation has to be brought in to do this work.

HEADHUNTER/HEADHUNTING The popular, slightly scurrilous and irreverent term for consultants and executive search firms, used synonymously and interchangeably in this book with executive search. As a term it is not particularly liked by its purveyors, but is more or less accepted by them. The verb (to be headhunted) refers to a change in job due to an approach by a search consultant, not just being telephoned. An executive is headhunted by a client, using the search firm as an intermediary; but one cannot be strictly headhunted without the role of a search firm.

HIGH-LEVEL SEARCH Assignments at the top level of the salary range – including high-flyers in the City – and in terms of areas of responsibility such as chief executives. These include searches at £80 000+, compared with middle-level search of between £45 000 and £80 000 and lower-level search of around £35 000 to £45 000 and below. These figures are approximate and subject to change.

HOME-GROWN BRITISH HEADHUNTERS/NATIONAL HEADHUNTERS Search firms originating in Britain who in some cases have opened branches or linked with associates overseas and who, like Norman Broadbent and GKR, are now strong competitors to the Big Four and other international headhunters.

HOMEWORK Research, usually carried out by researchers, for background information on candidates and sources before cold-calling, including research within the librarianship phase. Research-based search firms claim to concentrate on quality, in-depth homework before making approaches.

IBM WAY, THE The corporate code of behaviour promoted by IBM, in the book of the same name by Buck Rogers, discussed in Chapter 4. The aim of such publications are to instil a spirit of company loyalty and a strong business culture to resist the attempts of headhunters to poach from them. This phenomenon is more prevalent in the USA than in Britain.

IDEAL CANDIDATE A theoretical person exactly suited to the position to be filled, described in the job specification; drawing up a profile of the ideal candidate is a popular approach to headhunting in the USA.

INDIVIDUAL-ORIENTATED SEARCH FIRM The opposite of a teamwork-orientated search firm, where consultants work on their own assignments with a large degree of personal autonomy. Such a structure is favoured in firms where the earnings of consultants are directly related to the business they bring in and the assignments they carry out.

IN-HOUSE RECRUITING When a client decides not to engage a search firm and tackle its own recruiting problems, either through the old-boy network or by advertising. Not to be confused with internal candidates.

IN-HOUSE SOURCES The research facilities available within the offices of a search firm, including the internal data bank, and as opposed to out-housed sources.

INITIAL BRIEF A proposal letter from the search firm to the client, outlining their understanding of the assignment, and why the client should choose them; this is followed by either engagement to undertake the assignment or rejection. Four examples are quoted in Chapter 4. Not to be confused with the brief.

INTERNAL CANDIDATES Candidates for a position to be filled who are already working within the client company, sometimes in competition with external candidates for the job.

INTERNAL DATA BASE The in-house sources of a search firm accessible from desk-top terminals on consultants' and researchers' desks.

INTERNATIONAL HEADHUNTERS The Big Four and other firms with several branches – not associated firms – overseas, such as Egon Zehnder and Boyden.

INTERVIEW PROCESS/PROGRAMME Part of the search process in which the consultant then the client interviews the candidate. This can also include psychometric testing and graphology.

JOB SPEC./JOB SPECIFICATION An outline of the requirements of the ideal candidate including age, experience, qualifications, background and personal qualities. Also known as job description.

LATERAL THINKING A quality needed by third generation researchers in carrying out creative, efficient research, such as in cross-vectoring.

LIBRARIANSHIP PHASE This term refers to headhunting research – in books, the in-house sources and in on-line data bases – before cold-calling and working the phones. Desk-top research includes the librarianship phase and sometimes includes telephoning too.

LOW-LEVEL SEARCH Below medium-level search; for positions at the £35 000 to £45 000 level, when many clients are undecided whether to use search or not. Sometimes this part of a headhunting firm's business is hived off into another, separate firm.

MANAGEMENT CONSULTANTS Strictly speaking, those firms which merely offer advice rather than headhunting services too; but many search firms are also management consultants, or are within management consultancy organisations. In countries where executive search as such is not officially recognized, such as Germany, headhunters carry on their business whilst referring to themselves as management consultants.

MARZIPAN HEADHUNTERS Those search firms below the top level – the icing – who handle lower-level search and frequently advertise appointments.

MATURE SEARCH MARKET A business environment in which executive search is widely accepted and frequently used, such as the USA; Britain is rapidly becoming a mature search market too.

MEDIUM-LEVEL SEARCH Assignments for positions paying between £45 000 and £70 000; below high-level search and above lower-level search.

MINIMUM FEE The smallest sum for which a search firm will undertake an assignment. This varies between firms according to the level at which they work, but figures of £15 000 and £20 000 are frequently quoted by leading firms.

MOVEMENT OF TEAMS Mainly during the Big Bang, the headhunting of two or more people from one company wholesale to another company, often a foreign business where a group of people, already used to working together, are needed in a hurry. This phenomenon has received much criticism from non-participating search firms and clients in terms of the ethics of headhunting.

'MOVERS AND SHAKERS' The type of businessman or woman for whom headhunters spend most of their time searching within high-level search; these are the people who are going to make a major impact on a company.

NICHE A limited, closely defined area of a market which has been carefully explored and developed, either in headhunting or more generally in marketing, services or manufacturing.

NOT-FOR-PROFIT SECTOR An increasingly important area for executive search in the USA, including charities, hospitals, museums and art galleries; this sector is now growing in Britain.

OFF-LIMITS/NO-TOUCH Companies who are clients of a search firm who may not be seen as poaching grounds in which to search for candidates. Too many clients in a certain sector can produce the problem of blockage, or lack of searching-areas.

OLD-BOY NETWORK A system of personal contacts, based on knowledge of people one has met at school, university, the services and in social gatherings; a very random and inexact way of finding candidates for positions which is declining in relative importance with the growing acceptability of headhunting.

ON-LINE DATA BASES/ON-LINE INFORMATION Widely available sources, such as Textline and Datasolve, which are stored on large host computers and are accessed remotely using a computer located at a search firm's offices. Interrogated information can be selectively downloaded to computer 'hard disc' where it can be edited and merged into in-house documentation.

OUT-HOUSED SOURCES Sources such as specialist libraries and on-line data bases used by researchers outside the offices of the search firm, as opposed to in-house sources.

OUT-PLACEMENT A service offered by some marzipan headhunters and those involved in lower-level search by which displaced or redundant executives are helped in job-searching.

PA/RESEARCHER A member of staff of a headhunting form who combines PA work for an individual consultant or partner with basic headhunting research, as in the case of Alison Burnside of Korn/Ferry (see Chapter 4).

PARTNER The most senior members of a search firm, those who hold a share of the equity.

PLACEMENTS Successful assignments completed by a search firm, in which a candidate has been placed; many headhunters talk of the number of placements in a certain period as a measure of their amount of business.

POACHER/POACHING GROUND Although poaching from one's clients is un-ethical and inevitably bad for business in the long term, normal poaching is seen as very much part of the headhunter's job, in so far as it means approaching people within rival companies on behalf of a client. Ideal, but very difficult poaching grounds, are large companies famous for their good training schemes, with strong business cultures, whose people are very much company men and women, such as Xeroids or those exhibiting Unileverness. The problem of ethics arises when a strong degree of persuasion is involved; but, in the final analysis, the candidate can always refuse to entertain the headhunter's entreaties, and in any case the client may not appoint that person. A poacher, in the sense of being a headhunter can, of course, defect from a search firm to a company with whom he or she has had dealings, and become a personnel director or gamekeeper.

POLITICAL HEADHUNTING The term describing an assignment in which the client knows exactly who is required for a certain position, and wants the headhunter to act as middle-man in approaching him or her on their behalf, without searching; this is not necessarily welcomed by the leading firms.

POPULATION OF A SEARCH/POOL OF CANDIDATES The parameters of the search, the number of people suitable for a position, which can be very large or very small, depending on seniority and specialism.

POWER LUNCHES/BREAKFASTS The entertaining of clients, candidates and sources by headhunters, usually at some lavish and opulent establishment, with a view to gaining that person's interest in doing business; many of the leading firms officially deny that this practice is common, but evidence from many clients, candidates and sources suggest otherwise. Certainly some very expensive London hotels and restaurants do well out of it.

PROFILE OF THE IDEAL CANDIDATE See ideal candidate

PROJECT MAN An executive best skilled at solving specific corporate problems or setting up a new business, usually lasting a finite period, rather than handling more routine, static duties over a long period of time. Project men – or women – are not necessarily skilled at teamwork and building close relationships with colleagues over long periods.

PSYCHOMETRIC TESTS/PSYCHOMETRIC TESTING A device used by consultants and/or clients as an adjunct to the interview programme/process involving a battery of instruments to test particular, relevant skills. The psychometric tester may be freelance, employed by a firm of occupational consultants, or work directly for the search firm or client.

PURE RESEARCH Technically, this refers to the work of a researcher who is wholly dedicated to research without having to undertake PA work.

PURE SEARCH The method of conducting an assignment using only search methods, as opposed to selection and advertising.

REFERENCE CHECKS Investigation of a candidate's CV to ensure its accuracy; this term is also used in gaining outside references to a candidate's qualities and achievements, from people he or she has worked with in the past.

REFERRALS When clients will recommend a headhunting firm to another company, and that company subsequently commissions a search firm to undertake an assignment; a form of passive business development closely associated with firms who enjoy a large degree of repeat business. Also used in the context of enquiries to potential candidates in the initial search stages who may not be interested in the job described but are willing to suggest others in that company or among their circle of friends who would be suitable and might be interested, i.e. sources. These individuals are also known as 'Refers'.

REPEAT BUSINESS More assignments and work from existing clients of a search firm, seen as highly-sought after since working for an existing client, when the headhunter already understands the business culture, is easier than taking on a completely new client. Many search firms quote their percentage of repeat business; this will be higher in the case of consulting-orientated search firms than transaction-orientated search firms. It is also inevitably higher in the older-established search firms than in the newer ones.

RESEARCH ASSOCIATE/RESEARCH CONSULTANT A senior researcher, perhaps one being groomed to become a consultant, as in the case of Mike Goldstone of Heidrick and Struggles in Chapter 4.

RESEARCHER A member of the staff of a headhunting firm who undertakes research work as opposed to being a consultant. There are many different types, viz. PA/researcher, research associate, research consultant and research manager.

RESEARCH MANAGER A member of staff of a headhunting firm who has responsibility for its combined research resources, such as Robert Birkett of Merton Associates (see Chapter 4). The degree of involvement in other aspects of the research process of the research manager varies considerably between firms.

RESEARCH-ORIENTATED SEARCH FIRM A firm where great emphasis is placed on the importance of research, which employs a large number of researchers – perhaps even more than the number of consultants – and has the most modern and comprehensive research resources. Within such firms, it is not uncommon for researchers to become consultants.

RETAINER-BASED FEES Whereby a search firm is paid in stages within the search process, and where the payment of fees is not dependent on the success of the search in finding a suitable candidate, as in the case of contingency work.

REVENUE The total income of a search firm, including all expenses on top of fee income.

ROBBING PETER TO PAY PAUL A phenomenon occurring in an appointment within a nationalised or newly-privatised industry, such as that described in case study I in Chapter 5, when it is proposed to search for an executive within another nationalised industry. Should they be interpreted as poaching grounds, or are they off-limits? In this particular case, the headhunters were allowed to search in the nationalised sector.

SCREENING The process of sifting through a large number of preliminary candidates in order to arrive at a short list. Some screening may be carried out by cold-calling, or by contacting sources. Otherwise screening may be possible through detailed desk-top research and by obtaining candidates' CVs.

SEARCH BUDGET The amount of money allocated by a client to the search; an estimate of the total headhunter's bill should be ascertained from the outset. This term may also be used by the search firm itself, knowing that not all expenses are recoverable from the client, and mindful of its profit margins.

SEARCH PROGRAMME/PLAN OF ACTION The entire process to which the headhunting assignment is subjected, from the initial brief to the follow-up including the interview process and all the research input, as described in Chapter 4.

SELECTION A method of recruitment whereby a selection firm undertakes the shortlisting of a number of potential candidates through recruitment advertising and interviewing, as an agent of the client company, which then undertakes its own telephoning, referencing and further interviewing. Selection is sometimes offered by marizipan headhunters and those undertaking lower-level search.

SELECTION TESTS Within psychometric testing, a comparatively unsophisticated test usable by personnel officers in major firms to recruit their own staff.

Selection tests are normally either designed to test capacity, or attitude and behaviour.

SHOOT-OUT A competitive pitch for an assignment, nearly always at the client's offices, between a number of search firms – usually between two and five – whereby the client may judge which they prefer. Not to be confused with a beauty parade.

SHORT LIST The final list of candidates presented by the consultant to the client, all of whom have expressed real interest in the position, and in whom the client is interested. The short list may contain as few as two names or as many as half a dozen or more, but three or four possible contenders is most common.

SOURCE A person contacted by telephone by a consultant or researcher to suggest a possible candidate for an assignment; this may sometimes be interpreted as a roundabout way of approaching a potential candidate, but the leading firms do not favour this, and make clear when they make contact which of the two they consider they are addressing (see referrals).

SPECIALIST COMPANY/HEADHUNTERS A search firm or individual consultant who specialises in recruiting and searching in one particular sector, either by industry or function, who can ultimately face the problem of blockage and thus be restricted in terms of growth of volume business.

SUCCESS RATE The proportion of assignments successfully completed by a search firm, compared with those which had to be abandoned, either due to the failure of the search firm to find an acceptable candidate, or an unforeseen change in the job specification. Failed assignments and hence a low success rate are not always the headhunter's fault, but a good consultant will not undertake an assignment without having previously ascertained that it has a fair chance of success.

SYSTEM, THE A term used by some search firms to describe their own in-house data base.

TEAMWORK-ORIENTATED SEARCH FIRM The opposite to an individual-orientated search firm, where consultants work as a team and undertake assignments regardless of which of them has undertaken the necessary business development. This approach is more common in firms where consultants earn salaries rather than commissions on the basis of their work.

TRANSACTION-ORIENTATED SEARCH FIRM Those firms seeking to maximise their volume business in terms of number of assignments, who do not necessarily enjoy a large proportion of repeat business, and thus who attach a great deal of importance to Business Development.

TURNAROUND A dramatic change for the better in a company's fortunes, usually as a result of the appointment of a key executive, often from outside and frequently headhunted.

UNILEVERNESS A quality acquired by many people who have undergone a training scheme and worked for the Anglo-Dutch giant Unilever, a company with a particularly strong business culture. Many other such corporations are able to instil a uniform attitude to behaviour and work and their people are readily identifiable, such as Xeroids.

USERS OF SEARCH Clients who engage headhunters to work on an assignment.

WALK-INS Would-be candidates who literally walk in to search firms' offices asking for careers advice and how they can move on. Many leading firms will allow the 'walk-in' to talk to a researcher, to give them interviewing practice. Sometimes called 'drop-ins'.

WHITE KNIGHT A particularly aggressive and able businessman, brought in by a company – usually searched by a headhunter – to help that company fight off an unwelcome predatory take-over bid from a competitor.

WORKING THE PHONES A term used to describe telephoning sources and candidates, a task usually undertaken by a researcher, including cold-calling.

WRITE-INS CVs sent by hopeful would-be candidates to search firms.

XEROIDS People who work for the giant American photocopying business, Rank Xerox, clearly identifiable as a result of this corporation's powerful business culture.

ZANZIBAR A far-flung, unattractive and isolated posting for which it is difficult for a search consultant to find takers; this term is often used for any unusual and obscure assignment that is proving a tough nut to crack.

Bibliography

This section is a guide to further reading, first about the headhunting business in Britain and, to a lesser extent, in the USA, Europe and the Far East; and second, it acts as an introduction to basic headhunting desk-top research by indicating some of the most important reference works needed. It would be an immense task to list all relevant on-line material required as well, so the range of information given on Textline – one of the most popular data bases – is included as an example of the value of this source.

The first part of this bibliography is divided into articles in magazines and newspapers, books, and material published outside Britain, listed under author. These items are directly or indirectly about executive search, with some pieces written by headhunters themselves.

HEADHUNTING

Articles

Ian Ashworth, 'Schooling in the 1990s the Technological Way' *Comms Monthly* July/August 1987, p. 34

Simon Bartholomew, 'Small Businesses are now Attracting the Top Executives' *The Times* 24 September 1987, p. 31

Jane Bidder, 'Open Season in the Job Jungle' *The Times* 2 February 1987

Miles Broadbent, 'Future Trends' *First* April 1989

Malcolm Brown, 'The Hunt is hotting up for Money Managers' *The Sunday Times* 10 May 1987, p. 85

Tim Chevenix-Trench 'General Appointments: The Headhunter also needs to be Headhunted' *The Times* 15 October 1987

Barry Clement, 'Hunter who Banks on turning up Winners' *The Independent* 13 October 1986, p. 13

Nicholas Cobbold, 'Getting the Best' *First* April 1989

Fiona Cordy, 'Headhunters fill in the Gaps Other Firms cannot Reach' *Computer News* 10 September 1987, p. 18

Tessa Curtis, 'The Grand Headhunting Season' *Daily Telegraph* 23 October 1986

Allen Davis, 'The Accountants Helping to Create a Computer Gap' *The Times* 3 April 1987, p. 31

Clive Deverell, 'When Paper can't make People' *The Times* 20 August 1986

Andrew Dickson, 'Secrets of the New Headhunters' *Sunday Telegraph* 6 November 1988

Tim Entwisle, 'General Appointments: Follow the Rules of Recruitment and Pick your People with Care' *The Times* 10 December 1987

Frances Gibb, 'Headhunters in Room 12' (Legal & Financial Page) *The Times* 28 November 1987

Geoffrey Golzen, 'Headhunters Hit the Trail' (Horizons Page) *The Times* 26 March 1987

Geoffrey Golzen, 'Headhunters see Value in Highly-Placed Temps' *Sunday Times* 8 November 1987

Geoffrey Golzen, 'More Ways than One to go Hunting Heads' *Sunday Times* 31 January 1988

Geoffrey Golzen, 'The Right Candidate' *Forte* Winter 1988

Geoffrey Golzen, 'What to Do when the Headhunters ring up' *Sunday Times* 20 March 1988, p. E1

John Grumbar, 'The Search for the Euro-Executive', *The Living Market* (Report by Henley Management College) April 1989

Martyn Halsall, 'Headhunters Struggle to Cope with Regional Gap' *Guardian* 27 *May 1987, p. 27*

Stephanie Jones, 'Bait for the headhunters', *Daily Telegraph*, 29 June 1989, Appointments Section

Stephanie Jones, 'Executive Recruitment in International Financial Services' *Multinational Business* (Economist Intelligence Unit) Winter 1988–9

Stephanie Jones, 'Headhunters: The Costs and Benefits' *Management Accounting* December 1986, p. 16

Stephanie Jones, 'Headunters thrust Deeper into Jungle' *Sunday Telegraph* 2 August 1987, p. 25

Stephanie Jones, 'Headhunting for the Public Sector' *Local Government Chronicle* September 1988

Stephanie Jones, 'Headhunting's Covert Operations' *Management Today* September 1987, p. 94

Stephanie Jones, 'Heads for Hire' *Business Traveller* June 1987, p. 17

Stephanie Jones, 'Recruitment and Training' supplement to *Euromoney* September 1988

Stephanie Jones, 'Should Headhunters be Axed?' (headhunting in the property world) *Chartered Surveyor Weekly* 18–25 December 1986, Vol 17 p. 1158

Stephanie Jones 'Story of a Headhunt' *Cosmopolitan* April 1988, p. 32

Stephanie Jones, 'The Marzipan Headhunters' *Sunday Times* 11 November 1987, p. 97

Stephanie Jones 'Top of the Pecking Order' *Financial Times* 29 June 1988, supplement on recruitment

David Kimbell, '1992: A Single Market for Executive Search?' *First* April 1989

Nick Kochan, 'Headhunter with a Nice Line in Fold-Up Bikes' (about Stephen Rowlinson) *Guardian* 16 June 1986, p. 22

Laurie Ludwick, 'Hunters Lured by High-Priced Finance Heads' *Financial Times* 2 August 1986

Malcolm Macalister Hall, 'This Man could Fix you a £100,000 Salary' *Options for Men* May 1986, p. 30

Keith McNeish, 'Ensure Slim Pickings for the Headhunters' *Sunday Times* 20 July 1986, p. 74

Stuart Mansell, 'Tax experts scorn Revenue threat to City Golden Hellos' *Accountancy Age* 27 February 1986

Ian Middleton, 'The Hunters and the Hunted – Shipping joins the Game' *Seatrade* May/June 1988

J. M. Reid, 'Women who mean Business' (Letter) *Financial Times* 16 December 1986

John Richards, 'General Appointments: Restrictions to fend off Headhunting should be Replaced by Company Rewards' *The Times* 13 November 1986

John Roberts, 'International headhunters' *Business Life* (British Airway's magazine for business travellers) June/July 1986, p. 54

Stephen Rowlinson, 'Executives who want to Reach the Top must Plan their Job Changes' *The Times* 12 May 1988, p. 29

Stephen Rowlinson, 'Managers Manage Yourselves!' *Chief Executive* January 1987

Amanda Seidl, 'Recruiting the Best' *Business* February 1989

Pippa Sibley 'Unmasked – Britain's No.1 Headhunter' (David Norman) *Today* 5 October 1987, p. 12

Haig Simonian, 'Headhunters Stalk German Banks' *Financial Times* 25 February 1987

Geoff Slade, 'General Appointments: British Business often Fails in the Selection Process and the Effect is a Negative One' *The Times* 7 August 1986

John Spicer, 'A Lesson from John McEnroe' *The Times* 19 February 1988

John Spicer, 'How Personality Clashes Split the Boardroom' (Business and Finance Page) *The Times* 18 April 1988

Elaine Sunderland, 'Challenging for the Prizes in the Former Male Club' *The Times* 12 November 1987, p. 35

Pat Sweet, 'Jobscene: Headhunters Set their Sights on a new Target' *The Times* 9 December 1986

Michael Syrett, 'The Headhunters often bring in the Wrong Scalps' *Sunday Times* 22 June 1987

Patricia Tuddil (ed.), 'Headhunters Face Shake-Out' *Marketing* 3 April 1986

Stephen Wagstyl, 'Headhunting Japanese Style' *Financial Times* 21 September 1988

Nicholas Watkis, 'General Appointments: Executives on Lease' *The Times* 27 August 1987, p. 25

Clive Woodcock, 'Directors for Hire' *Guardian 5 May 1987*

Bert Young, 'The Importance of Decision-Making Chief Executives in British Business' *The Times* 22 January 1987, p. 25

Unattributed articles

'Secret Service – David Norman' *Sunday Telegraph* 3 Mary 1987

'Broad shoulder' (about the Duke of Edinburgh's non-executive directorships and role on the selection committee of Egon Zehnder's awards for MBA students) *Sunday Telegraph* 31 May 1987

'The Games's up for a Headhunter' (in the stockbroking business) *The Times* 26 November 1987

'Hunting the Head that Fits the Blot' (about Saxton Bampfylde's new brochure) *Marketing Week* 22 April 1988, p. 32

'Headhunters: Trophies Galore' *The Economist* 21 June 1986, p. 75

Books

Robert B. Baird and Jacqueline M. Hickson, *The Executive Grapevine* (London, latest edition, 1989–90)

John Byrne, *The Headhunters* (New York, 1986, with 2nd edition including new material on London, 1987)

John Byrne, *John Sculley: Odyssey* (New York, 1987)

Robert McKinnon, *Headhunters* (Newbury, 1982)

Robert H. Perry, *How to Answer a Headhunter's Call* (New York, 1984)

A. Taylor, *How to Select and Use an Executive Search Firm* (London, 1978)

John Wareham, *Secrets of a Corporate Headhunter* (New York, 1981)

American, European and Far Eastern material: a selection

John Alexander, 'Headhunters' *Australian Business* 9 April 1981, p. 44

Peter Bennett, 'Recruiting for China' *AMCHAM: Journal of the American Chamber of Commerce in Hong Kong* October 1985

Richard T. Bergsund, 'Executive Search – What is it?' *Underwriters' Report (USA)* 22 December 1977
Richard T. Bergsund, 'How an Executive Search Firm Works' *Underwriters' Report (USA) 21 December 1978*
Richard T. Bergsund, 'How to Work Successfully with a Search Firm from the Client's Viewpoint' *Underwriters' Report (USA)* 13 March 1980
Richard T. Bergsund, 'Selecting Your Executive Search Firm' *Underwriters' Report (USA)* 26 January 1978
Richard T. Bergsund, What to do When the Headhunter Calls' *Underwriters' Report (USA) 11 December 1980*
John Byrne *et al.* 'Forget the Old-Boy Network – Hire a Headhunter' *Business Week* 18 August 1986, p. 24
Stephanie Jones 'Asia's Traditions are a Challenge to Headhunters' *Far East Business* (Hong Kong) July 1987
Stephanie Jones 'Cazados Para El Exito' *Mercado* (Madrid) October 1987
Stephanie Jones, 'The Headhunting Business ... with a note on the Australian Experience' *Australian Corporate History Bulletin* August 1987
Beverly Gary Kempton, 'The Executive Woman's Guide to Headhunters' *Working Woman* (USA) April 1987, p. 110
Jim Kennedy, editor of *Executive Recruiter News,* published monthly since 1980 by Kennedy & Kennedy, Inc., Templeton Rd., Fitzwilliam, NH 03447, USA
Herbert E. Meyer, 'The Headhunters come upon Golden Days' *Fortune* 9 October 1978, p. 100
Richard Stengel, 'Manhattan's Hottest Headhunter' (Gerry Roche of Heidrick and Struggles) *Manhattan Inc.* September 1984, p. 72

HEADHUNTING RESEARCH

Books

This section lists a selection of a representative sample of basic annual directories and reference books used by headhunting researchers, in alphabetical order of title keyword, name of publisher and, where this is available, publisher's telephone number – all numbers are within London unless preceded by 0 – and later updated inserts.

Accountants in England & Wales Institute of Chartered Accountants 628 7060
Chartered Institute of Management Accountants CIMA 637 4716
Adhesives Directory Turret-Wheatland 0923–223577
Society of British Aerospace Companies Ltd, The Society of British Aerospace Companies Ltd 839 3231
Air Cargo Handbook UK (twice yearly) Herefords 441 6644
Bankers' Almanac and Yearbook (twice yearly), Thomas Skinner Directories Ltd 0342–26972
BRAD, British Rate & Data 434 2233
Brewery Manual and Who's Who in British Brewing and Scotch Whisky Distilling 1988, Municipal Publications 637 2400
Building Societies' Yearbook, Franey & Co 209 3322
City Directory, Woodhead-Faulkner 0223–66733
City of London Directory & Livery Companies Guide, City Press 0206–45121
Becket's Directory of the City of London, Becket Publications Ltd 736 3031
I.C.E. Civil Engineers' Yearbook (every two years), Thomas Telford Ltd 222 7722

Association of Consulting Engineers The Association of Consulting Engineers 222 6557
Consulting Engineers' Who's Who, The Association of Consulting Engineers 222 6557
Major Companies of Europe, 3 vols. Graham & Trotman Ltd 821 1123
Computer Users' Yearbook, Computing Publications Ltd 636 6890
Conference Blue Book, Spectrum Publishing Ltd 749 3061
The Creative Handbook, Thomas Skinner Directories Ltd 0341–26972
Debrett's Distinguished People of Today, Debrett 736 6524
Designer Directory, The Design Council 839 8000
Directory of British Associations, CBD Research Ltd 650 7745
Directory of British Importers, Trade Research Publications 04427–3951
Directory of Directors Thomas Skinner Directories Ltd 0342–26972
Electrical & Electronics Trade Directory, Peter Peregrinus Ltd
Fellowship of Engineering Yearbook, The Fellowship of Engineering 799 3912
Hambros Euromoney Directory, Euromoney Publications Ltd 236 3288
Key British Enterprises, Dun & Bradstreet, 377 4377
Kompass Regional Sales Guides 7 vols. Kompass Publishers Ltd 0342–26972
Kompass Register (UK), Kompass Publishers Ltd 0342–26972
Machinery Buyers Guide, Finlay Publications 0322–77755 £22
Market Research Society Yearbook, The Market Research Society 439 2585
Benn's Media Directory, Benn 0732–362666
The Municipal Yearbook, The Municipal Group 637 2400
The Packaging Directory, The Industrial Press Ltd 441 6644
Vacher's Parliamentary Companion (quarterly), A. S. Kerswill Ltd 0442–776135
Pension Funds and Their Advisors AP Financial Registers Ltd 458 1607
Personnel Managers' Yearbook, AP Information Services Ltd 458 1607
British Pharmaceutical Industry, Jordan Surveys 253 3030 £210
Willings Press Guide, Thomas Skinner 0342–26972
Retail Directory Newman Books Ltd 439 0335
R.I.B.A. – Directory of Members RIBA Publications 251 0791
R.I.C.S. Yearbook, RICS 222 7000
Sells Directory, Sells Publications Ltd 03727–26376
ABC Shipping Guide (monthly), ABC Travel Guides Ltd 0582–600111
Solicitors' and Barristers' Diary & Directory, Waterlow Publishers
Stock Exchange Members & Firms, The Stock Exchange 588 2355
The International Stock Exchange Official Yearbook Macmillan 836 6633
Times 1000 Times Books 434 3767
Top Management Remuneration Monks Publications 0371–830939
Trade Names (UK) Kompass Publishers Ltd 0342–26972
Unit Trust Yearbook, Financial Times Business Publishing Ltd 799 2002
Who Owns Whom, Dun & Bradstreet Ltd 377 4377
Who's Who A & C Black 242 0946

HEADHUNTING RESEARCH: ON-LINE

As indicated in Chapter 4, the amount of information available on-line for searches and business development is vast, and an exhaustive listing would be beyond the scope of this book. Yet to give an indication of how useful this source can be, the data available on Textline is summarised as an example. Textline – now owned by Reuters – is the simplest database to use quickly and effectively.

It is most useful as a news data base, containing abstracts from an extensive range of periodicals worldwide.

The material available is regional or by specialist industry and can by easily combined and cross-compared, over any time period specified. For example, abstracts – of all the editorial material except for the advertising – from several national newspapers for most countries are searchable. The specialist data bases currently cover eleven sectors: banking and finance; insurance and investment; property; marketing; retailing; chemicals; engineering; electronics and computing; accountancy and tax; construction; and travel. For the banking and finance sector, over 450 publications abstracts are available, covering most countries.

How useful is this material for the headhunting researcher? Textline can provide information on individuals and companies, on their past and current activities, for briefings for business presentations. It can track changes in personnel at higher – and in some cases, middle – levels. It can provide information on even the most obscure economic activities, by keying in industry codes and combining them with names of companies and countries. It can produce listings of conferences on major business themes, which will attract the top people in their sector. It can be used as a source for information on legislation affecting business and recruiting. It can even be used to examine the PR efforts of competing headhunting firms!

The value of Textline to the headhunting fraternity is attested to by the fact that a number of major firms are clients of this information service, including Egon Zehnder, Russell Reynolds, Heidrick and Struggles, Spencer Stuart, Korn/Ferry, Merton Associates, Norman Broadbent and PA.

Textline's latest charges are £75 per connect-hour with print-out rates of 10p for a short summary, 20p for an abstract, and 30p for more detailed material. An initial inspection followed by a print-out does not attract two sets of charges.

Many changes are taking place and will come into effect in the years to come in the field of telecommunications, which will permit a more efficient use of on-line data bases without the need for expensive modems. This could substantially improve access by headhunters to this potentially vital material.

Index

Note: names of executive search firms are printed in **bold** type.